A MODERN PLAYBOOK OF DIGITAL TRANSFORMATION

AMITABH MISHRA | ASHISH RANJAN

ATLANTIC

PUBLISHERS & DISTRIBUTORS (P) LTD

ATLANTIC
PUBLISHERS & DISTRIBUTORS (P) LTD

7/22, Ansari Road, Darya Ganj, New Delhi
Tel.: +91-11-4077 5252, 2327 3880
E-mail: orders@atlanticbooks.com
Web: www.atlanticbooks.com

Published by Atlantic Publishers & Distributors (P) Ltd 2024

Previously Published by SAGE Publications in 2019

Printed & bound in India by Atlantic Print Services

Advance Praise

'Lucid style with flowing conversations, making it incredibly simple to understand key technical concepts.'

Anand Laxshmivarahan, *Chief Digital Officer, Cairn Oil & Gas*

'A complete digital guidebook, with an excellent narrative and a storytelling style that will have you hooked from the first page itself.'

Amit Ved, *Senior Director, Gartner*

'A good reference book on digital/digital transformation journey, it covers the basics of digital, digital transformation, the associated technologies and success factors. While the journeys for different organizations could be different based on the business and organizational context, the steps outlined in the book can be a good reference for those looking to start their digital journey.'

Uma Mohan, Ex-Chief Information Officer, *GE Healthcare India*

'The authors use a gripping storytelling style to demystify digital strategy and execution for readers. The rich experience of the authors comes through in the nonchalance with which they simplify the complex subject of successful digital transformation.'

Amit Sethi, *Vice-President, Global Digital Experience,*
Baker Hughes, a GE Company

'This is an excellent showcase of digital transformation at work. The authors have articulated very well the entire gamut of digital journey, starting with the basics and navigating through successful recipes around complex execution with winning ideas. I find this book full of practical insights coming from the greats, hence a must read for all leaders embarking on a digital transformation journey.'

Sujit Senapati, *Head, Digital, Vedanta Sterlite*

'While reading it, I connected with the vocabulary and the thoughts instantaneously...thereby experiencing the power of storytelling. The narration style not only makes it enjoyable to read through, but also it provides answers to why, what, how and who of Digital construct. I will only say to the readers...enjoy & apply!'

Akash Jain, *India Digital Leader, Caterpillar*

Dedicated to technology professionals worldwide
who can't wait to get going with digital transformation
but don't know where to start

Contents

Foreword

Welcome to the world of digital transformation. If you're starting out, it's likely that fear, ambiguity and uncertainty levels are running high in your mind, and confidence and clarity of strategy are rather low.

Four years ago at Tata Steel, we were in the same boat. We tasked ourselves with a vision to increase employee productivity by 30 per cent, and ensure that 80 per cent of processes acquire predictability with zero safety errors. Eighty per cent employees' career path was impacted positively. That a net promoter score of 70 per cent was achieved, and that 80 per cent of our operations was mapped to the digital world.

We had to figure out the strategy, the steps, from scratch, literally.

How many business leaders want to be innovative, harness the power of digital transformation in order to propel business along a path of exponential growth, and keep oneself and the organization in tune with the latest, most powerful technologies?

That should be every one of you, if you're reading this book. Perhaps you want to create new business opportunities by re-imagining your business model in the digital world, or encourage your customers to adopt new digital interfaces that provide them a seamless Google™- or Apple™-like experience, or digitize the core of your business, for example, your supply chain or manufacturing processes.

No matter which lofty objective you harbour in your mind, you'll need to first develop a digital transformation road map, which is commonly understood across your organization, can be rigorously implemented and is simple, yet ambitious, in its scope. You'll need a robust security strategy that underpins such a plan not as a matter of hygiene but as a differentiator. You'll need to look to create opportunities to re-imagine supply chain, operations, sales and marketing. Legacy systems and silos that stand in your way would need to be demolished via an assertive change management program that strikes the perfect balance between patience and urgency. Importantly, you need to nurture and retain the talent that is required.

Before I took on my current role as the Chief of Business Transformation & Digital Solutions at Tata Steel in May 2016, I was the COO of Tata Business Support Services (TBSS). We'd been talking about digital for over a year. We'd started with the fundamental notion that digital had to be about business; you should have a business strategy which is supported and enabled by digital.

Another important notion was that digital had to be about value. Steel manufacturing as an industry was going through a difficult phase owing to the challenges of margin compression, talent and so on. Earlier, we had 7–8 years to exploit a trend or new business idea. That margin had now shrunk to less than two years. Unless you had the speed to quickly exploit something you are thinking of, from idea to impact, you would not be able to create adequate value. Digital, by definition, allowed you to do that.

Now, almost three years down the road, we have a road map to achieve more than 10 per cent annual EBITDA savings using digital means over the next three years, migrating over 80 per cent of our workloads to the cloud and developing 50+ algorithms built on machine learning (ML) that are driving value. The Aashiyana platform for Individual Home Builders (IHB) is a significant vertical market that we are proud of.

Through the years of my own journey in digital transformation, I have keenly felt the need for a practical book, a pragmatic guide that would pave the way for me so that I won't have to figure out the next steps on my own. Although lofty strategies are fine, there came a point when I didn't need a new strategy; I simply needed to know how to perform the unpretentious tactical steps on the ground to take the next step.

As you know, digital transformation is hard. One of the things I picked up in the journey is that people freeze when you mention 'transformation.' Just imagine telling a caterpillar to transform! It is much easier if you can guide the caterpillar through the steps of creating a cocoon, falling asleep, waking up, untangling itself, feeling and flapping its wings and then taking the challenge of failure and the joy of flight. I believe Amitabh and Ashish have provided that guidance in their book.

I've known one of the authors, Amitabh, for nearly 5 years. I consider him one of India's foremost digital thought leaders based primarily on two factors. First, his technology experience was forged in the digital organizations of three of the world's top corporations: Intel, SAP and General Electric. Second, his leadership philosophy was challenged and refined on the shores of North America, Europe and Asia. The cultural tenets that underpin his leadership style had to be pragmatic and flexible enough to perform under conditions of widely different organizational structures, cultures and political realities. The second author, Ashish, earned his leadership stripes at Accenture where he was a strategic go-to leader for some of the world's top corporations. In this book, Amitabh and Ashish have tapped into a rich vein of what I call 'digital gold,' the no-nonsense, unglamorous and unpretentious, but highly practical, steps that can get your digital strategy from 'thinking about it' to 'done and dusted.'

There are three reasons this book is significant and timely.

First, this book contains the recipe—namely a proven step-by-step strategy for successful transformation—that was successfully employed by the authors in their experience as digital leaders. This is the only book I know of that not only speaks of the strategy but also provides the list of the exact steps—just 20 in number—which, if followed faithfully, can be expected to result in success.

Second, this book outlines the step-by-step execution game plan, complete with tools, artefacts, lessons, pitfalls to avoid and best practices from industry. If you have a grand strategy but not the artefacts, you'll only go so far before the train comes to a grinding halt.

Third and most important, it addresses the softer side of transformation, the relationships aspect. It describes the softer nuances of people and stakeholder management and the internal functions of an organization that are prerequisites to successful digital transformation.

And here's why I feel this book couldn't have come about at a better time. Over the last 2 years, digital transformations have bubbled up from the periphery of organizational strategy to the centre of it. Organizations are investing in, and obtaining the requisite strategic input from, the Gartners, McKinseys and Accentures of the world, who're experts in formulating world-class digital strategies. However, the practical aspects of executing such strategies are not readily available to executing teams.

Up to 85 per cent of digital transformation efforts fail. Let yours be one of the 15 per cent that don't. Study this book, internalize the lessons and perform the easy-to-apply steps. If you follow a proven recipe, what percentage of the time can you expect to succeed? That's right; 100 per cent of the time.

Here's to your success.

Sarajit Jha
Chief, Business Transformation and Digital Solutions,
Tata Steel (featured in *Business Today*'s list of Top Executives Under 40, March 2014); Chairman, DX50, India's first Chief Digital Officer Organization, Jamshedpur

Preface

A few years ago, we were settling down into our roles as chief digital officers for two business lines of a $15B/year metals and mining conglomerate. Our first thought was: let's get hold of a 'how to' book for newly minted digital leaders like us. A book that would explain how to start a digital program from scratch, formulate a strategy, start an organization and successfully execute a first wave of digital initiatives.

We're still looking for that book, one that contains the recipe—namely a proven step-by-step strategy for successful transformation—that has been successfully employed by prominent digital leaders; that would offer practical insights into why digital transformations fail, and how to overcome potential pitfalls; that won't be afraid to delve into the 'how's' of the execution journey, not simply offer broad strategies; that would spell out the softer nuances of people and stakeholder management and internal functions of an organization that are prerequisites to successful digital transformation; that would describe how to achieve success against the backdrop of ambiguity and uncertainty.

Finally, and most importantly, we were looking for a *story*. We don't know about you, but we love reading stories. We love learning new concepts in a fun, interesting way: parables of soaring successes and heartbreaking failures of the protagonist who first stumbles and then redeems himself or herself, where real things happen, just like in real life. It is not a book of diagrams and theory but one of characters and their follies, just like us and everyone else.

What you're holding in your hand, however, may be the closest thing to such a book. Now, a word of clarification. There's no such thing as a successful digital transformation that's not a business transformation. Without a change in business processes, governance and mindset, no lasting transformation can occur. So, really, when you read 'digital transformation' in the pages of this book, think of 'business transformation using digital.'

Based on our combined 40+ years of experience in engineering and technology—specifically consulting and execution—we've perfected the practical aspects of how to execute technology strategies, in general, and digital strategies, in particular. We've worked with some of the world's top corporations, such as GE, Accenture, Intel, SAP, HP and IBM. We've directly worked in nearly 10 countries—with diverse cultures—around the world, in a variety of industries such as semiconductors, steel, natural resources, aviation, automotive, aerospace and defence, and pharmaceuticals.

All right, you may be thinking, this is all great. But why exactly should I read your book?

Here are four compelling reasons! First, this is an original story of private and professional struggle and victory, a modern parable that answers the quintessential question: What makes a leader great? Second, it contains a step-by-step execution game plan, complete with tools, artefacts, lessons, pitfalls to avoid and best practices from industry. Third, it contains detailed cultural strategies to ensure buy-in at all levels of the organization. Finally, the book explains key technological concepts in simple, conversational terms.

Who'll benefit from reading this book?

If you're someone entrusted with leading or participating in a digital transformation exercise *in any capacity*—CxO or manager, team lead or engineer—you'll find the concepts and practical ideas in this book very useful. If you're an IT leader looking to equip yourself with an understanding of digital so as to transition into a new career, you'll find the explanation of digital fundamentals most beneficial. If you're a manager or leader wishing to bring about transformation in your organization, you'll find the stories around culture and change management relevant and practical.

In short, this book is for everyone who's struggling to find his or her place in the digital world.

'Digital' technologies—artificial intelligence, machine learning (ML), Internet of things, sensors, analytics, cognitive computing—have permeated our lives and businesses. However, while 96 per cent of business executives, according to *Forbes,* acknowledge that digital transformation is 'critical or important,' 50 per cent of digital strategies are failing, and 20 per cent of the executives feel that digital transformation is a 'waste of time.'

Why the disconnect? The reasons are threefold: (a) a gap between strategy and execution, (b) the culture and (c) the mindset. Top corporations are adept at formulating world-class digital strategies. However, the practical aspects of executing such strategies are not well understood, documented or available to executing teams.

This book is written to address this critical gap. The book also answers the questions that bedevil every digital professional: How is digital different from IT? Is digital transformation different from digital? How do you explain the technology to senior leadership? Is it all about technology, or is there a mindset of success? How important is culture? Why are business leaders reluctant to allocate budget? How do you sell your vision? What are the top three reasons transformations fail? What are the seven factors that should be kept in mind in order to ensure success?

We hope you'll enjoy reading this book, and applying the lessons herein, as much as we've enjoyed writing it.

Let the journey begin!

Acknowledgements

A journey—such as the one you'll find described on the pages of this book—always has a purpose, a destination. For the two co-authors of this book, the writing of this book was a journey, whose purpose and destination were both deeply rooted in their respective families, leaders and close associates.

Amitabh humbly acknowledges the belief shown in him by senior leadership at the various corporations where he's executed CXO roles. These leaders wished to start something great in their organizations; they were willing to take a chance on a leader long on potential but short on experience.

Amitabh would also like to acknowledge with gratitude the love and belief of his mother, Saudaminee, and the spirit of love and egoless service exemplified by his father, Pradeep. Amitabh would also like to express his gratitude to his wife, Pallavi, and son, Sohum, for their patience and support which, at times, included the possibility of dad being away on the weekends, typing away on his laptop. (It may well be claimed that it's somehow fun being a writer, but no one can claim that it's fun to live with a writer.) His family kept him going, and the journey—and the resulting book—would not have been accomplished without their unconditional love and support.

Ashish derived his inspiration for writing this book from his grandparents and deeply acknowledges the love, patience, support and belief shown by his parents. He is indebted to his wife, Pragati, for her ever-encouraging support and for managing the show in his absence from home, many a time for months on end. He's also grateful to his son, Shaurya, who has kept him on the right side of the digital world, achieving a balance between technology and personal life.

Ashish very humbly acknowledges with gratitude the confidence shown in him by his colleagues from his past roles, and the senior leadership at the various corporations where he has executed CXO roles.

Amitabh and Ashish would be remiss if they were not to point out the crucial and timely encouragement and assistance of Manisha Mathews and Namarita Kathait, who kept the authors honest and accountable. Through the multiple editorial iterations, Manisha and Namarita kept up the communication and motivation; their assistance was as priceless as it was timely.

Introduction

Centre Court, Wimbledon, July 2018

Eight-time champion, Swiss maestro Roger Federer has just exited the Wimbledon tournament, stunned in the quarter-finals in a thrilling five-setter by South African Kevin Anderson. The audience accords a standing ovation to both players, especially Federer, who may arguably have played his last match at Wimbledon. He's almost 37, in a game where most top players retire in their early 30s. It's Federer, for goodness' sake, but even he'll lose to Father Time.

The players walk off the hallowed Centre Court and speak to reporters for a minute or two. Then, something amazing happens. ESPN plays a 3-minute highlight of the match. Why is this amazing? Highlights have been playing on TV since the 1930s, haven't they? Well, the match was over four hours long, and it's been just minutes since it ended. So, how could a program editor have edited a four-hour long video to turn out a 3-minute highlight reel in a matter of minutes?

It turns out artificial intelligence or AI went to work. Behind the scenes, a digital team worked to employ AI and pattern recognition to create a software that edited match videos, ranking and compiling the top moments of the match on the basis of factors such as the expression on the players' faces, crowd reactions, the length of the point, the culmination of points (e.g., players pumping their fists or raising their arms in a gesture of triumph) and emotional gestures (like a player walking over to the crowd and bowing).

The resulting 3-minute highlight reel is crisp and technically sound (e.g., the voice-over from the last amazing point merges seamlessly with the video of the next point). And it was done really, really quickly.

And technology made it happen.

Is AI Taking over the World?

If technology is this powerful, surely it can take over the world, especially if the technology learns on its own and evolves and becomes really all powerful. *Nineteen Eighty-Four,* George Orwell's dystopian novel, describes a world where people have become victims of, among other things, omnipresent government surveillance.

In theory, a government can track citizens and employ AI to control people using a system of rewards and punishments. Eventually, the AI technology will become so powerful, goes the thinking, it'll dump government and rule people on its own.

Although that line of thinking is a favourite of conspiracy theorists, AI is not taking over the world. On the contrary, it's freeing up people's time so that they could do something more creative, something a machine can't do yet.

However, technology is now part of the mainstream. If it can cross the moats of tradition and invade the last bastion of orthodoxy, the All-England Tennis Club, then, depending on your viewpoint, it's either doomsday, or it firmly establishes technology in the public consciousness. Certainly you can't get more mainstream than Wimbledon highlights on ESPN.

AI is changing your work, your company and the world. In fact, a group of technologies such as Internet of things (IoT), analytics, AI and ML—clustered as 'digital'—is removing obstacles and constraints, and generating thrilling new possibilities that impacts enterprises and consumers in profound ways.

Technology isn't new; the basic building blocks have been in the works for a few decades now. But the acceleration of innovation and the confluence of independent technologies have resulted in remarkable progress that is changing the world in front of our very eyes.

Digital Is Ready for Business, but Are Businesses Ready for Digital?

It's all well and good that we have powerful technology at our command. But will our businesses warm up to the possibilities? Are they ready to forsake traditional processes and embrace digital, given the risks of failure?

Expectations are high. The potential of digital is fairly well understood. Self-driving cars and human-like robots and augmented reality have captured business leaders' attention. However, the fact remains that the history of technology abounds with hype, exaggerated promises and high-profile busts. An enterprise resource planning (ERP) implementation failed spectacularly at Fortune 500 Company Hershey Foods, causing the stock to dip 8 per cent. MillerCoors sued a systems integrator for over $100M for a failed information technology (IT) project. Bridgestone sued a software OEM for a failed technology implementation.

Is it going to be any different with digital? Existing evidence clearly indicates that the answer is yes. Consider the following.

The Benefits of Digital

Real-life business benefits have already been delivered at some of the leading companies of the world. None of the technologies included in the 'digital' bucket is unproven.

In addition, unlike large IT implementations, digital implementations are more amenable to an agile, iterative, minimum viable product (MVP) approach, which enables corporations to scale up only those technologies that work, so the failures, if any, don't impact the organization significantly.

Finally, venture capitalists (VCs) are betting large amounts of funding on digital technologies such as AI and IoT (and the amounts have gone up exponentially between 2013 and 2018), which leads us to believe that the promise of such technologies has been realized to such an extent that VCs view the domain as a safe bet. VCs have been wrong before (anyone remember the dot com bust?) but as we explained earlier, the risks to corporations are smaller.

Consider a couple more examples of how digital (specifically IoT) can change the nature of our personal life and work in the not-too-distant future:

When you enter your hotel room, not only does the TV switch on but also options are provided of your favourite shows (e.g., football or crime drama). This is an example of smart personalization.

Siemens, the German manufacturer that builds heavy equipment for the likes of BMW, has a plant in Germany which is 75 per cent automated, with its 1,150 employees mainly operating computers and monitoring the processes. This has increased efficiency and reduced costs. There's no reason why the number can't go up to 90 per cent or higher.

Why Then Do Digital Transformations Fail?

Fair question. If digital is so full of potential, it must be getting implemented at a fast clip, right?

Wrong. *Forbes* ran a story in 2016 that said 96 per cent of business executives acknowledge that digital transformation (DT) is critical or important. However, a report by *CIO* magazine and Wipro Technologies in 2017 said 50 per cent of digital strategies were failing. A full 20 per cent of US-based senior executives in the study felt DT was a 'waste of time.'

Why is this the case that there's a perception that something is important and yet can't be made to work?

The first reason, we submit, is the gap between strategy and execution. Some of the top management and technology corporations of the world, such as Gartner, McKinsey and Accenture, are adept at formulating world-class digital strategies. However, the practical aspects of executing such strategies are not well understood, documented or available to the executing teams. How do you bridge the gap?

The second reason is a matter of mindset. For example, how do you focus the attention of the CEO and the executive council on DT? How do you overcome their resistance to change? How do you create a consensus on what leadership wants you to do (i.e., the prioritization), and how do you create awareness around how (i.e., people, process and technology) to execute the strategy? How do you in-source the right talent to sustain the digital function long after the transformation phase is done and dusted?

The Recipe Followed by Successful Organizations

Given the challenges, is there hope? Absolutely. There is a recipe.

There are certain characteristics that organizations that have performed successful DTs share. First, the executives in the leadership team have a shared, clear vision that every one of the leaders has bought into. Second, they have a robust prioritization framework that takes the hundreds of ideas around digital innovation and reduces them to a list of about 10 or so priorities that can add the most value in the short run. Third, they invest time and energy into developing an organization with the right kind of talent that sustains the momentum in the long run. Finally, they adopt the best technology practices such as lean, agile and DevOps execution models.

We discuss the practical aspects of each of these factors that are essential to success.

What This Book Will Do for You

The hard question now: why another book on DT? Aren't there 2 million of those out there already?

First, this book is a *story*. You love stories? We do too. In fact, the bigger the mission, the more critical it is for business leaders to be able to tell a story that communicates the message effectively. DT is a mighty important topic indeed (think 10% more sales and 15% higher operational efficiency), and we couldn't think of a method to tell you how to do it in a more fun, more interesting way.

Second, this a *practical playbook,* a leadership guide on how to execute DT. We provide an overview of the technology in a way you'd understand even if you don't have a technical background. We promise we won't talk of gateways and APIs and microservices unless we have to, and even then we'll provide a context and a definition.

We won't bore you with stochastic theories and success quadrants. Instead, we'll provide a step-by-step, simply explained approach of how to start from scratch and execute a DT strategy.

Organization of the Book

Here's how we've organized the book.

Chapters 1–2 introduce Dykstrand, a market-leading manufacturer of shoes that's rapidly expanding a retail segment of its business and is currently evaluating an execution strategy for digital. And we also introduce the hero of our story, Dillon D'Souza, who's facing a major technology crisis. We trace back his roots, his past, his challenges and how, through his trials and tribulations, he has uniquely qualified to take on the role of DT leader.

Chapters 3–5 provide a primer on digital: how technology has evolved over the last few decades; the definition and common understanding of digital; and nature of benefits that you can expect of digital. We include many illustrations of specific benefits from a number of companies in different sectors.

Chapter 6 addresses a central question: if digital is this good, why haven't more Indian companies benefited? The reasons are two-fold. We delve into the two reasons in substantial detail and show how you can avoid the common pitfalls that plague most DT efforts.

Chapters 7–9 describe all the tools you'll need to run the execution of a DT strategy at your organization, presented in the form of a real-life case study drawn from the transformation journey at Dykstrand Corporation.

Chapters 10–12 list the capabilities you need to develop in your team and your organization in order to carry out DT successfully, namely the technology architecture (TA), the agile mindset and the technical skills that you need to build.

Chapter 13 summarizes the learnings and culminates the story of our hero, who moves on to his next challenge. We describe the pitfalls of the digital journey, the key action steps that leaders ought to, and ought not to, perform. We also describe a secret to lasting success.

You've Got Questions? We've Got Answers

Some of the questions that'll be answered in this book are as follows:

1. What do you mean by Industry 4.0? How is it relevant to you?
2. What is digital? How does it relate to IT? How should you view digital versus Industry 4.0 versus AI versus IT?
3. What benefits can you realistically expect from digital?
4. What artefacts are needed to get your budget request approved?
5. How would you persuade your executive leadership to provide you the mandate you need?
6. How would you nail down the technology architecture (TA)?
7. What is the mindset your organization would need to adopt in order to pull off a successful digital transformation (DT)?
8. Is there a culture that's conducive to driving a technology transformation at your company?
9. How would you instil a culture of innovation in your organization?

Why This Style of Writing?

We've addressed this question a little earlier, but it bears further explanation. We've adopted what you may call a 'continuing narrative' style of representing a successful approach to DT. In other words, we've told a story rather than lecturing you. In our interactions with executives at some of the world's largest and most successful companies, we've found that storytelling as a means of instruction works much more effectively than dry presentations, no matter how comprehensive they are.

We have introduced a fictitious $2B company, amalgamated from the many corporations we've been part of or consulted with, that's aggressively positioning technology as the lever that'll help propel it to the $4B level in the next 3 years. We take you through the process as the organization deliberates and picks the top use cases that'll deliver the biggest benefit. We then take you through the 'inside story' of how a budget is drawn up, and resourcing and staffing are figured out.

We then provide examples of the frameworks, flow charts and models that would be required for the DT to be successfully executed. We provide details on the TAs that would be necessary to implement the strategy.

We also address the key issues: the mindset, culture and organizational set-up that would not only ensure a successful execution of the transformation but also enable the organization to sustain digital for the long term, ensuring that new technologies would be adopted and internalized, and enhancements would continue to be delivered in order to keep the company up to date with technological upgrade for years to come.

Who Are We? Why Should You Heed What We Have to Say?

We have a combined 40 years of technology experience and a 12 years of DT experience at some of the world's largest and most successful companies. More importantly, we have real-life, practical experience of execution on the ground.

While most, if not all, books on DT focus on broad digital strategy and benefits, this is the only book that provides step-by-step directions on how to go from strategy to execution, from ideation to full-scale roll-out. This includes how to craft request for quotes (RFQs) and internal notes for financial approval, work out a scope definition document (or statement of work [SOW]) and formulate other practical artefacts that are required to execute a strategy on the ground.

For example, at one of the companies where we worked, digital project proposals needed to have an essential component in order to be approved. At another, digital and IT organizations had to be structured in a certain way for collaboration to occur and execution to accelerate. What we've done in this book is to abstract some of our learning and provide you with a framework, and the constructs of the actual artefacts, that will expedite your own execution of the digital strategy.

All Right Then, Shall We Get on with It?

If there were one overreaching conclusion from this work, it will be: you ain't seen nothin' yet. By 2030, workers would be using augmented reality technologies to perform repairs in minutes rather than hours; virtual assistants with human cognitive abilities would free up humans to perform highly creative and impactful work; dashboards based on deep analytical capabilities would equip leaders to make real-time decisions on the fly rather than wait for monthly MIS meetings; and the world would be 'one'—as in, one interconnected entity made up of personal and industrial devices that will be designed to work together coherently to simplify our lives and businesses.

Becoming a digital trailblazer isn't easy, but there's never been a better time to get started.

Are you ready?

1

There's No Such Thing as One Crisis

The Cyberattack

'You're dead!' said the e-mail, simply. Dillon grimaced and turned around to pick up the coffee mug, but noticed it was empty. His head was buzzing, probably a natural reaction to three cups of coffee in a little under two hours. His desk was a mess. Crumpled paper lay all around; coffee cups were strewn.

Dillon buried his face in his hands. *Steady now,* he thought. He was in his late 30s but retained boyish looks—tall, short cropped hair greying on the sides, good-looking. The 'boy sage,' as his boss in California used to call him. He exercised daily, ate well—mostly—and got in his seven hours of sleep—on good days, and was a more than useful tennis player.

The tennis skills, the good looks and the large ears—especially the large, protruding ears—were what were distinct about Dillon. 'I've been made by nature to be a good listener,' he often joked about his ears.

He turned around to stare at the monitor. The e-mailer, known by his online handle 'Str4X,' had sent four e-mail messages in the last hour, each shorter than the one before. The last one, *You're dead,* had chilled him.

The day had started real early, at 2:38 a.m. Dillon remembered the time because he wasn't initially sure if it was 8:32, which would've made it very late, or really 2:38, which would make it crazy.

Turned out, it *was* crazy. The call was from Ankit, the senior cyber security professional on Dillon's team. 'Sorry, Dillon, there's been a situation,' he said. Groggy, Dillon sat up on his bed. His wife, Kavya, lay fast asleep next to him.

'What's it, Ankit? You know what time it is?' said Dillon softly as he got up, trying not to wake up Kavya.

'Sorry, Dillon. Sapna and I have been on this for the last couple of hours. Look, our customer database is gone!'

'What do you mean, gone?'

'Really .... someone's hacked into our system. It's bad. As I said, Sapna and I have been here since midnight. I'm mobilizing the entire security team. Sorry to ask, but can you make it here—like, now?'

'OK, alright, I'll come right over.' The sleepiness was gone. Cold water in your face in the middle of the night does the trick.

Dillon zoomed to his office in his car, his mind racing even faster. *Ankit had been telling me the team was noticing odd network behaviour for the last few days. It wasn't your regular malware. What was the term he used? Yes—it was advanced persistent threat or APT.*

'What is it, Ankit?' he asked, as he strode into the situation room, a biggish conference room on the fourth floor.

'Dillon, we're still figuring out. Orders aren't coming through. We've lost a lot of data. We were able to establish contact with the lead hacker.'

'Contact with the lead hacker? Aren't these villains supposed to just go away?'

'Not at all, Dillon. This attack seems to be a backdoor Trojan. The bad guys won't leave because once they own the system, there's only so much we can do.'

'All right, tell me more.'

'There seems to be a group behind this. The leader, who goes by "Str4X", reached out to me. I've received two e-mails from him, which I've already forwarded to you. Take a look.'

Dillon frowned as he read the first one: 'Hi, we have taken over your entire computer system. You can't access anything. Not your employee information, your orders or customer database. Nothing. Wait for further info.'

The second laid out the demand: 'You need to pay $2M in bitcoins. If you comply, we'll decrypt your encrypted files in minutes. Confirm how soon you can pay.'

'Should we respond?' asked Dillon. 'Not unless we want to pay,' replied Ankit. 'No, we aren't paying,' said Dillon. *We can't be paying,* he thought. *Heck, we don't even know how to pay using bitcoins! There's got to be a way.*

The third e-mail came before long: 'Not waiting around much longer. You need to tell us NOW if you'll pay. Reply within 10 minutes.'

And then a fourth, ominous one, after just seven minutes: 'You're dead!'

That was more than three hours ago. Now his cyber security team had stepped out after almost six hours of non-stop work. Ankit for his smoke, the rest of the gang for a cup of coffee. Dillon glanced at his watch. It was 6:43 a.m. *This has been one heck of a day,* he thought. The CEO goes in front of analysts in about two hours' time, and he doesn't yet know. Customers can't place orders! At some point in the next hour, I need to call him.

Damn! Dillon's head reeled. *How did I get here?*

His mind wandered to the lovely day in July when he was sitting in the CEO's office. It seemed as though it was a lifetime ago.

Welcoming the New Chief Digital Officer

Dillon had just reported for work at Dykstrand India, the Indian subsidiary of the $10B/year global footwear brand, Dykstrand Inc. The company, founded in 1947 in Budapest by Tadeo Kovács after the conclusion of the Second World War, and best known for its spiked running shoes, enjoyed its heyday in the 1990s with diversification into ski wear and women's yoga apparel. However, since the death of the founder's son, Thomas, in 2006, the company had fallen into years of stagnation and legal issues.

The Indian unit, started in 2008, was now mature and ready to take off. With a burgeoning middle class armed with spending power, India presented a bright spot in the company's fortunes.

The country headquarters were a rather sprawling facility at Siruseri, about 150 km south of Chennai, on the south-eastern periphery of India. The town, situated on the coast, but located in the centre of India's vast rain-sparse region, witnessed a boom after Dykstrand India set up a modern manufacturing plant in the late 2000s. It currently employed 1,300 people, with over 5,500 contract workers on its rolls.

Dillon made his way to the administrative building, located adjacent to the manufacturing unit.

'Welcome, Sir,' said the CEO's secretary, Aditi, shaking Dillon by the hand. After a few words had been exchanged, Aditi remarked, 'Your pronunciation is decidedly American! Did you live in the USA for a long time?' 'Well,' replied Dillon, 'In fact I did. I was born in Goa, but my family immigrated to the USA when I was 9. I grew up in Los Angeles. I lived in the USA for almost three decades. Hence the American accent, but I promise I'll reform!' They both laughed.

'Where did you go to college?' asked Aditi.

'The University of California at Berkeley. Played competitive tennis there. Fell in love with sports—especially American football and basketball. Then I worked for a top-4 consulting company in Boston for two years. Then—you probably know this—I joined Dykstrand's US offices in San Jose, California, and worked there for 11 years.'

'With distinction, I may add,' said Aditi. 'Your welcome e-mail said you were the youngest manager ever in that office, at 25.' Dillon smiled, blushing, not entirely without a sense of satisfaction at having risen to the level of head of operations—assistant to the chief operating officer—at the California plant, at age 32.

'You have your family with you?' asked Aditi.

'Yes, they have moved in with me. My wife, Kavya, is a former teacher—she taught in San Francisco for four years. We have a son, 9, a loving, bright kid—and our one major concern.'

'Why do you say that?' asked Aditi, puzzled.

'Well,' responded, 'he's a special needs child. We just don't know if there are any schools in Siruseri that can accommodate him. He needs an encouraging, supportive environment.'

Aditi was about to say something, but the CEO stepped out of his office and, broadly grinning and holding his hand out, welcomed Dillon into his office.

Meeting the CEO

Mr Eknath Iyer, the CEO, was a grizzled veteran of the manufacturing industry. At 57, he stood erect and tall, with a thick shock of salt-and-pepper hair, mostly pepper. His office, elegantly decorated, gave the impression of informality, which wasn't surprising since the CEO was a modest, soft-spoken man. When Dillon addressed him as Mr Iyer, he immediately corrected him, 'I prefer to be simply called Eknath.' He was well respected within the Indian apparel and footwear industry, having won a handful of technical and leadership awards over the years. His papers on the utilization of by-products in the apparel industry were cited by industry experts and academicians alike, culminating in the R&H Lifetime Apparel Leader award in 2015.

'Welcome, Dillon. We can't wait to get started on our digital journey!' said Eknath.

'Thank you, Eknath,' responded Dillon. 'I must say it was a pleasant surprise to be tapped as the digital leader at this factory, and a thrill to be able to hold a C-level position while still fairly young,' he added, smiling.

'Quite so. Speaking of hiring, what was your overall impression of our interview process? Did you get the feeling we were overly in a hurry?' asked Eknath.

'Probably so,' replied Dillon, 'in fact, I remember remarking to my wife that the whole process—from beginning to end—hardly took three weeks.'

'I'll share with you this, in the spirit of transparency,' said Eknath. 'While we were looking to hire a DT leader in the next 6–12 months, the immediate trigger for the hiring was that a critical manufacturing equipment, the upper preparation and stitching machine, went down for 25 days, causing a $200M revenue loss.

'Now, production problems are always going to be there. But this one hit us hard because a major customer cancelled its order. We'd been talking about using digital to predict and prevent equipment downtime, but we were slow to get moving. It hurt.

'As a result, rather than embarking on a prolonged external hiring process, we quickly interviewed three young up-and-coming executives, all insiders. And we tapped you to take on the newly created chief digital officer (CDO) role, banking on your technology business savvies. A sound digital strategy is now not anymore a good-to-have. We must get rolling.'

'I guess we can agree that I was at the right place at the right time, Eknath!' said Dillon, smiling.

The conversation then shifted to how Dillon was settling down in Siruseri, how he felt about moving to India, especially to a much smaller city.

'I'm looking forward to life in this town, just as I am excited about starting a new phase of my career as a digital leader,' Dillon asserted. 'The Bay Area was a great place to live in. It was arguably the place where the best and brightest minds of our generation congregated, owing to a number of reasons.

'Having said that, I'm more excited about settling into the peace and quietude of a small town. My family felt we didn't want to live in a major metropolitan area where the overcrowding and lengthy work commute could be major burdens.'

Dillon Takes Charge of IT

'Makes sense. Look, we're extremely bullish about digital and about you,' replied the CEO, 'and don't let the peace of this little town lull you into believing we're laid-back! Quite the contrary, we want to accomplish a lot and we're in a hurry. Well… you just joined today and will need to undergo your orientation and other formalities, but I must tell you about an unfortunate situation. Our CIO just left a couple of weeks ago due to personal reasons.'

Dillon listened intently.

'As good as he was,' the CEO continued, 'I believe our IT team had fallen into a bit of a rut for some time now. Now, it's not broken, but I don't think the IT team has really kept up with new-age technologies. I mean, ERP was the last big thing. So I'll tell you what: with you on the leadership team, we're not in a rush to hire a new CIO.'

Am I being also asked to handle IT? Dillon thought. *In fact, the reason I took up the CDO role was because I was hoping to have a CIO to lean on, someone to handle the IT headache while I worked on the cool stuff!*

'Now,' continued the CEO, 'IT is an area that requires stronger leadership. It's the Board's desire that you also take up the responsibility of the IT organization, at least for now, and we'll evaluate after six months.'

Dillon nodded unsurely.

'You see, Dillon, while we're excited about the upcoming DT, we believe we also need our IT strategy to be robust. IT is the foundation and digital is the fancy stuff on the third floor.'

'Of course,' Dillon said. Doubts streamed into his head: the move to India, to Siruseri, to a brand new role. *Can I handle Digital and IT?* He wondered. In a moment, however, the clouds of confusion drifted away, and he found himself regaining his composure.

'Absolutely Eknath,' Dillon said. He surprised himself with the level of confidence his voice projected. 'With your support, I'll accelerate the transformation of this business, specifically of the processes, competencies and even the business model, by leveraging technology.'

'You bet!' said the CEO. A call came in, and he excused himself. He then turned to the new CDO. 'Dillon, it so happens that our monthly management review meeting is scheduled to start at 11. Would you mind joining us? I'd like to introduce you to the rest of the leadership team.'

'Sure, I'd love to get started on my journey here, sir.'

Getting Acquainted with Senior Leadership

A short time later, Dillon was ushered into a roomful of senior leaders. It was a long board room, with exquisite detailing on the wood panels covering the walls end to end. The chairs were leather-upholstered. Wall-grazing fixtures provided a rich texture of stone, and display lights provided a rich highlight to beautiful artwork on the walls.

The first one to get up from his seat was a tall man in his early 50s. 'Hi Dillon, great to meet you face to face, finally! We're very glad you've joined us.' Then, noticing a little hesitation from the new leader: 'You remember me, of course, from our video call?' he asked.

Looks familiar, Dillon thought. *Of course, he's the HR head!*

'Hari?' he said, somewhat unsurely. *Must get better with names!*

'That's right, Dillon.' The HR head looked pleased. 'Welcome aboard and all the very best! I'd like to wish you, on behalf of the entire leadership team, a long and successful tenure with us.'

Hari was tall, thin and light-complexioned, with a broad smile. Dillon noted the similarity of his features with the British comic actor Mr Beans and chuckled to himself.

Seated next to Hari was a diminutive, attractive woman in her mid-to-late 30s, smiling mildly but making no attempt to get up or greet the newcomer. Hari stepped in to introduce her: 'Dillon, meet Falguni, our CFO. Be sure to keep her in good humour, or else your budget requests aren't going to fly!' He laughed heartily.

Dillon smiled and extended his hand. Falguni shook it weakly. *Not too excited to see me,* Dillon thought. *Not friendly in the least.*

Next to Falguni sat a stout man with a friendly, kind expression. He was almost completely bald, but looked sharp and dapper. He got up and shook hands warmly. 'Hi, I'm Prabhat, head of strategic projects. Welcome to Dykstrand!'

'Glad to meet you,' said Dillon. *Nice handshake,* he thought. *Confident man.*

Seated at the end of the table, chatting with another man, was a man in his early 40s, somewhat portly built, medium complexion, with a big moustache. Hari introduced him as Om, the COO. Om didn't look entirely happy. In place of a smile, he wore an expression that could be classified as half-bemused.

'It's good for you to fly in all the way from America to save us!' he said. Dillon smiled and shook his hand warmly. Om's expression didn't change. He quickly sat down at the table and went back to a conversation with another person, presumably a leader on his team.

Dillon observed this person—the one Om was speaking to—closely. He was listening intently, nodding and sometimes getting in a word or two. It wasn't as much what he was saying as it was Om's response to what he was saying that made Dillon take notice. Whenever he spoke—slowly and with emphasis—Om listened with respect and complete attention. Dillon wondered who this man was.

Presently, the management review meeting began. The CEO spoke first. Looking at Dillon, he said: 'It's with great anticipation that we welcome a new officer to our leadership team. He's Dillon D'Souza, our new CDO. By now, most of you have already greeted him. The rest of you please do take a moment to say hello to him afterwards. He's new to the town, and indeed to the country, but an old hand at Dykstrand.'

Dillon smiled and turned his head to glance at the entire table.

Operational Review

'Now, let's start with an operational review of last month. Srini, can you take the lead?'

It was the very same person Om had been speaking with. Srini was in his mid-40s, with aquiline features, large teeth, a kind expression and a generous-sized moustache. Every once in a while, he'd break out into a toothy smile.

But, as he began to speak, Dillon noticed he spoke sparingly, with calmness and assuredness, and got everyone to pay attention. *I need to know this person,* Dillon said to himself.

'Last month, our cost of production went up marginally, and here're the two reasons why,' said Srini.

The meeting followed a round robin format, with everyone providing a summarized review of the operations of the prior month. Most leaders had their top assistants in the room, seated on a second row of chairs behind the leaders at the table.

After the meeting was over, Dillon smiled at the others and lingered on in the room for a few minutes, chatting.

Presently, Srini walked over and extended his hands and a big smile. Dillon shook hands with him.

'Srini, impressive presentation. Glad to make your acquaintance,' he said.

'Mr Dillon, the honour is mine,' responded Srini. 'Out of all the places in the world, you chose to come to Siruseri. I appreciate that.'

'Thank you,' said Dillon.

'As a mechanical engineer, I always dreamt of going to UC Berkeley. You've done something what most Indians can dream of. I admire that,' Srini said.

Dillon was about to ask Srini how he knew that, when he realized the welcome e-mail had already gone out. He was nevertheless glad that Srini had taken the time to notice.

'Do let's catch up soon,' Dillon said. 'I need to understand a little more about living and working in Siruseri. I need an experienced hand to guide me. How long have you worked here, Srini?' asked Dillon as they began walking out of the room.

'Oh, 21 years,' responded Srini.

Twenty-one? thought Dillon. *How does anyone stay in one company for that long? Can I stay here for more than four or five years?*

'You see, Dillon, I started out in this company as a clerk, following in the footsteps of my father, who worked here as a maintenance worker. I was able to finish my education on the side, taking night classes, got married, started a family and here I am, 21 years later.'

'Incredible, Srini. It's been a pleasure to have met you!'

Back to the Present—The Cyberattack

'Dillon, we've identified the problem!' The words were uttered with excitement, accompanied by fist pumps.

Dillon came back to reality, with a start. 'I was just ... just lost in thoughts,' he responded, somewhat sheepishly. *Gosh, I hope I didn't doze off into sleep!* He muttered to himself.

It was Ankit, holding a few scribbled notes on a sheet of paper.

'We found a backdoor Trojan installed on about 12 computers on our system, and ransomware on two computers. It's the Kraken kind. We've isolated those computers and will take steps to eradicate the root cause.'

'How long will that take?'

'About six hours to fix the machines and get them reconnected to the network.'

'And the system to come back up?'

'Another two hours, so that's about eight hours from now. Is there a way you can speed it up?'

'Dillon, we need to physically copy from a backup. You know it's 3TB worth of systems data. Two hours is an optimistic estimate.'

'All right, Ankit, can you ask Sapna and team to start the containment and eradication process?' asked Dillon. 'They're already on it, Dillon,' responded Ankit.

'Any data lost?'

'Well, very little. As I said, we're going to rewrite production data from our backup system. Unfortunately, the jobs that were running—we'll have some partial updates to the database from those. However, considering it was Sunday night, the ordering activity was minimal, and I believe we'll not have any significant loss of data.'

'But there'd be some data loss, won't there?' asked Dillon, preparing to answer the inevitable questions from senior management.

'Probably not. But that's my best guess at the moment; I can only confirm in about two hours,' replied Ankit.

Dealing with the Aftermath

'All right,' said Dillon. 'Everyone, listen up!' he motioned with his hands for everyone to gather in the centre of the room.

'Team, we've just made a breakthrough, having identified the root cause. What I'd like Ankit to do is to lay out the exact steps for recovery of the data and ensure that the steps are meticulously followed and completed as soon as possible. In the meantime, I'm going to prepare the communication plan for updating our external stakeholders.

'Thanks, everyone. Let's get back to our seats! As the next step, I'm going to call the CEO. I'll just need Tarun to come sit with me until I figure out the communication bit.'

He'd barely finished before the phone rang. It was from the CEO's office.

'Dillon, where are you? The CEO has been receiving frantic calls from marketing folks since early morning!' said Aditi, the CEO's secretary. She spoke rapidly, clearly betraying a sense of panic.

'Aditi, good morning. I did try the CEO's number a couple of times, but it was unreachable.'

'He's in Mumbai, getting ready to meet the analysts. He must have been in the elevator or something. Hang on, I'll connect you now.'

Breaking the Bad News to the CEO

'Dillon, what's going on?' asked the CEO, sounding anxious. 'I'm going to take the analysts' call in about 30 minutes. I need to understand what the hell happened, and quick.'

'Sure Eknath. The team has been in the office since midnight, I've been here since 2:30 a.m., and we've got the situation under control.

'Here's a summary for you: we had an intrusion into our sales and customer relationship management software systems early today, around midnight to be precise. It's taken us about seven hours to perform the first two remedial steps, identification and containment. It's going to take us another eight hours to eradicate the issue and complete the recovery process.'

'That's—what—15 hours of customers not being able to place orders? You know what that does to our stock? On the day of the quarterly analyst call?'

'Eknath, I realize the timing could not have been worse. But we've been able to retrieve all our data. You'll be glad to know that we've thwarted a very sophisticated attack on our computer systems, and we haven't compromised any customer or financial information. Data leakage or loss would have had us run afoul of data protection laws, but I'm glad to report that that didn't occur.'

'All right. Here's what I need you to do. Send me a summary—no more than five talking points—and let's reconnect early this afternoon. In the meantime, I'm going to come up with some excuse and delay the analysts' call to 9:30.'

'Sure, Eknath, I'm on it.'

'Dillon, just one more thing—call Falguni and let her know. The analysts will want to know the financial impact. By 10 a.m., I may need to take Falguni on the call and have her address the revenue impact.'

Which Fire to Put Out First?

Thirty minutes later, Dillon was on his way back home, after having called the CFO and e-mailed the note to the CEO. He called his home number from the car.

'Honey, did Aaron leave for school already?'

'Yes, he did. Where on earth are you?' Kavya sounded irritated. *That's reasonable,* Dillon thought. *Who steps out of the house at 2:30 a.m.?*

'It's a long story. You know, we've had a cyber security incident!'

'What?'

'Someone broke into our computer system. I had to leave home just before 2:30 this morning. Didn't want to wake you up.'

'OK, I've got to deal with the servant now. She's waiting for instructions. Let's talk when you're back.'

Dillon reached home in about 20 minutes.

Kavya, who was busy in the kitchen with the maid, ignored him.

Nothing's changed, sighed Dillon. *She's indifferent—as usual—even though I had to leave at 2:30 a.m. and we're facing a crisis at work.*

'Serve breakfast?' asked Kavya, after a few minutes.

'Yes,' responded Dillon. 'And a cup of coffee, please. Make it in 40 minutes or so. I'll take a quick shower and a nap first, and then eat.'

'Nap?' Kavya sounded surprised. 'You said you went at 2 or something. Shouldn't you take the day off?'

'No, dear—we're facing a massive problem at work. All hands to the deck. I need to get back right away.'

'You should know Aaron's teacher called. She said Aaron again fought at school.'

'That's terrible, dear. Can you deal with that today? We'll discuss in the evening.'

'So your work is priority #1, is it? I guess I know the answer to my question, but you need to recognize when there are urgent issues with the family. I never get any support from my own husband!' Kavya looked away; looked like she was ready to sob.

Dillon was about to hug Kavya, but stopped. *She needs to understand this isn't the time to be emotional!* 'Dear, please try to understand. I've first got to put out this fire at work. We'll discuss in the evening, I promise.'

Containing the Fallout at Work

An hour and a half later, Dillon was back in the office.

Aditi knocked on the door. 'Dillon, CEO has fixed a meeting at 12:00 noon on the cyber issue.'

'Okay, Aditi. Please do me a favour. Also invite Ankit and Sapna as well. I'll need them in the room to reassure senior management, in case there are technical questions.'

'All right.'

Soon, the meeting began.

The CEO spoke first. 'Dillon, Avik Banerjee from Jefferies said he's going to recommend a downgrade to the stock. Analysts were very concerned, and if I were in their position, I'd be concerned too.'

'But sir, that isn't just about today's incident. Isn't it that we also reported a flat quarterly revenue?' interjected Prabhat, the head of projects. 'I'd say there'd be an adverse reaction on the call today even if the cyber security incident hadn't happened.'

'Right, but I think the incident psyched out the analysts. The timing couldn't have been worse,' said Om. 'I think our new technology leader should offer an explanation.'

'Om, I'll respond to you in a second,' responded Dillon. 'First, to the CEO's point—I share your concern, Eknath. Regardless of our other challenges, our technology infrastructure shouldn't even be an issue on the table.

Summarizing for Senior Leadership

'Coming to Om's point, here is what we know about the incident. There was an attack on our network late last night. The identification, containment, eradication and recovery processes were performed reasonably quickly. What I need to understand is how well prepared we are, and how we ensure this doesn't happen again.'

'Based on the evidence, I'd say we're not well prepared,' quipped Om.

'Let the team explain, Om,' directed the CEO. 'Finger pointing can wait.'

'Sir, we recovered fast,' said Ankit. 'We discovered the issue around midnight and quickly estimated the impact, the scope of the compromise and the effect on operations.'

'I understand orders were not getting processed for over 12 hours?' asked Om.

'That's right,' replied Dillon. 'We may have dodged a bullet because it was Sunday night, but I have a bigger concern.'

'What's that?' asked Falguni.

'That this may have just been a dress rehearsal. The real one—the *big* one—won't likely be on a weekend, I can tell you that,' said Dillon.

'We need reassurance, Dillon,' said the CEO. 'The way you're putting it won't make us or the investors very confident.'

'Absolutely, Eknath,' responded Dillon. 'I believe we'll need to buy the protection of a cyber insurance policy. But, to be realistic about the level of our preparedness, we'll review our security infrastructure, focusing mainly on whether as a company, we're prepared to deal with incidents such as these. Can we put a report out in the next three days, Ankit?'

'Yes, Dillon,' replied Ankit. 'Our primary focus today and tomorrow would be to ensure operations are back on track, but I'll put my team on the job.'

'Great, thanks! Any other questions, before I let my team go?' asked Dillon.

'Yeah—I hope the result of this review won't be a new budget request. I can tell you right now: we're spending way too much on IT already,' said Falguni.

'IT security, to me, is non-negotiable,' asserted Dillon. 'Let's say you buy an automobile. Would you put the insurance payment under "let's not buy it because we spent too much already" bucket?'

'I may,' retorted the CEO, 'especially after an accident has already occurred.'

'Point made,' responded Dillon. 'First let's review where we are, and if it turns out we need to buy something, I guess we'll have to. If a next attack happens, what I'll ensure from our side is that we're fully prepared.'

Dillon paused and corrected himself. 'Sorry, not if—but *when* the next attack happens.'

2

Tiny Steps towards Progress

Even the Manager Needs a Heart-to-Heart

'The biggest challenge, I'd submit, is not professional. It rarely is.'

Dillon was spending the late afternoon of his third day at Dykstrand, in the company of Srini, the senior operations leader. They'd finished discussing an operational issue with an equipment, on which Srini sought out the help of Dillon, who was an operations expert with deep expertise. Afterwards, Srini suggested they grab a cup of coffee and Dillon readily accepted.

'By the way, how're things at home? Have your wife and son settled?' enquired Srini.

'Well, things could be better,' responded Dillon. 'The truth is, things are quite complicated.' *In fact, they're a mess, and I'm not a happy camper at home,* Dillon thought. *Should I share?*

'Well, tell me about it. You may not know this, but I'm a certified counsellor. So I can handle it. Besides, I always like to be of help if possible,' said Srini.

'Well,' said Dillon, unsure of how to begin. Then he hesitated.

'There's no shame in sharing, Dillon. Remember you're talking to a counsellor,' said Srini.

'I appreciate that Srini,' responded Dillon. 'Out of all the senior managers on the leadership team, you may be the one who's most eminently qualified to listen to my rant. During my first week here, I've consistently observed you as calm and kind.'

'Thanks,' responded Srini. 'I appreciate how hard it is for most CxOs to handle their personal and professional lives, how they need to be playing multiple roles, almost juggling different personas, if you will.'

'Now, tell me about your situation.'

'Thanks, Srini. I would *indeed* like to seek your advice on a huge personal challenge.'

'Which is?'

'My marriage. It's been challenging for a few years now. In fact, I don't mind admitting it's more than challenging; it's on the rocks.'

Personal Issues Matter

'Please elaborate, if you don't mind. How was it to start with? What happened?'

'My wife's name is Kavya. She's in her mid-30s; attractive, a highly educated professional. We met almost 11 years ago at an event organized by our common friends. It wasn't quite love at first sight; in fact, we resented each other at our very first meeting. Over the little things, you know. She hated the fact that I was a smoker—I took two smoking breaks in the one hour we talked—and I resented the fact that she was a conservative type, a girl who had inhibitions about interacting freely with men. I wanted my girl to be a free soul, someone who was comfortable with men and women alike.

'They say opposites attract, so we became close. We saw each other regularly for about two months, and then informed our families. My family was OK with my choice, but Kavya's family was somewhat concerned because I smoked and drank. And because my family was from Goa, whereas her family was from Maharashtra.

'Eventually, however, her family came around and accepted me. We waited for almost nine months as Kavya wrapped up her PhD from Santa Clara University—she was training to be a university teacher—and I wrapped up my stay in Boston and relocated to the San Francisco Bay Area to be close to her.

'Things happened quickly from then on. We saw each other daily. By then, we'd saved up enough money to arrange a grand wedding in India. We travelled together to India during a Christmas break, got married and returned to the USA just after New Year's Day.

'We settled into the most blissful phase of our relationship. I started working at Dykstrand, and Kavya took up a job as an assistant professor at San Jose State University. We lived in Mountain View, our commutes were short and we were saving a ton of money. We hung out with friends on weekends and sometimes hiked and trekked in the northern California wilderness.

'After two years, our son, Aaron, was born. He was really a cherub, the loveliest addition to my family. Kavya took a year off from work to settle down into the new life of a mother; she did a fantastic job of adjusting to her new lifestyle.

'Meanwhile, I got promoted to the role of manager. I got a big pay raise; although the work hours went up significantly, I also relished the challenge. I had to lay off senior employees as a new manager, which was a very hard thing for me to do. I saw people older than myself cry, which was hard. Here I was, a new manager, letting long timers go, folks who had a family to feed.

'However, as a family, we couldn't be happier. And then ...'

Dillon paused.

'Dark clouds appeared on the horizon?' asked Srini.

'Well, yes. There were two big dark clouds,' responded Dillon, picking his words carefully.

'My son's medical situation came first, which was the first dark cloud, leading to a personal lapse on my part, which was the second. Let me elaborate.

'When Aaron turned a year and half old—no, I take that back—he must have been around two when we noticed the symptoms. He behaved oddly, but we weren't worried initially.

'Aaron won't make eye contact with us. He would smile and, in general, appear to be a perfectly happy child, but he won't look us in the eye. He'd also appear socially awkward. Although kids only develop social skills after they're older, Aaron's reactions and responses were what you may term as odd. For example, one time, I scolded him for some reason. Suddenly he broke into laughter and ran around the house.

'It was as though he was missing the social cues that are obvious to most kids. If I was scowling or frowning, he wasn't able to tell I was angry.

'As he became a little older and began to speak, he spoke in a flat, robotic way. We began to get alarmed enough to take Aaron to see a developmental paediatrician—the kind of doctor who specializes in developmental problems in children.

'Her diagnosis? Aaron had a mild-to-medium case of Asperger syndrome, a kind of autism. While it wasn't going to prevent our child from leading a normal life, it meant that my wife and I had to spend a considerable amount of time helping him with social skills training, speech language therapy, behavioural therapy and other types of specialized training.

'I was quite stunned at the diagnosis and went through a phase of turmoil. First came the denial: *the doctor must be wrong! There was nothing wrong with our cherubic child,* etc. And then came the anger and the self-pity: *why did it have to be us, why did I have to go through this,* etc. For some time, I went through these complex emotions and it gradually began to affect my work and my peace of mind.

'I'd be at work, in a meeting, and suddenly lose track of the conversation. It was as though a thread of thought was always working in the inner recesses of my mind, reminding me of our poor son. A couple of times my boss sent me home early. I was consumed with thoughts of how life was going to be different for us.

'Kavya's reaction to the situation was almost completely opposite to mine. From the beginning, her perspective was centred on our child: what does he need? What do we need to do for him? How do we need to change our routines to make it work for him? etc.'

'If you don't mind me saying this,' interjected Srini, 'your wife handled the situation quite maturely, probably a lot better emotionally than you did.'

'I realize it now, having the wisdom of hindsight, but at the time, it infuriated me.'

'Why so?'

'Well, Kavya was always a devoted wife and daughter. Now she became a completely devoted mother, and I, in my immaturity, thought her affections were exclusively for Aaron.

'Whereas I could understand, at a certain level, that Aaron was our top priority, I resented that my wife didn't have *any* time for me anymore. It was silly of me, of course. I was being completely self-centred, while my wife was setting an example of unselfishness right in front of my eyes.

'I began spending more and more time at work. I didn't have to look for excuses—at the time we were expanding our production capacity. But I began staying longer even when there was no need. It was almost as though I didn't want to return home.

'That's when I met Krissy.'

'Krissy?'

'Yes, a young MBA on the finance team. She may have been 22, 23, I have no idea. She was assigned to a project that I led, a task force on operational excellence that was mandated to spot inefficiencies and hidden value within the existing organization,' said Dillon.

'So technically she wasn't your direct report?' asked Srini.

'No, she wasn't. The thing about Krissy was she had an infectious zeal for life. She was fun-loving and interested in what I had to say—precisely those things I badly wanted from my wife. If she was a direct report, I know it would have been wrong for me to date her—the employee manual expressly forbade that—but she wasn't, which is why I didn't think it was wrong.'

'Professionally, perhaps, but certainly so from the moral angle?' asked Srini.

'Absolutely,' replied Dillon. 'But I wasn't thinking straight. When under stress, humans engage in self-destructive behaviour, and there I was, a prime exhibit. I began spending more and more time with Krissy. She was aware I was married, but either didn't care or couldn't help it because she'd gone through a breakup of her own. I guess I was the "rebound boyfriend" for her.

'Well, one thing led to another and we ended up having a torrid affair.'

'Did you tell your wife?' asked Srini.

'No, I wasn't in a state of mind to confide in her. Moreover, it got over in a matter of weeks; I ended the relationship. She had to move on to a different role that required her to move to Oklahoma, far from California. In a selfish way, I was relieved. I was beginning to realize my mistake, and having her move out was a convenient time for me to bid goodbye to the relationship.

'Except that there was a problem. Krissy had written me a loving goodbye note—sentimental, long, and very detailed: how we'd met, how she felt, what we'd told each other, etc. It was precisely the kind of note you don't want your spouse to see: the musings of a young woman in love. Sentiments don't last, but the memories can last a long time, if a careful and accurate journal is maintained.

'I should have shredded the note and thrown it away in the office. But I couldn't bring myself to do it. How could I destroy a note that was part of my history—however misguided—part of *me*? Long story short, my wife found the note in my shirt pocket one evening as she was preparing clothes for laundry.

Even the Best among Us Falls Apart

'Kavya took this very hard. That's one surprising change that I'd noticed in her lately. After our son was born, Kavya had become more impulsive, emotional, moody.'

'Modern science doesn't find that surprising,' said Srini. 'Research has shown that during pregnancy women's brains undergo significant remodelling that can last for years after childbirth.'

'Well, science and research were farthest from my mind that evening when Kavya confronted me. I'd never seen her that so angry, so *hurt*.

'"How're you going to manage without your darling Krissy?" she demanded. I stammered out some response, which I frankly don't recall, but she insisted upon the truth.

'"Well," I said, "she was a colleague. I didn't particularly have a close relationship with...." Kavya interrupted me. "How much closer could you have gotten? You slept with her!"

'"Kavya dear, I love you...."

'"Don't—don't. Just *stop!*" she screamed. With that, she stormed into the bedroom and closed the door behind her.

'That was almost seven years ago. We're still married, but there's been a sense of emptiness ever since. To add to the injury, every now and then Kavya would accuse me of not being a good father to Aaron.'

'Any specific reasons that your wife has alluded to?' asked Srini.

'She said I'm not mentally present when I'm home. That I kept bringing work home, I took too many calls at home, etc.,' replied Dillon.

'Was that true?'

'Well, yes. It was true for about two years after the Krissy affair, but I changed. Slowly but surely, I developed better work habits. I made it a point to be "in the moment" while at home. I attended events at Aaron's school. We spent time together on weekends—father and son time.

'Despite all that, I don't think Kavya ever forgave me. Many times we'd be sharing a tender moment, and all of a sudden, a change would come over her. She'd withdraw physically, as though touching me reminded her of my indiscretion. Of course, I was remorseful, but there was nothing I could do to change the past.

'Now we share a hollow relationship. Don't get me wrong—we live together, but I can't help feeling we're together simply for the sake of Aaron. We go places, visit our parents' homes, celebrate family dates, but there's a sense of aloofness. She cares for me, but in a mechanical sort of way.'

'All right, Dillon,' said Srini. 'Let me chew on this a little. I think you've gone through a lot, but the fact that you're still together tells me there's hope. Marriage is like a dance. Even if you don't know initially how to dance, you can learn the steps and become an effective dancer—if you have the desire and keep working at it.'

'I realize that, but I wish I knew how to ....' Dillon trailed off. He gazed down, lost in thoughts.

Srini put his hand on Dillon's shoulder.

'Even the best among us slips when under great stress. Now we are defined by our choices, and you made a terrible choice. But, based on what you've told me, I think you've paid the price for it. Your wife, on the other hand, has many admirable qualities. I have no doubt in my mind you two can get back into this together. Just give me some time to think.'

'I can't thank you enough, Srini,' Dillon said with genuine gratitude. Even though Srini hadn't provided a solution, it felt like a big load had been lifted off Dillon's shoulders. *Venting really works,* thought Dillon. *Maybe Srini is that confidante that I've needed all these years.*

'Of course. In the meantime, don't forget we have a very important meeting tomorrow morning,' Srini said, with a wink.

The Management Review Reveals Trouble

'Of course,' responded Dillon. 'The business diagnostic session, as the CEO termed it. What exactly is this all about?'

'Well, every quarter, after the analysts' call and the quarterly reports, we review our numbers. The CFO leads the discussion. We review the state of the company, but we don't get to the details; that is done at the level of our teams. Since you're new, this will be a great opportunity for you to see where we stand,' Srini explained.

'I'm looking forward to the discussion,' said Dillon, 'and to identifying opportunities for DT!'

The next morning, Dillon reached the conference room about five minutes before the start of the management meeting. His evening with his wife and son had been well spent. He'd been "in the moment", genuinely interested in what his wife and son had to say. Not surprisingly, he felt energized, more positive than he had in a while. He was determined to give his personal relationships a fresh start.

Prabhat was already there. 'Morning, Prabhat. How are you?' asked Dillon cheerfully.

'Fine, and you?'

'Quite well. Looking forward to my first quarterly review in this company!'

'And I'm looking forward to my 60th or so,' said Prabhat, chuckling. 'Honestly, I lost count after 25.' They both laughed.

Not long afterwards, Falguni called the meeting to order. 'Let's get straight down to it, folks,' she said.

'You're aware that we just finished a financial year. While I could just display the last quarterly and annual results, the CEO suggested that I consolidate and display the last four years' worth of data. That way, we can have a broader discussion around the health of the company.

'Which is not to suggest that the immediate results are not important. In fact, I have distributed the printouts of our Q4 and yearly results for your reference. You can see that our Q4 sales, costs and earnings were roughly similar to those for Q4 of last year.

'Please take a moment to review,' Falguni said and paused.

After a minute, she added, 'However, as I said, we want to focus on business diagnostics, the numbers and trends that tell the bigger story.'

With this, she projected the following numbers on the screen. 'All numbers are in USD, millions,' she said. 'To help you, I've taken the entire balance sheet and reduced the information to the three or four key parameters that reveal the health of our business. I've found that it's a simpler and more effective way to analyse the health of a business.

	4 Years Ago	3 Years Ago	2 Years Ago	Last Year
Sales	2,180	2,200	2,195	2,130
Market share (%)	28	27	24	19
Cost of production	1,264	1,320	1,273	1,278
Other Expenses				
Salary	283	308	373	362
Rent/Utilities	153	176	176	213
Insurance	22	44	44	53
Total Expenses				
	1,722	1,848	1,866	1,906
EBITDA	458	352	329	224

'What comes to your mind when you see these numbers?' Falguni asked.

'I think our sales folks may be wrongly incentivized,' said Prabhat.

'You're getting ahead of the class, Prabhat,' said Falguni, smiling. 'Let's just share our observations, to start with. Then we'll get to the causes.'

In a room full of business leaders, should I, the technology leader, speak up? Dillon thought. *Heck, I'm going to speak up, even if I'm wrong!*

'Well, the sales are flat, but profits are trending downward, so far as I can see,' Dillon said.

'Sure,' observed Falguni. 'Anything else?'

'Sales are flat while our market share has clearly suffered,' said Srini. 'I'd say we've not kept up with the competition in terms of innovation and product choices.'

'I'd venture our sales people may be focused on hitting sales targets and not on selling the right products,' said Falguni. 'Sort of what Prabhat alluded to.'

'Our expenses have been going up,' said Om. 'We've hired a substantial number of employees, and our other expenses have been going up too.'

'All right,' said Eknath. 'What's the leadership's overall assessment of the health of our business?'

'I'd say we're not in good health, sir,' replied Srini. 'We're limping along, but not running at a speed we're capable of.'

'That's right,' responded the CEO. 'We've got several challenges on our hands. First, sales: we've got to find ways to sell more. Second, costs. Our costs have been creeping upwards. Third, our market share is in danger. Fourth, our headcount may be going up too fast compared to our plans.

'There can be several reasons for this. Like one of you said, we may not be innovating enough. Or our sales people may be wrongly incentivized. Or our machines and equipment may not be as reliable as they were earlier. Or our hiring strategy may need to be reconsidered.

Opening Doors for Digital Technology

'In my view, technology needs to play a big role in all of this. I'm glad you're here, Dillon. Your timing could not have been better. Let me elaborate.'

Dillon smiled. He opened his notepad and got ready to take notes as the CEO spoke.

'Traditionally, in any business, you always look to increase revenue and reduce cost,' continued the CEO. 'However, those metrics, while important, cannot continue to be the sole metrics that drive our strategy. In order to build a stronger business, we need to look for ways to increase our efficiency in our supply chain and operations. Fundamental improvements to those will make a huge impact. More importantly, we need to improve consumers' experience. We must give consumers what they want. For that, we'll need to consider insights from big data and AI on fashion trends and customer preferences.'

Dillon jotted down on his notepad: (a) increase operational efficiency, (b) increase supply chain efficiency and (c) improve consumer experience.

'Count me as a skeptic,' said Falguni. 'In my view, we shouldn't consider fancy technology such as digital or big data unless there's a clear return on investment (RoI).'

'Of course,' asserted Dillon. 'RoI is key to deciding which digital technology we employ. That should be fairly obvious.'

'Perhaps obvious to you,' bristled Falguni. 'I'm sick and tired of technical leaders who assume the whole world is tech-savvy. I'd say, focus on the basics. Digital can wait. If we don't use our ERP fully and our basic reporting is messed up, digital is a waste of money. You're talking about what fancy features you can deliver on the 20th storey, while our ground floor is shaky and needs urgent attention.'

'Let's not bring IT into this,' retorted Dillon. 'You don't want to get me started.'

'Get *you* started?' asked Falguni rhetorically. 'Boy, that would be something, won't it? I'm waiting with bated breath to hear what a tech leader, completely out of touch with the realities of what it takes to run a business, has to say!'

Is Digital Technology Here to Stay?

Dillon could respond to this from about 20 different angles, and while he was deciding on which one would be best, Prabhat chimed in: 'All right, boys and girls, let's calm down. I would suggest that we focus on digital for the purposes of this meeting. Dillon is right that IT is a separate discussion. However, Falguni's got a point too; that the IT foundations need to be shored up before digital can take root.

'Having said that, I'd still absolutely bet on technology. RoI is a given; we'd not be in business if every one of our investment didn't make money for us. But here's how I look at it. I invest a substantial amount of money to send my girl to one of the best schools in India. However, there's no RoI on my investment now. In fact, my wife and I may not see any return for years. Does that mean we'd not support her? No, we invest even though the return can't be quantified conclusively or takes years to materialize.'

Srini spoke up. 'Agree with Prabhat. In my view, digital technology isn't something we should even be debating. The benefits are clear and have been proven in every sector, including the consumer sector. I would rather focus on what our priorities should be, rather than debate whether we should be investing.'

'I agree; digital technology is here to stay. I support using technology to help us fix our problems,' said Om.

Dillon thought he saw Falguni sneer.

'I hear you all,' said the CEO. 'While technology will have a very important role to play, I'd like to emphasize to each one of you that technology, by itself, won't be the panacea. There are extraneous factors unrelated to technology that we'll need to address urgently. For example, if our business process is messed up, if we just automate it, we'll get an automated, messed-up process.

'However, since Dillon is on board, I'd like this team to spend the next few minutes to set a broad agenda for him,' Eknath said.

Aligning DT with Business Imperatives

Om spoke up first. 'Thanks, sir. Let me take a crack at this. One way in which technology could help us is with product cycles. You see, we aspire to become a market leading fashion retailer. For that to happen, what we need is to predict what the market needs. If we knew precisely what consumers need, we won't end up with bad product cycles. We have too many bad product cycles, where we have to significantly discount our inventory and later figure out how to move the inventory out. Since our price points are low, it's very expensive for us to recover from bad purchase or production decisions.'

'Let me ask a clarifying question,' said Dillon. 'Is it fair to say that our objectives are a flexible supply chain, faster response to trends and consumer demand, and a way to feed the data to inventory management and pricing?'

'Precisely,' replied Om. 'I'm glad you're seeing the business side of things, Dillon. Our last CIO wasn't quite as good. We need our technology leaders to speak our language.'

Dillon smiled and made notes.

Prabhat said, 'One area where we're pushing for automation is in our warehouses.'

Om nodded.

'Currently, most of the warehouse activity is manual, which means we can't reach the customer quickly,' Prabhat continued. 'Our vision is to have next-day delivery of 90 per cent of our consumers. We believe we can do it by a combination of robotics and radio frequency identification (RFID) technology.'

'Agreed,' said Dillon. 'And we'll also need software, specifically computer algorithms that administer loyalty programs, shipping and returns.'

Prabhat was now excited about the topic. 'Gone are the days of clipboards and spreadsheets,' he continued. 'With modern software systems and warehouse automation technology, we can reap the benefits of increased accuracy and efficiency. Technology will help us prevent lost items, shipping errors and other mistakes that not only increase expenses, but worsen the consumer experience.'

Digital Themes and Objectives

By now, Dillon had made a table in his notepad. On the left-hand side, he had a column that said 'theme,' and on the right, there was a second column entitled 'objective.' He updated his table with the information that Prabhat shared.

'One important area for us is to improve end customer experience even further,' said Eknath. 'When a customer walks into one of our retail stores, we need to know everything about him or her. What their demographics are, what their ordering history is, which products they prefer, etc. Based on all the information, we should be able to offer them something that they're likely to buy.'

'Correct,' said Dillon. 'In fact, computer algorithms should be able to help sales people offer highly personalized options to the consumer. And if the customer picks a certain product that is not available in the right size or colour, the system should help tell him or her if the product is available in a different store or online.'

'I'm an old school guy,' opined Om. 'End-user experience (UX) and personalized service be damned; I just want operational efficiency.

'First, I'd like to understand our overall equipment effectiveness (OEE). Is it 90 per cent? 85 per cent? A lot of this information gets calculated manually. Different managers measure these numbers using different methods. I would like a system to not only calculate the OEE but also provide the number in real time.'

'Understood,' said Dillon. 'Taking it one step forward, in addition to monitoring performance, do we also want to optimize machine performance? If we're able to simulate the operation of an equipment, we can make a machine perform at the highest level.'

'That would be great,' said Om. 'In addition, one particular struggle for us is predicting when a piece of equipment is going to go down. Unscheduled downtime is the biggest killer of production.'

'We can fix that,' said Dillon. 'There are models that can be build that not only predict, with a high degree of accuracy, when an equipment is going to fail but also what remedial measures we should undertake now, in order to prevent the equipment from going down later. It's called *predictive maintenance.*'

'I like where this discussion is going,' said Falguni. 'Improving our machine effectiveness and reducing downtime increase our revenue from the increased production and predictive maintenance reduces our costs.'

'That's right,' said Prabhat. 'In fact, each one of the need areas, or themes, we have discussed so far, impact our revenue, costs and customer experience. For example, supply chain efficiency enables us to increase the sales as a result of our being able to respond to trends and consumer demands, and reduce the costs as a result of our being able to manage the inventory better. Automating our warehouses enables us to reduce costs by cutting manual labour.'

Dillon made some further notes in his notepad and here's how his table looked:

Theme	Objective
Increase operational efficiency	(a) Measure equipment effectiveness (OEE), (b) optimize OEE by simulations and (c) perform predictive maintenance
Increase supply chain efficiency	(a) A flexible supply chain, (b) faster response to trends and consumer demand and (c) a way to feed the data to inventory management and pricing
Improve consumer experience	(a) Use algorithms to administer loyalty programs that keep track of shipping and returns and (b) offer consumer personalized choices and options based on the individuals, and offer shipping options from other stores or online
Automate warehouses	(a) Use robotics to automate shipping and returns and (b) provide real-time updates to consumer to improve satisfaction

As the meeting concluded and Dillon started walking out of the conference room, Srini caught up with him.

A Hero's Dilemma

'Looking pensive, Dillon?' he remarked. 'Something the matter?'

'Well, to be completely honest with you, I'm feeling a little overwhelmed,' replied Dillon.

'Let's grab a cup of tea, and maybe a bite to eat?' asked Srini.

'It's lunch time already, didn't realize that,' admitted Dillon. 'Tell you what, give me 15 minutes, and we can grab a quick lunch in my office. How does that sound?'

'Make it 30 minutes; I'll be in your office at 12:45,' replied Srini.

Can I do this? Thought Dillon as he walked back to his office. He called the office boy and asked him to deliver a lunch for two in his office, continuing his chain of thoughts. *I've never done this before—this whole digital thing. They think I'm the expert; I'm barely a step ahead of them.*

'You know, Srini,' started Dillon, when Srini had settled down half an hour later, 'the way I see this, there's a lot on the plate. Digital, analytics, the whole nine yards. I'm facing a tall order; I'm not only expected to lead the IT organization, I'm also expected to implement long-term digital strategies that rule out unexpected downtimes of the major equipment, improve operational efficiencies, reduce costs, help reverse the recent mediocre performance of the company and bring about the technology to help improve the customer experience.

'That's a pretty demanding mandate for any leader, leave alone a brand new CDO with zero experience and serious family issues. Wouldn't you agree?' said Dillon forlornly. It was obvious he was full of self-doubt. There was food on the plate, but he wasn't eating.

'We do it one step at a time, Dillon,' said Srini smiling, as he bit into an *aloo bonda*. 'Like, for example, taking a bite of your food, to start with,' he said, smiling.

'Look at it this way, Dillon,' Srini continued, as Dillon perked up a little and bit into his sandwich, 'DT is new not only for us but also for you; I understand it's a challenge to pull it off. Moreover, you're having to deal with your personal relationships that are—for lack of a better word—suboptimal. The deck is stacked against you.

'And yet, it's your best opportunity. You know why? You have nothing to lose and everything to win. You don't make a reputation doing the easy stuff. You make it doing the hard stuff. But if you pull it off—and

I don't just mean the work bit—you'll be a better man, a better leader and a successful transformer.'

'You make it sound like a battle, Srini,' said Dillon, smiling, feeling a little better already. 'I'm hoping I'm the good guy though.'

'In a way, it is a battle,' responded Srini. 'We're in the daily battle called life. If we make good choices, we win. If we make bad choices, we lose. The sum total of the results of the daily battles makes our character. At least that's how I see it. However, I believe you're ready to go—to make some good choices. What says you?' asked Srini.

'I'm ready!' replied Dillon, his spirit uplifted. 'Let's go and do battle!'

The men shook hands and Srini left. As Dillon sat down at his desk, he recalled his greatest challenge, his father's untimely death when Dillon was 11. How, as the 'man' of the house, he'd rallied his mother and younger sister, working odd jobs and raising the money needed for school. And how, at the age of 17, he was rejected by virtually every college he applied to, until the University of California took a chance on him, a poor immigrant kid.

He could almost smell the stuffy, dingy house they lived in when he was in his teens. Clothes torn in places, stitched up by a hapless mom. Living in Los Angeles—the city of dreams in the most prosperous country in the world—and yet, barely getting by with two square meals a day. The going was tough, but Dillon had made it, based, in no small measure, on a strong measure of self-belief, and love and support from his mother and sister, and a helping of the good old fighting spirit.

I didn't give up then; I'm certainly not going to give up now, Dillon thought. *I can do this! Let's go!*

3

Going Back to the Basics

'Coffee with CDO' is how Dillon built up the weekly meet-and-greet at Dykstrand India. It happened to be sparked by a conversation with Srini.

'Congratulations on setting up a digital team! I heard many employees are excited about the journey ahead, and rightly so,' said Srini one day, while they were both waiting to meet the CEO.

'But I do have a concern,' he added. 'What're you going to do about the fact that we don't know much about digital—and, in fact, about technology? How do we build a basic level of awareness, so that when we discuss what we're going to do, we don't tune people out?' he asked.

'Good question, Srini,' replied Dillon. 'There is an urgent need to build a common understanding of technology, a culture of transformation at my new company. Dykstrand USA wasn't too bad—the culture already existed when I joined there. After all, in Silicon Valley you don't have to sell technology to anyone. India is a different story, however.'

'That's absolutely right,' said Srini. 'Although India is a market where rapid growth can be reasonably expected, it'll still take focus and effort in order for Dykstrand India to grow at the desired rates. Technology, as the CEO said, is to be a primary driver.'

'How's the culture?' asked Dillon.

'Staid, laid-back,' replied Srini. 'Bureaucracy is an issue; anything worth doing takes about three dozen approvals before it can take off. Last year we evaluated a process that had 37 steps in it.'

Dillon chuckled. 'No kidding?'

'No, really. We got the department heads together and deliberated over a dozen meetings. And you know how many steps we got it down to?'

'No, maybe 5?' Dillon guessed.

'No, 24. 24!' Srini sounded exasperated. 'That's when I realized we couldn't hope to simplify our processes unless we had technology that automated manual paper flow and approvals and signature. I figured we could get the process down to five or six steps if we had the right tool.'

Neither spoke for a minute.

'All right,' Dillon said, finally. 'The need for technology education is probably more urgent than I realized. How about this: build a little excitement into the mix—stir it up a bit—by providing an open forum where young engineers and technologists could come together and discuss technology?'

'You got it,' said Srini.

'Let's start from the basics, as in the basics of technology. Let's establish the basic words and phrases we use, so that members of the digital team begin to speak the language and gradually the lingo spreads to the rest of the organization,' said Dillon.

Evangelizing Technology

The first in the series called 'Coffee with CDO' occurred about a week later, in the cavernous main cafeteria hall. About 60 young, excited employees filled the hall. Srini and Hari too joined after a few minutes.

'I know some of you are here for the coffee and samosas,' Dillon began, to the laughter of the audience. 'However, no matter what brought you here, you'll be a little more tech-savvy by the time we're done today. Gone are the days when IT or technology was simply a separate function within an organization. Today, everyone, especially all leaders, is expected to understand technology and exploit technical advances in order to drive growth, reduce cost and enhance customer and employee experiences.

'I believe that, despite our stated focus on technology, we don't really understand the topic too well, which obviously doesn't move our agenda forward if we want to leverage technology to do it. We need to be educated and then transmit that knowledge to the rest of the organization.

'In other words, this team can be the change agent for propagating technology.'

Some of the members of the audience smiled and looked at one another. Clearly, they were excited. This sounded like quite a good opportunity.

'We need the entire organization to speak the same language,' said Dillon. 'When anyone around here says "analytics" or "cloud", we want them to mean what they say and say what they mean. Lack of common understanding is a major reason why technology transformations don't work.

'Again, change agents can be the drivers of common understanding and language.'

A hand went up from the front row. It was Hari, the HR leader. 'What do you mean by "change agent"? I guess I'm asking because we in HR talk about it all the time. We just need to make sure we are aligned.'

How to Be a Change Agent?

'You mean whether a techie speaks the same language as HR?' interjected Dillon, chuckling. 'On a serious note, however, that's a good question, Hari. In my book, here's what it means. Actually, it means three things. First, you naturally like change and believe in change. Not only that, you know your facts, persuade people to change, are trusted and have a record of standing for and implementing change. In our context, you'd be promoting technology-related change.

'Second,' Dillon continued, 'you are a continuous learner. You're always looking for external knowledge and trends. You attend seminars, you network—both online and offline—and you are curious about goings on in the world of technology.

'Third and final, you're good with people. You may not yet be a manager, but you're good at leading people, and hiring and training. You are able to engage with people.'

Hari smiled and made a thumbs-up gesture. Dillon smiled back. He loved establishing a common understanding of the basics.

'Does it mean we have to be extroverts?' asked a young professional seated next to Hari, presumably a young HR manager.

Dillon pondered for a moment. 'No,' he replied, 'but you have to be able to effectively mingle with people. If you're like me, your natural inclination may be to pick up a book and a cup of coffee and retreat to a comfortable sofa in the corner of the room, but nevertheless you'd still be willing to become genuinely interested in others if it helped you accomplish a greater good.'

Dillon paused. 'Having said that,' he continued, 'since today's meeting is about the fundamentals of technology, because that's going to be requisite knowledge in our journey in this company in the months to come, we should get on with our main course for this afternoon. Let me explain the basics in the simplest way I can. A disclaimer before I begin: I'm not an electronics engineer. In other words, I'm not the expert here. However, I've done my reading, and I'm ready.'

Everything Comes with Risk, Even Technology

'To paraphrase Charles Dickens, the age of technology is the best of times, it's also the worst of times,' continued Dillon. 'It is the age of connectedness; it is also the age of the dangers of connectedness. It is the age of information; it is also the age of that information falling into the wrong hands. It is the age of the greatest of technological accomplishments; it's also the age of the greatest fear of what that technology can do to harm us.

'DT has been happening to us for quite some time, although we only may have given it a name now. Imagine a future where your house, car, fridge, TV, security system and all other appliances are connected to your phone. Your fridge automatically places an order for milk and eggs, when it "senses" that you're running out of them. The car drives itself and all you do is to chill in the back seat, or catch up on a movie. Your TV, knowing what kind of a day you had and what you typically want to watch, shows you just that perfect something that you need to relax and recharge. The audio system knows when it's time to play your preferred music before you plop off in bed, and, of course, your phone reminds you of the schedule for tomorrow and sets the alarm to go off at 6:00 a.m.'

'Question,' said a voice from the back of the room. 'Is technology good news all the way through, or do we need to worry that something could go wrong?'

'Unfortunately, we do need to worry,' replied Dillon. 'Take self-driving cars. While one is likely to be thrilled that a ride in the future may not involve the drudgery of looking up the destination address, the actual driving and the parking, it's not hard to imagine a scenario where a hacker can break into the system—the car's "electronic brain"—and hijack the car. Consider another scenario: a power generation plant, running super efficiently and completely free of human intervention, is taken over by a malicious individual or organization that wishes to disrupt and destroy, commit an act of war.

'Let's suppose we connect our equipment to the ubiquitous IoT, which is the name given to the network of smart, or intelligent, machines, appliances and equipment that enables us to monitor and optimize performance. In theory, someone could hack into the IoT and disable a critical piece of equipment, or worse, use it as a weapon to cause harm.'

A young engineer, sitting in the front row, spoke up. 'Sorry to force you back to the basics,' she said. 'But you haven't yet told us what exactly is meant by "technology". We hear the term all the time; I could never tell if it referred to computers, software or something else. Could you perhaps recap the history of technology for us?'

'Sure,' responded Dillon. 'Let me start by explaining what technology is,' he said.

Evolution of Technology

'The history of tools and techniques is as old as the history of humanity. Can all of those tools and techniques be called "technology"? It turns out, the answer is no. The root of the word is the Greek word *techne,* which refers to arts and crafts, and the common suffix, logos, the word used to describe, well, the word, or specifically, the word of God.

'So "technology" literally means the word describing arts and crafts. However, the meaning has been subverted and now refers to that which describes the advancements and changes which affect the environment around us, or more precisely, "the means or activity by which man seeks to change or manipulate his environment."[1]

'So technology is not some hairy monster, it's just a fancy word to refer to that which brings about change.'

A smartly dressed young man in a back row raised his hand. 'To tie this back to your point about change agents,' he asked, 'are all change agents, then, technologists?'

'That's a good question,' replied Dillon. 'Not *all* change relates to technology. For example, you could be advocating changes to environmental policy or the school curriculum. I guess you could say effective technologists are change agents, but not all change agents are technologists. Does this make sense?'

The young employee nodded.

'Let's now talk about the history of all this,' said Dillon.

Dillon continued, 'Don't worry, we're not harking back to the beginnings of recorded history, aka the Stone Age, but to the more recent times when a device known as a computer was put together for the first time. That computing device, it's commonly agreed, was the ENIAC, released in the year 1946 as the first general purpose computer.[2]

'The reason we can assume that technology started with computers is because that's the first time *tasks useful to common people* were performed using technology.

'In the 1940s and 1950s, a number of computers were developed for use at universities in America and Europe, but these computers employed vacuum tubes, which generated huge quantities of heat, were bulky and were susceptible to malfunction. However, these computers were programmable, that is, they could perform a number of useful, computational tasks.

'The age of digital could be said to have started when computers began to use transistors in place of vacuum tubes. A transistor is a semiconductor device that amplifies or switches electronic signals. It's the basic building block of computer hardware. What is digital about it? Well, electronic switches can only turn on or off, and cannot exist in a state other than on or off. See this picture? Transistors were small, radiated little heat and were much more reliable than the bulkier vacuum tubes.'

Dillon projected a picture on the screen.

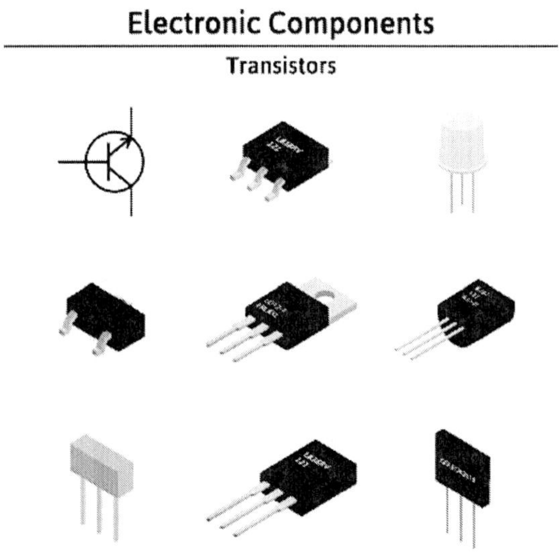

Transistors[3]

The young employee who'd asked the last question shot up his hand again. 'But we don't use these devices anymore in computers, do we? When did the technology change? What was the trigger for the move to modern, smaller devices?'

'To answer that,' Dillon responded, 'we'll have to turn our attention to something which all of you probably have heard of, the microprocessor.

Small Gets Smaller: Microprocessors

'How small are microprocessors, the brain of your phone, computer or pretty much all major electronic appliances, for example, washing machine, fridge or car?' asked Dillon.

'Just a few millimetres long and wide. How can you pack all that intelligence into such a small area? Here's how. If there's one essential aspect of modern technology, this is it: the race to faster and smaller. You don't have to look further than the size of the phone you're holding, or that of the laptop you may be using.

'Electronic circuits follow what's known as "Moore's Law". Gordon Moore, the cofounder of Fairchild Semiconductor and Intel, famously predicted in 1965 that the number of components per integrated circuit would double every year. It's really more of a prediction than a rule or law.

'How is it done? Well, at the heart of every computer is a "gate", which is the root of the definition of digital, because an electronic gate, just like its physical counterpart, can be open (on) or closed (off). Electronic gates are special types of transistors that are made by a controlled oxidation of silicon. Now, these gates are such that their area and the heat they generate (which comes from the electrical power they produce) can always be scaled down with the advancement of design techniques.

'That renders the basic building blocks of computers continually smaller, and consequently, the devices that use computers can be made smaller as well. The smaller the "computing brains", the smaller the device,' Dillon said and paused to sip from his glass.

Then he continued, 'Nowhere is it more evident than in "microprocessors", the brain of every electronic device today: phones, laptops, workstations, cars and all kinds of home appliances. It was in 1968 that the world's first microprocessor arrived, courtesy Intel's C4004. Check out this picture,' he said, as the projector showed the following picture on the screen.

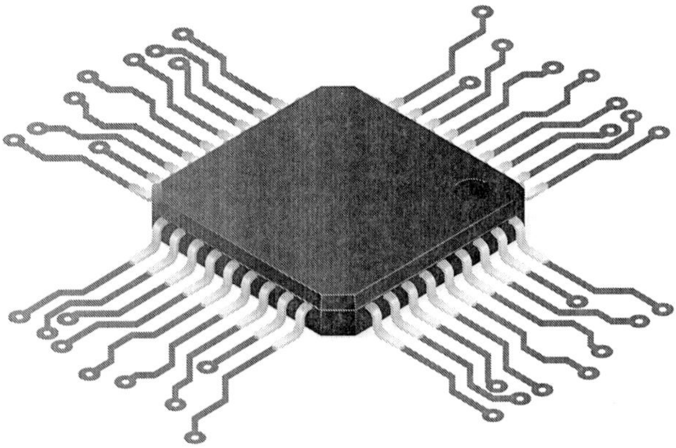

Intel C4004 Microprocessor[4]

'How small is small? Well, try this for size: today's microprocessors, measuring less than a square inch, can pack up to 2 billion transistors per square millimetre.'

'Are microprocessors prefixed with *micro* because of their tiny size?' asked the young HR manager. 'Could there be other types of processors?'

'Good question,' replied Dillon. 'In the early days of processors, yes, you could say a processor would be prefixed with *micro* in order to distinguish it from others. However, these days you don't have any types of processors other than the *micro* type.'

'Would you say that the advancements in technology were a prerequisite for the IT boom?' asked the young woman sitting in the front.

'Absolutely,' replied Dillon. 'That's a nice segue into what I was going to describe next. Thanks!'

We Need Information, Please: IT and Computers

'Man has been writing,' continued Dillon, 'or putting thoughts on a medium, for at least 5,000 years. Storing, transmitting or retrieving information is a common human need, and humans from the times of the Mesopotamia culture have been at it.

'However, the phrase IT is quite modern; it was coined in 1958 in a seminal *Harvard Business Review* article. It meant a technique by which information could be systematically used to aid decision-making and higher order thinking. The elements of IT, namely data storage (1930s onwards), databases (1960s onwards) and data retrieval and transmission (1970s onwards) have been around for a while, but it was only in the 1980s that IT as an industry gathered momentum.

'It can be argued that IT was a natural step in the evolution of technology; if not for transistors and microprocessors, there won't be IT as we know it. Today, IT has transformed the way people live and companies operate; it contributes trillions of dollars to the world's economy, and millions of professionals are engaged in the field. Vast swathes of towns and cities in the world's developing economies have grown by over 300 per cent since the 1980s. A case in point is the city of Bangalore in South India, which was considered a retirees' paradise until the 1980s, with about 3 million people living. Today, nearly 13 million people live and work in this megacity. Much of the population growth can be attributed to the explosion of the IT industry.'

'Is IT the same as computer software?' asked a young man sitting in a middle row.

'Not quite,' replied Dillon. 'Most laymen would equate the two. However, there is a crucial difference. The software that goes into IT—think database, operating system, enterprise resource planning or ERP—is not all that there is to software. There are other kinds of software in use, for example, mechanical design engineering software, commonly known as CAD or CAM, 3D modelling software for home interiors, and so on.

'Additionally, IT encompasses areas other than computer software, for example, hardware, servers, telephony, information security, etc.

Hardware refers to the "hard" components of a system, such as electronic circuits mounted on a board, a screen or a monitor, an input tool such as a keyboard, etc. Software, as you all know, means code or programs. Servers refer to programs that process requests, and the hardware that provide the computing means behind the programs. Information security refers to the securing of IT systems. All these fields are traditionally considered part of IT.

'I hope that you can see that IT and software are different animals. In summary, IT is software, hardware and a bunch of other tools and systems. Software means programs and systems, which includes IT software and software systems used for other purposes.'

'Let me bring in another common phrase we hear these days,' said someone. 'That is Industry 4.0. What is it? Is it software? Is it digital?'

Industrial Age

'To answer that question,' responded Dillon, 'you have to go all the way back to the history of industrial automation, or the way that industrial—or factory—work has been automated over many decades, or centuries, to be precise.

'Industrial revolutions have been few and far in between. The first, the original "industrial revolution" that started in Great Britain, consisted of the transformation of manual—meaning hand production—methods to machines, especially in the field of textiles. This period lasted from about 1760 to roughly around 1830.

'The second industrial revolution commonly refers to mass production in the form of assembly lines, no better illustrated than by Ford's automobile manufacturing lines in Detroit, and the generation and distribution of electrical power that took off in the early decades of the 20th century, led by General Electric (GE). The third revolution is the one brought about by computers and robotic automation. Think automated back office processes made possible by IT, and robotics-assisted assembly lines.

'Take a look at this picture; it'll help you understand the concept better,' said Dillon as he projected the following picture.

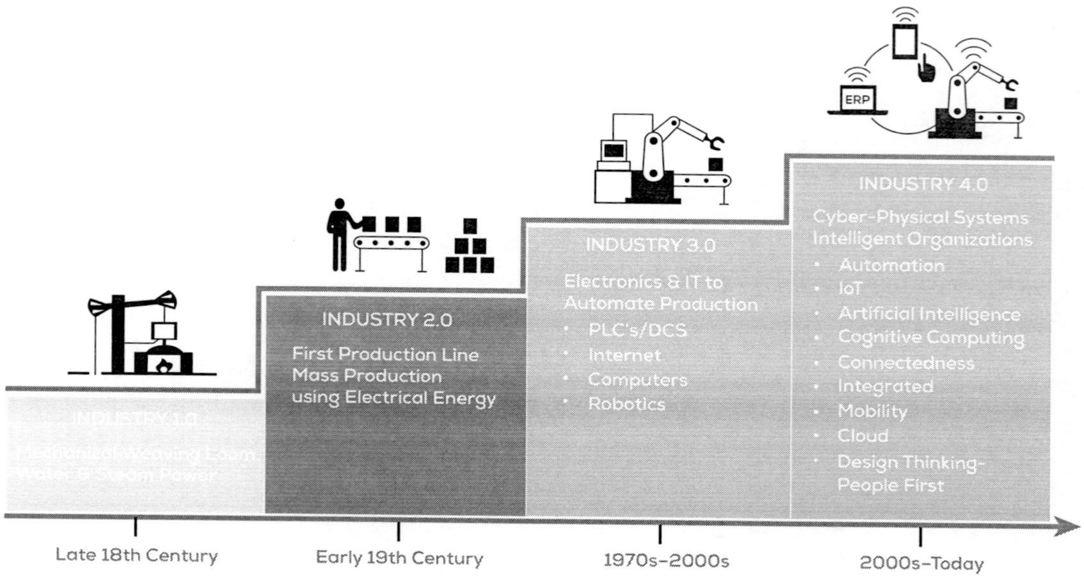

Industry 4.0: Timeline and Main Advancements

'Now, to get back to your question,' continued Dillon, 'the phrase "Industry 4.0" originated in the German government and referred to the computerization of manufacturing. Specifically, it consisted of greater automation using robotics and the control over the overall manufacturing processing with the use of computer systems.

'The rate and pace of change of technology in the past two decades have outpaced those in the past two centuries. What is different now is the convergence of technologies that are attuned towards meeting the rapidly growing needs of businesses and consumers, thus thinning the line between the digital and the physical worlds.'

'When you say computerization of manufacturing, what do you mean?' asked the HR manager. 'I guess I'm just trying to understand Industry 4.0 a little better.'

Industry 4.0—A Primer

Dillon responded, 'Think robotic manufacturing, or quality control through computers. However, Industry 4.0 is not *just* computerized manufacturing.

'In the years between 2011, when the phrase was coined, and 2018, "Industry 4.0" has acquired additional scope and now refers to the following broad areas.[5–7]

'The first is robotics and automation, as in industrial robotics with sensors and standard interfaces, for example, a robotic crawler in use at a metals major that measures the linings of an acid tank and transmits the data to a back-end IT system, saving $2M annually.

'Next is big data and advanced analytics, which mean comprehensive collection and evaluation of data from a variety of sources, namely ERP, SCM, CRM, social/unstructured, machine/sensors, for example, an African gold mine used sensor data obtained during leaching in order to increase yield by 3.7 per cent.

'Next is 3D printing, which aids the manufacture of spare parts and even critical components, reducing costs and increasing reliability, for example, blades in use at GE's GE9X engines that spin 2,500 times per minute amidst searing heat and pressure. 3D printing reduces manufacturing cycle times by 30 per cent or more.

'Also included is augmented and virtual reality, providing a digitally enhanced experience to facilitate repair, maintenance and logistics, as well as provide training for hazardous tasks. For example, a metals major reduced occurrences of serious injuries by 40 per cent by using AR and VR to train operators dealing with hazardous working conditions.

'Next up is modelling and simulation, which means using digital models, or simulations, of the physical world which includes equipment, material and humans. This allows engineers to optimize processes and equipment settings, increasing throughput and asset life. For example, turbine and aircraft engine maintenance technicians can reduce root cause analysis times by up to 90 per cent.

'Next is the IoT, which refers to connected equipment and devices with embedded computing, allowing them to communicate with one another and humans to control and optimize production and efficiencies. For example, by connecting high-end boilers and furnaces to an IoT, a major industrial company was able to maintain the equipment predictively, reducing unplanned downtime by up to 75 per cent.

'Next are two important components, cloud computing and cyber security. Security threats assume greater importance with increased connectivity between systems and machines. These heightened security risks must be managed.

'The final piece is system integration, which means the integration of data across functions and verticals, and the provisioning of a fully integrated, single source of truth. For example, a mining company increased sales by $12M/year by creating a single view of the data from various functions in the production chain, such as sales, marketing, finance, treasury, etc.'

'Phew—that's a lot of information,' exclaimed the young female engineer. 'I guess you never bothered to explain some of the words you used in Industry 4.0!' she added in mock anger.

'Fair point, but you may relax,' replied Dillon. 'We will go over all of these ideas to the extent that you need to know the concepts in order to formulate and drive a technology strategy effectively.

'Today, we achieved something important,' Dillon continued. 'We touched upon a few of the major milestones in the journey of technology's advancement. Clearly, we didn't cover the details, because that would be beyond the scope of today's meeting. Additionally, it would have kept you in the office for about eight more hours,' he added, smiling.

'However, here's the good news,' Dillon continued. 'In order to understand and employ what we call "digital", you don't need to understand everything, for example, what's on the inside of microprocessors. You simply need to understand the pieces of technology that constitute digital, how the pieces work with one another and how to formulate a strategy that can deliver real, significant business benefits.

'You don't need to know everything, but *enough,* in order that you may begin to deliver a DT.'

'I do have a fundamental question, however,' admitted the young engineer. 'Why would a company implement digital in the first place? I guess the decision has already been made for us, but I'd like to hear from you why digital is needed. Why isn't IT enough?'

Why Digital?

'OK, let's take a step back,' replied Dillon. 'Why isn't IT enough? Why should we consider digital? In fact, why *must* we consider digital?' he asked rhetorically.

'To answer the question, we must first understand what digital encompasses. But I'll start by listing some of the things IT *cannot* do. Can your IT system enable robots—both mechanical and electronic—to optimize physical tasks and answer common queries? Can IT provide an alternate kind of reality that makes it possible to train workers, reduce exposure to hazards and help in repairing equipment? Can an IT system help you hook up big machines and equipment to a network that can monitor and optimize their performance? Most importantly, can IT provide you with a system that *learns and improves over time*?

'I'll answer that one for you,' continued Dillon. 'The tools and systems that are usually considered part of IT cannot do any of the tasks I just mentioned. The capabilities are most certainly digital.'

'I'd nevertheless say we have some apprehensions about digital,' said Hari. 'We had a bad experience while implementing an analytics product in this company about 18 months ago. Whether it was because our vendor wasn't up to the task, or it simply didn't pick the right tool, or we were up against a different type of risk we were unaware of, I don't know.'

'Your concerns are absolutely normal,' responded Dillon. 'In fact, I am planning a lecture to cover the two major reasons why the majority of Indian companies haven't still benefited from digital. In that talk, I'll cover lessons learnt, pitfalls to avoid and best practices.

'However, at the moment, we have to take a step back,' Dillon continued. 'This team first needs to understand the basics of digital.

'What exactly is digital after all? Isn't it the same as IT? If they're different, how do digital and IT work together? And is Industry 4.0 the same thing as digital?

'I'm sure you have all these questions in your mind. It so happens that day after tomorrow I'm addressing an audience in the local chamber of commerce on these topics, from four to six in the evening.

'Why don't you join me?' asked Dillon. Many in the audience nodded. 'How many of you are planning to attend?' About 15 hands went up.

'Great,' said Hari. 'We'll arrange the transportation. Just make sure to sign here, on this sheet of paper, so we can keep track of who wants to join us.'

'Hold on, everyone,' said Dillon. 'I'd suggest that you fill out an electronic survey, which I'll e-mail to all of you to indicate your participation in the chamber of commerce event.

'The digital journey starts now,' he added. 'No more paperwork unless it is absolutely unavoidable! What do you say to that, Hari?'

Why Meditation?

'Srini, do you have a few minutes? Really ... I'd appreciate it.'

To Srini, it sounded like an SOS. He knew the new CDO well enough by now to guess the criticality from his tone.

Fifteen minutes later, Srini and Dillon were sipping tea.

'Last night, I was still high from the night's session, Srini,' Dillon started. 'I tossed and turned all night. This morning, my mind was racing; I found it hard to concentrate at work for the first hour or so. All because I was excited, in a good way. Fast forward a few hours. This afternoon, I experienced the opposite kind of emotion. I had a little bit of an unpleasant conversation with my boss, the CEO. This served to agitate my mind and excite it to a level of despair.

'How do I overcome these intense emotions? Not only at work, even at home? On being praised, I tend to float on cloud nine, and on being criticized, I sink into doldrums. How can I become—what's the right word now—*equanimous*, which means equal in joy and despair?'

'You've got to be a rock,' responded Srini. 'Don't let criticism fluster you, and don't let praise get into your head. Stay grounded; stay humble; stay consistent.'

'That's all well—but *how do I do it*?'

'In order to prevent your mind from suffering from turmoil, you need to meditate,' replied Srini. 'Meditation stills your mind; it reduces your agitation. The goal of meditation is to still the mind, to make it thoughtless. This helps you overcome sorrow, kill your ego and achieve peace, according to spiritual masters. It takes months of effort—it isn't achieved overnight. I can say in all humility, but with the conviction of my own experience, that it took me about six months of daily meditation, often for as little as two or three minutes, to start reaping some of these benefits in my own life.'

'But isn't it hard work?' asked Dillon. 'I hear about meditation, and the first question that comes to my mind is, can I do it? Others may be able to, but can I—with my excitable personality?'

'Nothing in the world is too hard, including meditation,' replied Srini. 'Easwaran said "The Lord will never put on your shoulder even a pound more than you can bear. But he won't put one pound less, either, for then you won't grow!"'

'Well, but the next question is: *when* should I meditate?' Dillon asked, sounding doubtful.

'There's almost universal agreement on the best time to meditate,' replied Srini. 'It's early in the morning. Why? Because in meditation, you're trying to still your mind, and early in the day, the mind is already calm. Imagine trying to meditate after drinking your cup of coffee or tea, reading the news from the newspaper or the Internet and checking your e-mail. Imagine your mind as still water over a bed of mud. Performing the activities I've listed earlier would muddy up the water.'

'How *long* should I meditate? How long do I have to meditate to derive the maximum benefit out of the experience?'

'My guru recommended 15 minutes,' replied Srini. 'Serious spiritual aspirants spend considerably more time, but in my opinion, a few minutes a day is best for most of us. Try to still your mind for a minute at first and then increase the duration gradually.'

'All right, Srini, I'll follow your suggestion for a week and then report my progress to you,' said Dillon.

Scheduling Regular Outings with Family

'There's one more suggestion I have,' said Srini. 'Schedule regular breaks with your family. Take them out; do something fun.'

'Oh yes, of course,' responded Dillon. 'We do that all the time, especially on Sundays.'

'That's good, but you can do more,' said Srini. 'As a family, you should slot "create a memory" trips and events into your calendar.'

'What're those?'

'Look, the main reason why we schedule outings is not because of the fun, which of course is nice. The more crucial reason, especially for a family going through relationship challenges, is to create memories. The memories hold the family together; they provide a shared, common past. After all, our life is a series of intertwined experiences, like a quilt. The higher the number of "family time" patterns, the stronger your family.'

'This makes a lot of sense. Thanks, Srini!' said Dillon, thoughtfully. *No wonder my family isn't close-knit,* he thought. *We just haven't created enough beautiful memories, no matter what the reason: lack of time, initiative or whatever.*

The next day, at breakfast, Dillon said, 'Honey, any plans for the upcoming long weekend?'

'No, why?' replied Kavya, surprised. It wasn't in Dillon's nature to plan ahead for vacations. Usually Kavya was the one that would bring up the topic, before Dillon would express his inability due to important meetings or a report that needed to get done over the weekend.

'Nothing—I was just thinking if it wouldn't be nice to grab a vacation at Trevan Hills, and spend a couple of nights there.'

'Are you serious?'

'Of course—why do you ask?'

'You know why I'm asking! We haven't had a vacation like that in ages. Don't you have important meetings lined up next week?'

'I do, but all those can wait.'

'And any reports to be submitted Monday?'

'No, not really. Let's just go, honey!'

'Are you all right?' asked Kavya, somewhat incredulously. 'I mean, seriously?'

'Yes, absolutely. Haven't felt better in a while....' replied Dillon, his voice trailing off.

References

[1] Buchanan, Robert Angus. 1998. 'History of Technology.' *Encyclopaedia Britannica*. Available at https://www.britannica.com/technology/history-of-technology (accessed on 12 April 2019).

[2] Light, Jennifer S. 1999, July. 'When Computers Were Women.' *Technology and Culture* 40: 455–483.

[3] Transistors. *Getty Images*. Available at https://www.gettyimages.ca/photos/transistor?sort=mostpopular&mediatype=photography&phrase=transistor (accessed on 12 April 2019).

[4] Microprocessors. *CPU World*. Available at http://www.cpu-world.com/CPUs/4004/index.html (accessed on 12 April 2019).

[5] Brunelli, Jacopo, Vlad Lukic, Tom Milon and Marco Tantardini. 2017. 'Five Lessons from the Frontlines of Industry 4.0.' Boston Consulting Group White Paper. Boston, MA: Boston Consulting Group.

[6] Baur, Cornelius and Dominik Wee. 2015. 'Manufacturing's Next Act.' Available at https://www.mckinsey.com/business-functions/operations/our-insights/manufacturings-next-act (accessed on 12 April 2019).

[7] Othman, Bahrin. 2016. 'Industry 4.0: A Review on Industrial Automation and Robotic.' *Jurnal Teknologi*, 143. Available at https://www.researchgate.net/publication/304614356_Industry_40_A_review_on_industrial_automation_and_robotic (accessed on 10 June 2019).

4

What's Digital After All?

Fresh Trouble Knocks on the Front Door

Scheduling regular outings with the family, as per Srini's suggestion, had the desired effect on Dillon's family life. Dillon was grateful; a peaceful, contented wife and an engaged child can work wonders in the life of an overstretched executive.

But it didn't last long. Life has a way of jarring you when you least expect it, and for Dillon it came at the end of a draining, but productive, day at work.

'You know what, honey?' he asked as he pushed open the front door at his home, with Kavya facing the other way while peeling vegetables. That she didn't turn to welcome him should have warned him, but Dillon wasn't looking.

'The CEO has asked me to make a presentation to the Company's Board next month!' he announced, excitedly, as he put down his computer bag on the carpet. 'Can you believe that?'

'Believe what, that men who continue to cheat on their wives would be entrusted with bigger responsibilities at the company?' she asked, turning to Dillon to reveal a dismayed countenance.

'No, not that. What I meant was.... wait a second,' said Dillon, as he realized what had just hit him. 'What was that—men who cheat on their wives? What're you *talking* about?'

'Someone from this house is going to Oklahoma to meet with an ex-lover, and it isn't me or Aaron who's going,' said Kavya.

It took Dillon a few moments to digest the question. 'Oh,' he said, finally. 'I understand. You noticed I'm traveling to Oklahoma at the end of this month, and you assumed I'm going to meet with Krissy?'

'Of course!' Kavya responded. 'What else could take you to Oklahoma, of all places? I mean, what's there to do in Oklahoma, for God's sake?'

Dillon smiled. 'I was about to tell you. You may not believe this, but there's plenty to do in Oklahoma,' he replied. 'For starters, the new plant we're building is in the town of Erick. You know, Dykstrand's brand new, fully automated plant is going up in Western Oklahoma. So far as Krissy is concerned, the last time I checked, she lived in Tulsa, which is nearly 400 km away! For the company to fly me business class from India to Oklahoma so I could meet with my ex-sweetheart is a little too much, don't you think?'

Hitting the Reset Button with the Wife

The hint of a smile appeared on Kavya's lips.

'And I have been stupid before, I'll admit that,' said Dillon. 'But *even I* understand not to do something so obvious!' Saying this, he gave his wife a little hug. Kavya didn't respond, but she didn't push him away either.

'OK, I may be foolish,' Kavya said, as she resumed peeling the veggies, 'but my womanly intuition told me you were up to serious mischief when I saw your travel reservation documents on your study desk. I know you won't have left it there if you wanted to hide the whole thing, but nevertheless....'

'Your imagination is just way too active, Kavya,' Dillon said. 'In fact, my trip to Erick was precisely what I wanted to discuss with you. The CEO said that I would address the leadership at the new plant and, upon my return to India, update the board next month on our technology strategy. That's exciting, because we're finally raising the profile of our technology team.'

'Good for you,' said Kavya, a faint smile appearing on her lips. *My wife smiled at me,* Dillon thought. *It's been a while since it happened last!*

'No, good for the family—for you and Aaron as well,' Dillon said, drawing closer. 'My journey as a business leader is nothing if I'm not a good father or husband.'

'We'll see about that,' Kavya said, with a sombre expression. 'When you had that affair, you broke my trust. It's going to take time.'

'But it's been seven years!' exclaimed Dillon.

'These things take time,' responded Kavya. 'A lot of time,' she muttered under her breath. 'Now I've steeled myself so I won't be hurt again like I was hurt last time,' she continued, a little louder. 'The wall I've erected around me is pretty high.'

'I know, but I can't be always on trial forever,' said Dillon to no one in particular.

Progress Is Possible in Relationships

The next morning, Dillon narrated the previous night's story to Srini.

'Thanks for sharing, Dillon,' said Srini. 'I believe you're making important progress. The fact that you both handled a potentially serious misunderstanding shows that you both want to make reconciliation happen.

'You have to *believe progress is possible* for progress to happen,' he continued. 'When you think something is impossible, your mind starts figuring out all the reasons why it won't work. When you believe the opposite, your mind goes out of the way to figure out how.'

'That's right,' Dillon said. 'But I'll tell you what—there's something even more fundamental. There's got to be *desire* first. First you got to have the desire to make something work, then you'll have to believe that progress can be made.'

'Agree,' said Srini. 'Your wife's got the desire to make your relationship work, or else she'd have walked out by now. What you may want to do is to keep reiterating that progress is important, and that progress needs to be continually made. Speak faith into everything you do. Even when things become rocky, speak words of faith, of love. Repeat expressions of faith often.'

'Faith….' Repeated Dillon. 'Faith in the unknown. But I'll choose to *believe*. Thanks, Srini!'

What Is Not Digital?

'What on earth is "digital"?'

The scene was the local chamber of commerce, a couple of evenings later. Dillon was the featured speaker at the event at the modest two-storey building near Siruseri's municipal headquarters.

'In technology strategy meetings around the globe in recent years,' Dillon said, 'it's only a matter of time before a senior leader asks, "What the heck are we doing in digital? I've been hearing this term in our company for a while now, but I'm not sure we've done anything about it! I'm not even sure I know what 'digital' means!"

'At which point, the answers are various, and reflect, to a varying extent, the person's understanding and area of responsibility,' said Dillon. 'Let me ask you this: what do *you* think digital is?'

'It's analytics,' replied someone.

'No, it's AI and all the new stuff,' opined another.

'Yes, in fact I'd say it encompasses all new technologies, like block chain.'

'No, it's a mindset, not a new technology. Been around for years.'

'I'd say it's something IT teams need to take up.'

Dillon smiled. 'Reminds us of the story of the elephant and the blind men,' he said, as he projected the following picture on the screen. 'Most of us are like the blind men in the story, only relating a new concept to what we've experienced.

'But it's a fair question, really: what exactly is digital after all? Isn't it the same as IT? If they're different, how do digital and IT work together? And is Industry 4.0 the same thing as digital?

The Children's Story[1]

'Pertinently, what is DT? Do people sometimes mean DT when they say digital, or vice versa? Let me give you all a hint: the answer is yes.

'Let's get to the heart of this.

For Starters, Digital Is IoT

'The foremost benefit offered by digital to the world of manufacturing is machine connectivity, the central idea being: "Get connected, get insights and get optimized".[2] Digital is about connecting devices and equipment—in other words, your assets—to the IoT, in order to collect performance data and readings of key process parameters. Once you collect and analyse the data, you can drive productivity, reduce equipment downtime and enhance production and profitability.

'Right now, if a part fails, the OEM, or original equipment manufacturer, would have to send a technician and a part to fix it. However, by implementing an IoT strategy, you'll be able to monitor and control the machine's performance and potentially eliminate unexpected failures. That's the direct, obvious value. But the greater idea is this: it will also allow us to obtain new insights into making the machines work better in the future.

'I hope the following picture clarifies IoT.

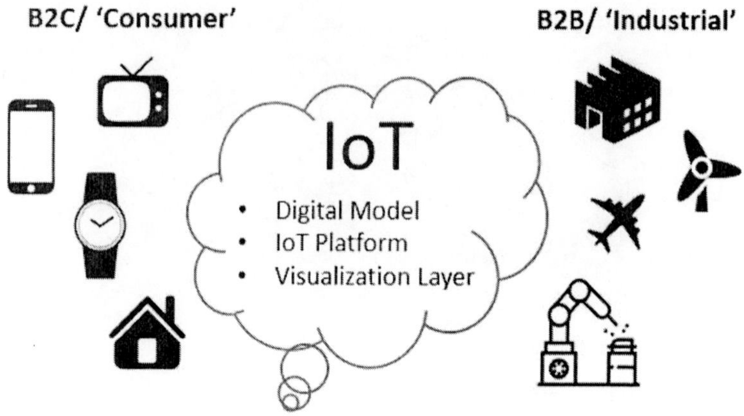

What is IoT?

'The illustration indicates that IoT has applications in both B2C and B2B domains,' Dillon continued. 'Let me address both in turn.

'First up is consumer/B2C: Interconnecting end consumer devices. An example is a consumer's phone instructing his or her TV to start recording a specific show. Consumer IoT devices may include phone, wearable devices, TV, home appliances, home monitoring system and home automation system.

'Next is industrial/B2B: Connecting heavy equipment and machinery. An example is an operator analysing and optimizing the performance of a wind turbine based on the data transmitted by the turbine, and the analysis of the data in the IoT cloud. Equipment in the B2B IoT category includes factory machines, health care devices, robots, heavy machinery and vehicles.'

A hand shot up from the back. 'Which technology components make up an IoT system?'

Dillon replied, 'Well, an IoT system may consist of three technology components listed below. Most major industrial automation organizations such as GE, Siemens, Honeywell and ABB, among others, offer these technology solutions.

First, there's the Digital Model or 'Twin': this refers to the engineering or physics model of the equipment, such as a waste heat recovery boiler or rectifier. Example: the digital twin of GE's aircraft engine. When the equipment is connected to the IoT, the digital twin enables the operator to monitor the performance parameters and potentially optimize the output by manipulating the parameters.

'Second, there's an IoT layer: Equipment or devices, represented by their respective *process models*, may be connected to a platform that allows the broad monitoring of overall parameters, for example, ABB's "Asset Vista". Process models are not as detailed as engineering models. The platform enables operators to perform condition-based maintenance (CBM) of equipment. This includes real-time monitoring, modelling and controlling of parameters, including "what-if" analyses.

'Finally, there's the visualization layer: There is typically an analytics or visualization layer on top of the IoT platform, which allows data to be modelled and displayed in a way that answers queries and aids decision-making, for example, Siemens' MindSphere.'

Digital versus IT

'But how is this different from IT?' someone asked.

'Well, in IT, the only "connected" device is the computer. Digital goes beyond computers: it integrates physical assets, machines, industrial equipment; in fact, anything with a microprocessor chip inside it.'

'And who owns the function?'

'Good question,' replied Dillon. 'Is this something IT should own? Not really, unless the current functional responsibility of IT is enlarged. IT, in its present form, primarily drives automation, for example, the automation of data generation and transmission during shop floor execution in a manufacturing or service shop. What used to be written on a piece of paper and passed on to the next machine operator for processing now gets entered into a software system, thereby reducing manual errors and establishing a single source of truth.

'But digital ventures beyond IT, namely in the vertical and horizontal integration of systems. For example, in most organizations, there is little to no integration between finance, sales, marketing, treasury, procurement, supply chain and other critical functions within the company. And we're talking about corporations already using an ERP system. In organizations which don't have a robust implementation of ERP, the integration is even more woeful. Consequently, decision-making gets bogged down in phone calls, e-mails and the hunt for paper documents.

'Digital provides robust integration between these diverse systems.'

'But the broader question still remains, on what constitutes the essential difference between IT and digital,' asked a young woman seated in a middle row.

'In technology conferences around the world,' replied Dillon, 'I hear this question all the time, including one I attended in Mumbai two weeks ago.

'It's best to summarize the broad differences in the form of an illustration,' Dillon added, as he projected the following picture.

Differences between IT and Digital

Facet	IT	Digital
Definition	Computer systems that support internal operations, compliance and legal	A set of technology capabilities, architectures and mindset that provide coverage beyond computer systems
Examples of technologies	ERP, CRM, cloud, storage, information security, infrastructure, etc.	IoT, analytics, machine learning, artificial intelligence, block chain, etc.
The team	IT department, built of internal resources and managers of contracts with vendors	Most commonly: multi-function teams, reporting to a Chief Digital Officer
Objective	IT operations—'keep the lights on'	Business goals—cost, revenue, UX, etc.
Typical project	Automate payroll and planning	Improve end-user experience; increase volume

Digital Is Also Analytics, but Wait—Isn't That IT?

'Thanks, Mr Dillon. How about analytics? Is that part of digital?' asked a middle-aged man sitting in the front row.

'I was coming to that,' replied Dillon. 'An essential aspect of digital is analytics, which refers to insights resulting from the systematic analysis of data. To be precise, it's the use of data in order to provide you with *actionable* insights that deliver *quantifiable* benefits. In the 1990s and 2000s, analytics used to be known by other terms such as data warehousing (DW) or business intelligence (BI). But the difference between those and analytics is that in the latter, you have the ability to integrate and read data not only from software systems but also machines and equipment, and the possibility of using tools and platforms that are much more powerful and sophisticated than anything that existed before. For this reason, analytics is, strictly speaking, not entirely a part of IT.

'What is the fuel for analytics? Data, of course. Jorge Perez, a data leader at GE, puts it this way: "Immediate access to a rich data set is the biggest problem. Data is the biggest supplement to innovation." If we provide "good" data in the hands of technology teams, good things will happen. Hunting for the "right" data, in fact, is a draining challenge for most data leaders.'

'Can you provide examples of data that would be useful to an organization?' asked someone from the back.

'Here's a list of example "data sets" that would be useful to an organization,' replied Dillon. 'They are:

- Service customer
- New sales customer
- Price
- Reliability
- Cost
- Performance record
- Loyalty (deferred accruals)
- Suppliers.'

'What is analytics, by the way?' asked a woman sitting in the front. 'I've heard the term thrown around all the time, but I've never had it defined simply.'

'Sure,' reassured Dillon. 'It's not too hard to define the term. As I explained just a little while ago, analytics refers to the extraction of insights from the systematic analysis of data; it's something that helps you continuously improve systems and practices.

'Here are the components of the analytics technology stack:

- RDBMS: The database layer at the bottom, such as Oracle, SAP HANA or MS SQL
- ERP: The ERP system, such as Oracle, SAP or Salesforce
- Data modelling: This layer is needed to build a view of the data that's useful, for example, R, Python or Qlik
- Scripting: This layer lets you build complex logic using the data, for example, R, Python or Qlik
- Visualization: This is the front end that displays the data in the form of interactive charts, histograms, etc., for example, Tableau, Lumira or Business Objects.'

'Do you have any pointers on what we need to keep in mind as we pursue an analytics agenda at our companies?' asked a young woman sitting in the back.

'Yes, in fact I do,' responded Dillon. 'Talking to the data leaders at world-class organizations, a wish list emerges:

- Democratize the data. In other words, don't restrict access to it, or make folks jump through hoops to lay their hands on the data. Data lake is a great technology to do it. Data lakes are systems or repositories of data in their natural format, typically a single store of all enterprise data, most of it raw. The reason we want to have a data lake is because we cannot make all our data sources uniform (e.g., a single version of an ERP).

- Accelerate education. Make sure your folks are trained on data lakes and the latest visualization technologies. An example of a data lake is the distributed file system used in Apache Hadoop. Some of the most widely used visualization tools and platforms are Tableau, Qlik and Microsoft Power BI.[3]
- Develop cross-SBU user cases (SBU stands for strategic business unit). One of the most common challenges is that data exists in silos across business units, which limits its usefulness. Instead, seek data that spans factories and businesses. The goal is to avoid being restrictive. For example, an insight such as "which business units incur the biggest transportation costs for movement of parts or products between them?" cannot be gained unless the data spans the said business units.'

Digital Is Also AI

'How about AI? Is that considered part of digital?' asked a man from the middle of the room.

'Digital,' replied Dillon, 'is inextricably linked to AI. When we use insights derived from machine data and systems to formulate analytics, and influence and enhance the behaviour of the machine—such that the machine *learns* over time—we have just injected machine intelligence, or AI, into our technology.

'Some of the largest companies in the world, including Siemens, GE, Intel, NVIDIA and Microsoft, are using AI/ML approaches to improve several important aspects of manufacturing.

'For example, Fanuc, the Japanese industrial robotics major, is employing ML techniques as follows. Its industrial robots train themselves by performing the same task again and again, refining their learning with each iteration of the task, until they achieve a predefined level of accuracy. Fanuc works with NVIDIA to enable multiple robots to learn together. As a leader said, "The idea is that what could take one robot eight hours to learn, eight robots can learn in one hour."'[4]

'The examples you provide are all from industrial-type companies. How about consumer-oriented businesses?'

Dillon replied, 'It's not just manufacturing companies that are employing AI/ML in order to make a big dent to their costs or revenue; consumer-focused corporations are using the technology to revolutionize several aspects of UX and for upselling or cross-selling. Forbes reports that 84 per cent of marketing organizations are implementing or expanding AI and ML, and 75 per cent of enterprises report increases to customer satisfaction by more than 10 per cent.[5]

'Improving end customer experience is an important goal; enhancing employee satisfaction is another. For example, based on the direct experience of one of the authors, a large mining major is using chatbots and virtual assistants in order to improve employees' job satisfaction by more than 10 per cent by enabling them to engage in two-way conversations with top leadership.'

'What are the major components of AI?'

'AI consists of the following broad elements,' replied Dillon.

- 'ML: Computer algorithms that improve automatically through experience, for example, industrial robot mentioned earlier.
- Natural language processing: The ability of machines to understand human language, for example, voice recognition technologies to operate digital models of machines, or even the machines themselves.
- Perception: Ability to use input from sensors to deduce aspects of the world, for example, speech recognition, facial recognition (to control access to high value equipment) and object recognition.
- Motion and manipulation: Robotics and mobility, for example, robots moving products in warehouses. It's important to mention Moravec's Paradox: "It's comparatively easy to make computers exhibit adult level performance on intelligence tests or playing checkers, and difficult or impossible to give them skills of a one-year-old when it comes to perception and mobility." Why? Because physical dexterity has been a direct target of natural selection for millions of years.[6]

- Social intelligence: Being able to predict the actions of others by understanding their motives and emotional states, thereby allowing an agent to make better decisions, for example, virtual assistants that help customers make product selection in department stores.'

Isn't All This the Same as Industry 4.0?

'Wait a second—all of this sounds very similar to Industry 4.0, does it not?'

'No, digital and Industry 4.0 are different in one fundamental aspect,' replied Dillon. 'Industry 4.0 relates to the *automation of manufacturing*. What digital covers, in addition to manufacturing automation, is end-user experience. How do we give the consumer a world-class experience? How do we *simplify* their experience? How do we enhance the experience of employees? These questions collectively point to what is called the "soft side of digital."

'In fact, there is confusion on whether DT, Industry 4.0 and AI are one and the same thing.[7] They are not. The illustration would probably help clarify that the relationship is as follows: AI is a subset of Industry 4.0, which, in turn, is a subset of digital. Analytics may be considered to be the overlap between digital and IT,' concluded Dillon as he projected the following picture.

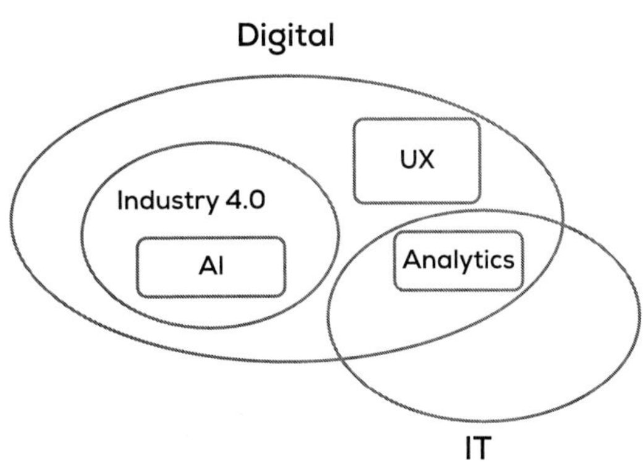

Digital versus Industry 4.0 versus AI versus IT

Is DT the Same as Digital?

'I have a question that may be silly,' said a young man sitting in the front. 'I hear the terms digital and DT more or less interchangeably. Do you think they're one and the same?'

'No,' replied Dillon. 'DT refers to the process of the transformation of an organization with little, or no, digital capability, to one having substantially more digital capability. It's relatively quick, and business-altering, which is what you'd need to justify the tag of "transformation." On the other hand, digital doesn't necessarily imply transformation.

'In fact, DT "is the profound transformation of business and organizational activities, processes, competencies and models to fully leverage the changes and opportunities of a mix of digital technologies."[8]

'It's probably best to consider the two side by side,' added Dillon. He showed the following picture on the screen.

Clarifying DT

Aspect	Digital Transformation	Digital
Transformation? Profound change?	Yes	No
Speed	Words such as 'speed' and 'acceleration' are relevant to a transformation journey	Not relevant
Boundary	Journey with a starting point, end point and intermediary goals	Not a journey
Disruption	Transformations are disruptive	Not necessarily disruptive
Capabilities	No long-term capability building	Capabilities need to be built for long-term sustainable digital momentum
Organizational culture	Supportive culture essential for carrying out transformation	Culture is important, but not critical

The Digital Mindset (i.e., Digital Isn't Only about Technology)

'Does digital simply mean the implementation of technology?'

Dillon pondered for a moment and replied, 'No, it's more accurate to describe it as "the integration of technology with a shift in mindset."[9] A top manufacturing company CxO put it best: "Digital has to change the way we do business: the way we think, the way we operate and the way others view us."

'A digital mindset entails the following:

- Start by defining what digital means. When senior leadership at most organizations refer to digital, they mean the implementation of new technology (e.g., IoT or AI)—but it's really the integration of technology with a shift in mindset. Unless there is a common agreement on the objective, that is, what the organization wishes to accomplish, the effort would likely be ineffective. The importance of this step cannot be overstated. Without senior management agreement, your digital initiative simply isn't going to work.
- Inculcate the culture that establishes a shift in the mindset.
    - Organizational buy-in from the top: A digital mindset needs to be driven from the top. Typically, you won't see a successful DT where the CEO hasn't enthusiastically championed the cause. Digital cannot be successfully driven by a CDO unless a broad buy-in is mandated by the CEO or chairman. In case of Domino's, "organizational buy-in from the top was critical", leading to a $4B sales in digital, and a 7,000 per cent appreciation in stock price in 10 years.[10]
    - Agility: The central idea is to test new concepts and ideas, "fail fast" (i.e., rule out approaches that don't work) and be collaborative. It also means the organization needs to adopt an agile technology development mindset, which includes a DevOps model, continuous integration and delivery (CI/CD) and an iterative approach of delivering a solution (MVP).

- o Think digital first: Successful digital organizations instil a culture of challenging any and all processes and practices. For example, why do we have a paper-based approval? Why can't we automate the registration process? etc.
- o Customer centricity: Successful organizations involve customers in their strategy. For example, if the objective is to replace the production chain or supply chain with a digital core, they require input from customers (e.g., how they would pay, how they'd register, etc.).
- o Belief in the process: The best digital organizations believe in the process even though the results may not be visible instantly. For example, Domino's management patiently backed an ambitious DT strategy using a mobile-first philosophy, which has today yielded it impressive market leadership using their "order from anywhere" approach.'[10]

- Take a holistic view of people, process and technology. How do employees need to be reskilled? What sort of an organization structure best supports digital? How can processes be optimized using analytics? Which technologies do we want to start with?
- In-source critical skills: The most successful companies bring in front-end developers, product designers and product managers, rather than rely on technology vendors. This allows them to easily align their technology team with business process owners and derive greater benefits from digital. A case in point is the DT journey of Sprint.'[11]

What Does This All Add up To? What's Digital Again…?

'Thanks, this is really useful,' said a middle-aged woman in the front row. 'Do you have a definition of digital—a way to encapsulate all that you've explained about it?'

'Certainly,' replied Dillon. 'Digital may be defined in two phases: First, digital is a crucial business need, a combination of technology, culture and mindset that provides key organizational capabilities, enabling a business to obtain a competitive advantage.

'Second, digital challenges status quo, enables a paradigm shift, asks the tough questions on major business processes and even redefines the business model itself.

'Done right, digital enables B2B and B2C businesses to improve their revenue, reduce their costs and improve their productivity. But, in time, digital will cease to be the enabler, it will be the function, the purpose of the company.'

'I do have a question—when you say "crucial", what do you mean?'

'The reason we term digital as a crucial business need,' replied Dillon, 'is because DT is now "a matter of survival"[12] just like ERP software which was, at one point in time, considered a tool for providing a competitive advantage but is now considered a must-have.'

'I work for a textile manufacturer,' said a man from a middle row. 'Is it too late for us to start our own DT? Have we missed the bus?'

'No,' replied Dillon. 'Every company, no matter what the industry, can, and should, get on a DT journey as soon as possible. No matter where they are, they need to take their digital capabilities to the next level. Digital masters—companies that use digital technologies to drive significantly higher levels of profit, productivity and performance—do exist, but they're rare. [You] may be tempted to believe you can wait. ... [but that kind of thinking] is wrong.[13]

'A question I often hear from business leaders is "Technology has been around for a while. What's different about this 'wave' of new technologies you're calling digital? Why should we care?" While business leaders are understandably wary of anything that may later be exposed as a fad, here is the main reason why digital has a tremendous potential to do well.

'Although technology has been around for ages, but what's new about this wave is the convergence of a number of revolutionary new technologies at one time (IoT, AI, ML, etc.), each of which is powerful enough to disrupt industries on its own. What's likely to occur is a seismic shift in how corporations do business. Additionally, technology today is about the experience of end users whose profile is changing rapidly. Millennials constitute the biggest consumer segment; we have a workforce in organizations who'll simply not accept the "old way" of doing things.'

The next morning, Dillon bumped into Srini in the break room. 'I heard rave reviews of your session of last night,' Srini said. 'A young engineer from my team told me although the session was planned for an hour, it lasted nearly two hours, and yet the audience stayed for the full duration. That's impressive! A lot of the folks at these events usually turn up to check a box. Clearly, your audience felt benefited.'

'Thanks, I appreciate the comment,' remarked Dillon. 'I think we have the start of something great here. Our focus should be to continue selling the concept while getting started on execution. I now believe our team has a working understanding of digital. Let's go and do it!'

References

[1] My Wonder Studio. 2012, October. *The Blind Men and the Elephant.* Available at http://www.mywonderstudio.com/level-1/2012/10/3/the-blind-men-and-the-elephant.html (accessed on 15 April 2019).

[2] Murphy, Kimberly. 2016, October. *Are You Ready to Get Connected? Get Insights? and Get Optimized?* Available at https://www.linkedin.com/pulse/you-ready-get-connected-insights-optimized-kimberly-murphy/ (accessed on 15 April 2019).

[3] Davis, Jessica. 2016, June. '10 Visualization Tools to Bring Analytics into Focus.' *Information Week.* Available at https://www.informationweek.com/big-data/software-platforms/10-data-visualization-tools-to-bring-analytics-into-focus/d/d-id/1325679?image_number=4 (accessed on 15 April 2019).

[4] Walker, Jon. 2018, May. 'Machine Learning in Manufacturing.' *Tech Emergence.* Available at https://www.techemergence.com/machine-learning-in-manufacturing/ (accessed on 15 April 2019).

[5] Columbus, Louis. 2018, February. '10 Ways Machine Learning is Revolutionizing Marketing.' *Forbes.* Available at https://www.forbes.com/sites/louiscolumbus/2018/02/25/10-ways-machine-learning-is-revolutionizing-marketing/#7ea133525bb6 (accessed on 15 April 2019).

[6] *The Economist. 2018,* April. 'IKEA Furniture and the Limits of AI.' Available at https://www.economist.com/leaders/2018/04/21/ikea-furniture-and-the-limits-of-ai (accessed on 15 April 2019).

[7] Buskell, Matt. 2016, July. 'Is Digital Transformation, Industry 4.0 and Artificial Intelligence the Same Picture taken by Different People?' *AI Business*. Available at https://aibusiness.com/is-digital-transformation-industry-4–0-and-artificial-intelligence-the-same-picture-taken-by-different-people-by-matt-buskell-of-rainbird/ (accessed on 15 April 2019).

[8] iScoop. 2018, June. *Digital Transformation: Online Guide to Digital Business Transformation*. Available at https://www.i-scoop.eu/digital-transformation/ (accessed on 15 April 2019).

[9] Lipman, Victor. 2017, July. 'Practical Tips to Help Companies Develop a Digital Mindset.' *Forbes*. Available at https://www.forbes.com/sites/victorlipman/2017/07/19/practical-tips-to-help-companies-develop-a-digital-mindset/#779060ec7fe5 (accessed on 15 April 2019).

[10] Wong, Kyle. 2018, January. 'How Domino's Transformed into an E-Commerce Powerhouse Whose Product Is Pizza.' *Forbes*. Available at https://www.forbes.com/sites/kylewong/2018/01/26/how-dominos-transformed-into-an-ecommerce-powerhouse-whose-product-is-pizza/#6368b81d7f76 (accessed on 15 April 2019).

[11] Abramovich, Giselle. 2018. 'Inside Sprint's Digital Transformation Journey.' *CMO.com*. Available at https://www.cmo.com/features/articles/2018/1/25/inside-sprints-digital-transformation-journey.html#gs.EcAkAUw (accessed on 15 April 2019).

[12] Ismail, Nick. 2017, July. 'Digital Transformation is Now a Matter of Survival.' *Information Age*. Available at https://www.information-age.com/digital-transformation-matter-survival-123467460/ (accessed on 15 April 2019).

[13] Westerman, George, Didier Bonnet and Andrew McAfee. 2014. *Leading Digital*. Brighton, MA: Harvard Business Review Press.

5

Digital Augurs Well

How Have Organizations Benefited from Digital?

'Can I join the party?'

It was Hari, the head of HR, who peered inside the conference room from near the partly opened door. 'I'm noticing a systematic attempt at minimizing the influence of HR,' he said, smiling.

'A conspiracy? Nothing of the kind,' replied Dillon. 'At the request of the CEO, we're simply meeting to make sure our leaders are on the same page so far as our understanding of the benefits of digital are concerned. Please do join.'

'Actually it was my idea to ask the CEO that we need a session like this,' said Falguni, the CFO, seated at the head of the table. 'I'll tell you up front, you must convince me of the value before I sign off on any budget request.'

'Count me as a skeptic, too,' chimed Om, the COO, who sat next to Falguni. 'I'm not questioning your ability, Dillon, but I must say I'm wondering how someone who doesn't have direct experience in working in an Indian organization can pull this off.'

Then you are questioning my ability, Dillon thought. 'Sure, I understand where you're coming from,' he said. 'All I ask is that you listen with an open mind.'

'Let the leader have his say,' said Prabhat, the head of projects. 'We can judge for ourselves whether we agree with his vision or not. Go ahead, Dillon.'

'Well,' began Dillon, 'a close friend, a senior technology executive at a large consumer electronics retailer says,[1] 'We are leveraging digital technologies such as virtual reality to enhance in-store customer experiences and drive sales. At the same time, we are using digital to optimize our operations and achieve higher operational efficiencies.

'In general, however, we need to take a step back and start with the end in mind. Start with the why. Why do digital at all? What do organizations want out of digital? And more importantly, what are the quantifiable benefits that can be delivered using some of the technologies we've discussed so far?

'It may be said that the "bottom line" reason an organization wants to leverage technology is because it wishes to achieve one or more of the following objectives:

- Increase free cash flow (FCF)
- Reduce working capital (WC)
- Increase earnings, specifically the EBITDA

'Based on the aforementioned objectives, five major need areas or themes for digital may be listed as follows:

- Enable greater operating efficiencies (i.e., reduce cost)
- Unlock new sources of growth and revenue
- Improve health, safety and environment (HSE)
- Enhance customer and employee experiences—the soft side of digital
- Enforce compliance, statutory and legal requirements'

'I don't know about you all,' said Hari, 'but I like stories. While this abstract information makes logical sense, Dillon, I think it'd be far more effective if you have examples—stories—of how you envision digital making a real difference to a company's bottom line.'

'That's right,' added Falguni. 'Ever since the two failed ERP implementations I was involved with, I'm not sure I'm very open-minded about technology projects that come with big tabs. Show me the success!'

'I'll be glad to,' retorted Dillon, 'if you can open up your mind. Just because two ERP projects you were involved with failed, that doesn't render technology a failure. I'd say you found two ways in which not to approach an ERP implementation.'

'Putting it differently doesn't make it better, Dillon,' said Falguni. 'I need cold, hard facts. Success stories. Real benefits.'

'Okay,' responded Dillon. 'Let's take a look at a few success stories of organizations that have benefited from adopting digital. Huge benefits are available to corporations that create significant operational efficiencies or innovative and compelling customer experiences. The corporations listed here represent a sample of those organizations that have been the leaders in their space; there are doubtless many others in the respective spaces who're either leading or following the digital revolution.

JetBlue Wants to Be #1 in Customer Service

'JetBlue Airways, I'm sure you know, is one of the largest airlines in the USA, with over 21,000 employees and over $7B in revenue. It also has a history of technology breakthroughs, including live TV in seatbacks and the first satellite-based, on-board Wi-Fi.[2]

'The mission of JetBlue's technology organization is to "bring humanity back to air travel."'[3] The most important, specific objective being *simplicity*.

'The following specific initiatives have allowed JetBlue to achieve its digital objectives:

- Their near-field communications (NFC) system allows the elimination of "the often laborious check-in process, essentially allowing a kiosk to identify a customer and profile the minute he or she walks up to it".[2] Additionally, biometrics-based boarding processes are being rolled out in order to enhance the travel experience.

- The team is implementing more AI and ML technologies into the company's customer service processes in order to get to know the customer very well.
- The team is also working to enhance the employee experience. The IT team has equipped airport-based teams to access weather and flight information using iPads. The devices are also carried by on-flight staff in order to access personal information and preferences of passengers, so that the service is personalized.'

'Doesn't personalization of services require personal information of the user? Won't there be privacy concerns?' asked Hari.

'Absolutely,' replied Dillon. 'As with any other type of technology, end users will have the final say in how much of their personal data they'd like to share. The more they share, the more personalized their service would be, for example, being able to watch their favourite movie during a flight, or reading their favourite magazine, but not all travellers are willing to share personal data, until they're convinced the data won't be shared without their permission.

'Is the airline industry the only space where deep personalization is relevant? Not really. Next I'd like to highlight another domain—restaurants—where digital is creating a huge opportunity.

Domino's Digital Sales Are $4B and Growing

'Domino's is an American pizza restaurant chain founded in 1960,' continued Dillon. 'In February 2018, the chain became the largest pizza seller worldwide in terms of sales.

'Domino's digital sales last year? $4B, including $2B in the USA.[4] *Forbes* calls Domino's an "e-commerce powerhouse."'[5] Domino's stock price, meanwhile, went from about $3/share in 2008 to about $210/share in early 2018.

'Let me ask you this,' said Dillon. 'If you owned a pizza chain, how would you leverage digital?'

'I guess the first thing I'd do,' Prabhat said after a brief silence, 'is to enable multichannel sales.'

'Bingo, you got it!' exclaimed Dillon. 'But that's not all. Here are a few highlights of Domino's digital program:

- Consumers can place orders from any computing device; this is "among the most progressive in the US... the company's AnyWhere platform allows you to place orders through any internet-connected device, including smartphones, smartwatches and smart TVs, by entering orders into the Dominos website, and by tweeting and texting emojis".[4] The key feature here is *choice* of ordering channels, which millennials love.
- Consumers have logged more than a million orders through the voice bot, Dom, since 2014. Natural language processing and AI-based tools enable consumers to order using a smartphone. The order is taken by a virtual assistant, using natural language processing algorithms. Given how complex it can be to order a pizza (think combinations of toppings, a side order and a soda)—not to mention the multitudes of accents and speech patterns employed by customers—and you have an idea of the magnitude of the task.
- The digital team ensures agile delivery of digital services using a strong DevOps culture. The team turns out several iterations of apps and services throughout the course of a day, thanks to an approach built on CI and CD. Iterations are quick, enabling developers to catch and fix software bugs quickly.'

'I guess the last benefit you mentioned related to internal IT processes,' remarked Falguni, with a superior air. 'I can't see how it would benefit the business.'

'It would cut costs, Falguni,' responded Dillon. 'If I told you I can get a new feature out the door in six weeks versus six months, what would it do to IT costs?' Om and Prabhat nodded.

'Operational effectiveness is a key focus area for digital. Aside from the two businesses we've considered so far, there are others where *understanding consumer behaviour* can drive large gains in revenue. Let's look at one such business.

Sprint Figures out Big Data to Increase Sales and Service Revenues

'Sprint, the American telecommunications company and Internet services provider, is one of the largest mobile telephone operators in the USA.

'Sprint officials were faced with a conundrum. Consumers would get on the Sprint website to browse, purchase phones and upgrade their existing products and services. However, for some reason, the consumer would abandon the transaction. In order to figure out the "why" of abandoned transactions, the digital team had to analyse data: lots of it. In fact, about 50 terabytes of it.

'In order to analyse such vast quantities of big data, Sprint turned to open source analytics.[6] This was a marked change from their earlier approach, which depended on individual application teams to monitor the performance of its own software. By analysing the sequence of the breakdown, the team was able to pinpoint the root cause of abandoned transactions, and thereby improve new sales revenue and service income.

'In addition, the digital team created a Hadoop-based data lake to analyse customer data, in order for the system to make a personalized recommendation to the consumer. For example, a 10-year user of Android phones would receive Android phone offers.'[6]

Om raised his hand. 'We have only discussed end-consumer-focused organizations that have utilized digital in order to improve customer satisfaction, sales and service. However, what does it mean for companies like ours, which have as much a manufacturing flavour as they have an end-consumer one? Frankly, I believe digital may not have any direct benefits to offer in our industry!'

'How can you say that?' said Dillon, with some indignation. 'I'm not even done talking through my next success story!'

'Whatever,' shrugged Om. 'Count me as a skeptic. I don't see any evidence that digital isn't just a bunch of hyped-up phrases that has never worked for real, manufacturing-oriented industrials like us.'

'I have a completely different perspective and experience,' stated Dillon with some force. 'In the manufacturing space, where there are no direct "end consumers", digital nevertheless makes a huge impact to revenue, costs and operational efficiencies. We consider such an example next. Have you heard of GE?

GE Uses Digital to Save $100M (and Counting)

'GE was cofounded by Thomas Edison all the way back in 1897. GE just finished the single longest continual tenure on the Dow Jones Industrial Average (111 years) and is in the middle of what *Forbes* calls "one of the most dramatic transformation initiatives of any major company".[7] Between 2010 and 2017, GE went from an industrial company with a large financial services arm to a "digital industrial" company with $7B in software sales.

'Here are a few examples of how digital is reshaping the way GE does business:

- Big industrial conglomerates such as GE order parts worth hundreds of millions of dollars from a large number of suppliers. Often, the orders to such suppliers can come from multiple business units within the same business, for example, health care or energy. GE sought to use digital technology powered by ML, in order to integrate supplier data and consolidate orders, saving over $80M. GE Digital's Bill Ruh said,

  'The supplier data integration was a big win. It's easy for suppliers to charge different prices for the same product when you can't compare them across business units. We might spend $250 million a year on nuts and bolts, but that only becomes salient when you look across business units and see if they're coming from the same suppliers. If they are, you are in a much better position to negotiate.'[7]

- GE's Aviation unit used the "digital twin" model of its CF34–10E engines in order to predict, with 95 per cent accuracy, when the engine may suffer from "nozzle distress". This reduces the frequency of service shop visits for the engine and helps GE fulfil its time-on-wing service level agreements (SLAs) with customers such as British Airways or Singapore Airlines. The digital model predicts dust accumulation, the resulting metal temperature and trailing edge distress. The direct benefits from such a digital twin technology may be hard to quantify, but given that GE Aviation makes 90 per cent of its money from its service businesses, the extra insight provided to its customers may benefit it to the tune of several tens of millions of dollars.
- At the Ramagundam power plant, the largest in South India, GE Power is reducing the CO_2 emissions by 924 megatons by a combination of hardware and software enhancements, specifically analytics. GE has developed software that can analyse data coming from 10,000 sensors on the power plant's equipment and help the operators gauge precisely the right amount of coal to burn and just the right temperature to maximize efficiency. The software can also predict when the utility should take the plant offline for maintenance and reduce unplanned downtime by as much as 5 per cent.'

'I do have a question,' said Om. 'When you say the software can predict when an equipment or plant needs to be taken offline, is that what's also known as *predictive maintenance*?'

'That's correct,' replied Dillon.

'Well then, what's the use of simply predicting when maintenance would be required? Wouldn't it be more useful if the software also told us what the operator or engineer would need to do, in order that the situation may be resolved?'

'You're spot on,' said Dillon. 'What you're describing is what we call *prescriptive maintenance*, that is, a highlight of what's coming up, and also what needs to be done in order to deal with what's coming up.'

'Won't it be useful if the equipment's memory remembered what types of maintenance activities were performed on the machine over the years?' asked Prabhat.

'Absolutely,' remarked Dillon. 'You're all getting good at this. In fact, a software or digital product that did what you just suggested would be said to have performed *prescriptive maintenance with AI* because due to the events recorded over time, the history of the equipment would reveal a highly specific course of action to be performed in a given situation. In the past, a similar maintenance may have occurred, from which lessons got learnt and the equipment now can benefit.'

Dillon paused, in case further questions arose.

'So far, we've looked at businesses that have reinforced or strengthened their existing business models using digital,' he continued. 'However, the truly revolutionary usage of digital technologies has been in the area of the "shared economy", where technology has created multibillion dollar industries from scratch. Let's consider one such example next.

Zipcar Reinvents a Business Model

'A company reinventing itself, or even the industry, is a tall task. However, when such an exceptional event does occur, very often, the means of reinvention is digital, specifically the use of technology to enhance the UX. The examples of Apple (digital media on iPad, iTunes, iPhone, etc.), Uber (transportation) and Airbnb (hospitality) are noteworthy. These ventures are complex and risky, but the returns when they do work out are quite incredible.

'Another company in the same pedigree, that you may never have heard of, is Zipcar, the car-sharing start-up. This company allows customers to rent a car for an hour or a day, and is a brilliant example of the *sharing economy*, which builds on the premise that the majority of cars sits unused for the greater part of the day. Founded in 2000, this company enables consumers to perform the following tasks[8]:

- Consumers can use their credit cards or phone to reserve a car for a duration and gain entry into the car. Cars are conveniently parked in lots that are distributed throughout the town, so the basic challenge of having to travel to one of the few rental locations is eliminated.
- Once consumers pick a car, they can access the vehicle quickly because rental paperwork, registration and check-in are automated.
- Once the car is used and returned, the financial transaction is completely automated; there is no time spent in charging a credit card manually or printing receipts.

'Using this simple, but powerful, concept of sharing, Zipcar built up a nearly million strong membership network by 2013 and offered 10,000 or more vehicles in several countries in North America and Europe.'[8]

'That's quite impressive,' opined Falguni. 'Digital seems to be enabling end consumer-focused businesses to perform fundamental transformations to core business processes. However, I still have to see evidence that industrial businesses, like ours, can benefit, except the GE example which you cited a little while ago.'

'Of course,' replied Dillon, 'the GE example, in fact, is a great example of industrial companies making the digital leap. There are, in fact, other businesses like ours which can make DT work for us in ways that result in even starker changes. Let's go over one more of those.

Roy Hill Mines Greater Profits from Its DT

'Roy Hill, a major Australian mining operation, implemented a digital solution to enhance their end-to-end operational visibility and optimize their mining value chain.[9] The mine was "greenfield", that is, it was a brand new iron ore mine. Each of its handful of infrastructure components were designed to help it meet its overall capacity of 55 million tonnes per annum (mtpa) of iron ore.

'Most mines, typically old industrial houses, are conservative, loathe to move to use technologies that aren't grounded in decades of success. Roy Hill was a new mine with this old problem; it struggled to hit its targets without encountering operational issues and losing profitability.

'After much brainstorming, the company identified a digital solution for the four broad themes or problem areas[9]:

- Demand chain planning and scheduling
- Inventory tracking and quality management
- Delay accounting
- Capacity simulation model

'The instrument of choice that delivered these benefits to the company was a Remote Operations Centre (ROC) in Perth, Australia. In this location, teams working on different processes and technologies came together in order to devise solutions to the problems listed earlier in a state-of-the-art tech centre, achieving risk mitigation, real-time visibility of the entire value chain from scheduling to planning, controlling mine and plant processes and almost all aspects of operations.'

'So the fundamental idea here was to simulate and optimize processes using a digital platform? I mean, if you can recreate a process on a computer, you could, in theory, tweak and maximize productivity?' asked Prabhat.

'That's correct. In addition, the company enabled full visibility of its demand chain, providing the real-time numbers to planners and schedulers,' explained Dillon.

'In this case,' opined Om, 'Digital capabilities were built into a greenfield operation. Are there any examples of how an already-valuable brand using digital to further distance themselves from the competition?'

'Yes, there are a few of those. Let me talk about one of those venerable brands,' replied Dillon.

Nordstrom Wants to Provide the Ultimate Customer Experience

'When I first made my thousand dollars in the USA, I fulfilled one of my childhood dreams: buy a sports jacket from Nordstrom. For a century, this store has prided itself on providing customers with an elegant and top-line customer experience. Growing up poor in the USA, while walking past a Nordstrom store, I always imagined being pampered and made to feel special. *What would it feel like,* I thought, *to enter into one of these stores?*

'Turns out, the company was one of the early digital leaders in its space. In order to maintain and further strengthen its brand, Nordstrom embarked on a bold digital journey in the 1990s.[10] The stated objectives were as follows:

- Innovating customer experience: A system that linked sales to customers' unique needs. In addition, the company developed social apps around the brand, a checkout option on mobile phone, the ability to send a text to a Nordstrom employee and a personalized clothing service on the cloud.
- Seamless UX: The store provided the same look and feel on the cloud (website) as it did in its physical stores, which meant the consumer experienced a "sameness" of experience in the bricks-and-mortar and virtual stores. Since this can only occur if the consumer experience on the cloud is as "rich" as possible, you can't provide the ability to feel the material on the Internet.

'Using the aforementioned innovations, revenues have grown by over 50 per cent in the last five years. What I personally find to be the most striking feature of Nordstrom's strategy is that their leaders understand that they need to continually evolve, or risk losing their leadership, in the luxury retail space. Erik Nordstrom, co-president, said:

> The way customers are choosing to shop in a more digitally-connected world continues to change, and we know we need to find ways for our stores to evolve with them. This is a challenge, but we also see a tremendous opportunity to leverage our stores in ways that will allow us to serve customers into the future better than anyone else.[10]

'Any questions?' asked Dillon. After a pause, he continued, 'Assuming lunch is now a more urgent initiative than digital, let's have a break.' Hari and Om chuckled.

'Before we do that, however, let's summarize the digital technologies used, and the benefits, from these representative examples.' Dillon projected the following summary slide.

Business	Digital Technology	Benefit
JetBlue	Facial recognition, biometrics, AI, ML, mobility	Customer service; user experience
Domino's	Virtual assistant, chatbot, AI, agile DevOps, mobility	$4B in digital sales; customer service
Sprint	Big data, analytics, data lake	Increased sales and service revenue; customer service; personalized service
GE	ML; digital twin; analytics	Inventory and spare parts optimization; customer service SLA; reducing unplanned downtime
Zipcar	IoT, mobility, RFID reader, embedded IT	Customer service; new business model
Roy Hill	Software to automate demand planning, inventory tracking, quality management and capacity simulation	Reduced costs from operational optimization
Nordstrom	Point-of-sale software system, mobile apps, customer–employee texting, cloud	50% increase in revenue in five years

'I hope the illustrations we discussed today persuade you that the benefits are real, that organizations of various sizes and in a variety of domains are reaping the substantial benefits of technology, and that, in some cases, entirely new business models can be developed and grown using technologies that are quite mature,' said Dillon.

The leaders nodded and filed out. Om gave a thumbs-up sign, and Falguni smiled and shook hands with Dillon. 'It's good,' she said. *The ice is melting,* Dillon thought. *Finally.*

Kids Spell Love as T-I-M-E

'So when are you taking Aaron out for basketball?' asked Kavya, the next morning, a bright Saturday, but cooler than normal, with a slight breeze. 'The weather couldn't be better.'

'I know, Honey, but sorry that I can't make it today. I have to prepare the budget draft, and then…'

'Dillon, you're impossible!'

'Why? I'm just saying I have some seriously important stuff on which I need to get caught up. You need to understand!'

'Oh, I understand you all right. In fact, *we* understand you quite clearly. Although, on the outside, you appear to be making efforts to become a better father and husband, in reality you're a self-centred man, too preoccupied to realize your duties towards your family. I expect a little love, at least for our son, but clearly that's too much to ask!'

And Kavya walked into the bedroom in a huff, slamming the door shut behind her.

Don't I really love my family? pondered Dillon. As indignation slowly built up inside him, thoughts of self-pity came to the fore. *No one appreciates what I have to do for the family*. Dillon's eyes welled up.

And then suddenly he remembered something Srini told him a few days ago—that kids spelt love T-I-M-E. In a flash, he saw it all: how in his eagerness to make an early start to the work week, he'd been regularly bringing work home in the weekends, spoiling the time he could otherwise spend with his family in creating beautiful memories.

'Aaron!' he hollered. 'Dad?' said Aaron as he walked slowly in. 'I didn't do anything wrong, I promise!' he added, with fear writ large on his eyes. Normally Daddy didn't summon him unless he needed to be punished for some mischief.

'No, son, you didn't do anything wrong!' Dillon said, as he hugged his son. 'Get your basketball—let's go balling this wonderful Saturday morning!'

'Yeah!' shouted Aaron as he dashed into his room.

Expressing Gratitude

'I'm really glad you spent most of the weekend with your family,' exclaimed Srini, with genuine excitement, on Monday morning.

'Thanks!' Dillon muttered. 'I gained a lot more playing with my son than I would've by working on my presentation.'

'There's one more important element for your happiness, isn't there?' asked Srini.

'I know what you're driving at, Srini,' replied Dillon. 'But I haven't been meditating regularly. I've been a bad boy.'

'There's nothing to be remorseful about,' said Srini. 'Perhaps I can help you. Tell me what's holding you back.'

'Well, I'm sold on the value of meditation,' said Dillon, after some thought. 'But I'm confused about the process—the how.'

'I can help you with that,' replied Srini. 'Would you like to know how I've refined my meditation practice over the years?'

'Of course!'

'First, start by expressing your gratitude for a minute or two. If we train ourselves to become grateful, it leads to a feeling of serenity. If our mind is agitated with the desire to get something, we lose our peace of mind. I started by expressing my gratitude as a matter of rote, but pretty soon, I was getting an incredible amount of peace by simply saying thanks, such as, "Thanks for my beautiful family. Thanks for my good health. Thanks for the health of my parents."

'Next, with emotion, say self-affirmations. Affirm, with emotion, that you are overcoming whatever your current challenge is. If you tend to get angry, for example, say, with belief: "I never get angry. With your help, God, I am overcoming anger". I use a set of about 10 self-affirmations including ego, the unity of creation, divinity in man, ahimsa and love for all. For example, "I see you everywhere, O God—I feel your presence in every atom of this world."

'Finally, focusing your mind on an image of God, still your mind. Or meditate on a mantra or an inspirational message. The goal of meditation is to reach thoughtlessness. However, it takes sustained, consistent effort to get there. Just as a child learns swimming with an inflatable "swim tube" draped around him or her, so you learn meditation by using a mental crutch: an image of God or a saintly figure such as

Mother Teresa, Gandhi or a spiritual guru. Then, by using the full force of your will, slowly still your mind. If that's hard to do, here's an alternative: repeat a spiritual or deeply inspirational message very slowly, for example, the prayer of Saint Francis of Assisi. I cannot begin to tell you how many times my soul has been soothed by simply repeating one simple line from St Francis' prayer, over and over: *It's in giving that we receive.*

'How did I realize I was making progress in meditation? I made an important discovery. All my life, I'd been conditioned to react to people and situations in a certain way: if threatened, I'd fight back. I'd always look after my own interest—*the other person is trying to take advantage of me!* I'd always give back in kind: love for love, hatred for hatred! Now, in meditation, I was reprogramming my mind—to be precise, my subconscious mind.'

'Thank you, Srini!' remarked Dillon with some emotion. 'I can't tell you how much it means to me that you're pouring your heart out to me. I do have a concern though. What if I do all this, and still don't achieve progress in meditation?'

'That's an easy one to answer,' responded Srini. 'Eastern spirituality believes that a step of forward progress is never wasted in the journey to peace. Even if you take a single step forward—say, meditate for a single day—you'll be closer to achieving peace than if you took no step.

'So my dear Dillon, march forward and waste not a thought in remorse or regret.'

References

[1] Accenture. 2018. *Reinventing Business with Digital—A CDO Handbook*, page 8. Dublin: Accenture.

[2] Watson, Brian P. 2016, December. 'JetBlue CIO Drives Innovation through IT's "Toolkit."' *CIO Magazine*. Available at https://www.cio.com/article/3149511/digital-transformation/jetblue-cio-drives-innovation-through-it-s-toolkit.html?nsdr=true (accessed on 15 April 2019).

[3] High, Peter. 2017, September. 'JetBlue's Head of Technology and Digital Also Runs the Company's Venture Arm.' *Forbes*. Available at https://

www.forbes.com/sites/peterhigh/2017/09/05/jetblues-head-of-technology-and-digital-also-runs-the-companys-venture-arm/#64bc5b7e6e48 (accessed on 15 April 2019).

[4] Boulton, Clint. 2016, August. 'Why Domino's Virtual Assistant Struggles to Understand Your Orders.' *CIO Magazine*. Available at https://www.cio.com/article/3111947/digital-transformation/why-dominos-virtual-assistant-struggles-to-understand-your-orders.html?nsdr=true (accessed on 15 April 2019).

[5] Wong, Kyle. 2018, January. 'How Domino's Transformed Into an E-Commerce Powerhouse Whose Product Is Pizza.' *Forbes*. Available at https://www.forbes.com/sites/kylewong/2018/01/26/how-dominos-transformed-into-an-ecommerce-powerhouse-whose-product-is-pizza/#6368b81d7f76 (accessed on 15 April 2019).

[6] Boulton, Clint. 2018, February. '16 Real-World Digital Transformation Success Stories.' *CIO Magazine*. Available at https://www.cio.com/article/3149977/digital-transformation/8-top-digital-transformation-stories-of-2016.html (accessed on 15 April 2019).

[7] Davenport, Bean. 2017, June. 'How AI and Machine Learning are Helping Drive the GE Digital Transformation.' *Forbes*. Available at https://www.forbes.com/sites/ciocentral/2017/06/07/how-ai-and-machine-learning-are-helping-drive-the-ge-digital-transformation/#6aa0640b1686 (accessed on 15 April 2019).

[8] Westerman, George, Didier Bonnet and Andrew McAfee. 2014. *Leading Digital*. Brighton, MA: Harvard Business Review Press.

[9] McMullen, Joseph J. 2018, June. *Roy Hill: A Digital Mining Transformation & Digital Strategy Success Story*. Available at https://sw.aveva.com/blog/roy-hill-a-digital-mining-transformation-digital-strategy-success-story (accessed on 15 April 2019).

[10] Dodson, Ian. 2018. 'Digital Leadership: 6 Examples of Brands That Reign Supreme.' *Digital Marketing*. Available at https://digitalmarketinginstitute.com/the-insider/08–03-17-digital-leadership-6-examples-of-brands-that-reign-supreme (accessed on 15 April 2019).

6

Why Some Things Don't Work Out

If Digital Is This Good, Why Haven't More Indian Companies Benefited?

'Can I come in?' Dillon asked, knocking on the door of the CEO's office.

'Oh, yes,' said Eknath, taking his reading glasses off and smiling. 'The reason I needed to have a quick word with you,' he continued, 'is because the board would like you to give a presentation on the progress on digital at the end of the month.'

'I'd love that,' said Dillon, smiling. 'If I get the board to buy in, it would mean a lot to the team.'

'That's all good, but I'm a little worried. You know KV—the senior board member who was the past chairman at Sterling Bank? I ran into him at the Mumbai board meeting Friday. He made a surprising comment about digital. I'd like you to address the concern right away, or else the board presentation could turn nasty really quickly.'

'What did he say?'

'Well, you may be aware that KV is also on the board at Maset Steel, which is one of India's largest steel manufacturers. He was saying Maset was running digital proof-of-concept (POC) projects for five years. *Five years!* He said LNH Consulting, which ran Maset's digital projects for three years, was booted out in favour of Ascent Solutions, which hasn't had much success with digital either.'

'I've heard about it.'

'Citing a McKinsey study,[1] KV said 70 per cent of DT projects fail, and quoting from a *Harvard Business Review*,[2] he said that some of the best companies in the world ran failed DT projects. One of the largest industrial conglomerates, GE, ran a DT project that was deemed a failure by the stock market. Lego, Nike, Procter & Gamble, Burberry and Ford all ran DT costing millions of dollars "only to encounter significant performance challenges and often shareholder dissent."'[2] Some of the CEOs leading digital were asked to step aside. Gartner says 83 per cent of leaders struggle to make meaningful progress on DT.[3]

'In India, KV said the number is higher, based on anecdotal evidence, such as the case with Maset Steel. I'm now quoting KV verbatim: "I've heard about a lot of pilot projects and POCs, but I haven't heard of too many successful DTs", he said. And then he said something for which I had no response. "If digital is this good, why don't we hear of more success stories? Why haven't Indian companies benefited like American and European companies have?"'

'I wouldn't entirely agree with his line of thinking. While I agree there are real challenges that have slowed the adoption of digital among Indian companies, there have been quite a few success stories as well. I can recount several successful digital interventions at Tata, Mahindra & Mahindra and Vedanta Sterlite.[4] At Mahindra Finance, the team achieved quicker turnaround times. Vedanta's Sterlite unit ran a program to eliminate fatalities. And Tata Steel created over $35MM in value using analytics.'

'You may be right,' said Eknath. 'However, we must prepare for this line of questioning. Facts are needed to counter strong opinions or narratives. At the last board meeting, KV killed our French unit's quarterly report with a sceptical comment that the rest of the board picked up on. What I'd like you to do is to prepare a slide that refers specifically to this concern.'

Not an Event, but a Journey

The next Monday, Dillon was closeted in a conference room with Cyril and Dinesh.

'Before we begin, I'd like to say thanks to the two of you,' said Dillon. 'As I explained on Friday when I bumped into you, the CEO wants us to prepare a slide explaining the lack of digital success, especially among Indian companies. I thought I could count on Cyril's skills with PowerPoint and Dinesh's ability to ask questions, and get this done over a working lunch today. And don't worry, I've ordered the best-quality pizza for us,' added Dillon, chuckling.

'Bepo's Pizza?' asked Cyril, hopefully.

'That's right!' responded Dillon.

'All right, Dillon, thanks for your confidence in us,' said Dinesh. 'I guess I'd like to start by asking you what, in your mind, is the top reason why Indian companies haven't made as much progress as some of the others.'

'Here is the top reason. Most senior business leaders believe that they can buy a piece of technology—"digital technology"—and implement it and start seeing the benefits in a matter of months. To start with, there is not one piece of technology that's digital; it's a combination of several technologies. In addition, DTs require time because of several reasons.[5]

'First, digital requires complex changes to be made to processes and people. These changes are interrelated in ways that sometimes can't be totally predicted and planned for. For example, digital may enable a process to be compressed, which means a planned on-premise ERP implementation may need to be scrapped in favour of a simpler cloud solution. That would, in turn, require a completely new private cloud strategy.

'Second, some digital technologies need several years to bear fruit, by definition. For example, a digital twin of an engine, which may be expected to depend on AI technology to predict and prevent failures, wouldn't work very unless two or three years' worth of data—most of it newly generated—accumulates in the system.

'Third, digital technologies are not as commoditized yet as, say, ERP or CRM software, which means, a pharmaceutical company implementing AI technology for expediting clinical trials, or a metals and mining company executing an IoT project for optimizing equipment performance, may not have too many precedents. They'd be at the bleeding edge of new technology implementation and not realize it. This means they can't predict the pains and challenges that derive out of the complexity of that project, which would then mean that their implementation would take longer as they sort out the issues.'

'OK, I'm beginning to get a sense of what you're driving at,' said Cyril. 'What would you like the first bullet point on the page to be?'

'I'd say, DT *is not an event, it's a journey.* It may take 5 years, or even be a 10-year exercise.[6] You'll find that the digital journey never ends, although the transformation phase of it may get over in three years or so.'

'Great, Dillon,' said Dinesh. 'The reason this is important is because it sets realistic expectations in the mind of leaders and reduces the chances of unmet expectations in terms of time and money. Question: is this more of an issue with Indian business leaders than, say, American leaders?'

'Based on my experience of working in the USA and in India,' replied Dillon, 'I'd say the answer is yes. When I consulted in Boston for a top-4 consulting company, I was the strategy consultant for some of the top US-based conglomerates. I found that while leaders were ruthless in terms of the commercials and project timelines, they were also realistic about timelines once they were mutually agreed upon. In India, however, I notice a sense of impatience, a constant attitude of questioning whether a payback was realized yet, even though the project may have been in flight merely for a few months.'

'What next, Dillon?' asked Cyril.

Digital Is No One's Salvation

'The success, or failure, of DT cannot be determined as though it were a disconnected, independent endeavour. Usually, there are many factors that weigh in on a company's performance, such as the economy, product design or government policy and regulations.

'Suppose a company grew from $100M to $1B in annual revenue while aggressively investing in IT. Can it then be said that the company grew tenfold simply because of IT? Perhaps it was IT that contributed significantly, but it's unlikely that it was the only reason.

'In a similar way, digital cannot be the deliverance. 'No managers should view digital—or any other major technological innovation—as their sure salvation.[2]

'Here's another reason the expectations from digital need to be realistic. Digital is not something you can purchase and plug into your company's operations. It requires a multifaceted approach involving execution rigour, an agile mindset and a carefully nurtured culture. Cyril, you don't need to type so furiously; I'll discuss these aspects in more detail shortly.'

'Thanks, Dillon,' said Cyril, looking relieved. 'But what does this mean, in terms of action items that the organization needs to perform?'

'What it means,' replied Dillon, 'is that an organization needs to move carefully towards digital and allocate budget after thoughtful deliberations. Sometimes, in fact, the overall digital investment needs to be diminished in favour of a few, carefully selected digital initiatives that are aligned with higher value activities, as was done at Nike in 2014.'

'Is it accurate, then, if we summarize this point as follows?' asked Dinesh. '*Digital initiatives should not be undertaken unless they're closely aligned to organizational strategy and provide a clear value. DT shouldn't be run because it's viewed as sexy or as a salvation.*'

'Perfect,' responded Dillon.

The Execution Gap

'The next major reason,' replied Dillon, 'stems from the fact that while digital strategies are fairly well established, there haven't been too many successful executions.'

'Interesting that you bring this up,' remarked Cyril. 'As you were speaking, I ran a search on Amazon for "digital strategy", and I found over 10,000 hits. When I run a search for "digital execution", guess how many hits I get? Precisely 86.'

'Gosh,' remarked Dinesh. 'So it's over a 100 times easier to locate strategy?'

'While it may simply be a case of using the right keywords for search,' said Dillon, 'here're a couple of reasons executions are not as easy as formulating strategies. For one, well, talking is always easier than acting. And in addition, I don't see the willingness to stick to the rigours of project management. This is more of an issue in India than in the USA for reasons unknown to me.

'I'll give you a few examples. Budgeting the cost of DT into the annual business plan, in some cases, is an afterthought, because digital is not yet a permanent line item in the CIO's or COO's budget. Since the technologies are not yet a commodity, as opposed to say, those for ERPs, the cost varies widely. For example, the cost for an IoT solution for a boiler varies between $80,000 and $700,000. Given such uncertainty, sometimes the CxO doesn't put the right number in, or doesn't put any number in, because it's taking forever to get an accurate quote.

'Second, most companies don't know how to put together a proper and actionable RFQ or request for proposal (RFP). You can't be vague in specifying digital requirements. Since the technology is relatively new, one needs to be very specific on the scope: which equipment? How much benefit? How about payment terms? Would the partner only be paid if benefits kicked in? If so, what percentage would be linked to delivery? How would the proposed technology integrate with existing ERPs, programmable logic controllers (PLCs), supervisory control and data acquisitions (SCADAs) and other existing systems? Would existing data historians be reused? These are just examples, mind you, but we may safely agree that the amount of specificity required is high.

'Third, there are other important documents that hold the key to successful execution, such as the note for approval (NFA), which enables executive management to sign off on the proposed digital investment and the SOW that precisely defines the scope of the work, timelines and division of responsibilities between the partner and the client.

'I consider all these documents as part of the execution phase. Now, even if these are in place, the rest of the steps of execution need to be followed quite faithfully. For example, can you execute a digital strategy if you don't have a formal vision and mission and a strategy document? Or if you don't have a digital advisory board, or don't perform the digital maturity assessment? Or don't prioritize the digital themes and outcomes, or hold value discovery workshops?'

'How about the choice of the partner, and the tools and technologies? Wouldn't those, too, determine the likelihood of success?' asked Dinesh.

'Of course,' agreed Dillon. 'Additionally, whether one adopts execution methodologies such as Agile and DevOps would also influence the likelihood of a successful outcome.'

'These steps,' concluded Dillon, 'tedious or formulaic as they may appear, nevertheless hold the key to a successful outcome. So the third bullet point on your presentation may be, *beware the execution gap, which results from shortcuts that eliminate critical documents or steps in the execution process. Discipline pays.*'

'This is excellent, Dillon,' remarked Cyril, as he typed into his laptop. 'Is there a bullet point #4?'

The Agile Mindset

'Oh yes, there's a Number 4 and more after that,' replied Dillon. 'There are a few concrete reasons why DTs fail. If we communicate it in a way that resonates with the board, it enhances their perception that this team understands the pitfalls and, therefore, must know how to deal with those.

'I mentioned Agile a few moments ago. Let me elaborate. Over the years, business leaders have come to view technology transformations as multiyear, multimillion dollar endeavours. A case in point is ERP and other complex software applications such as manufacturing execution systems. However, you have to think differently with digital.

'While business and IT leaders agree that DTs are disruptive, while being crucial to the future of the organization, they should insist that the IT team not boil the ocean and instead come up with an agile, measurable roll-out plan. GE undertook a massive DT journey and realized after 8 years and $4B that the stated objectives hadn't been met.[6] In business speak, it tanked.

'In the new world of digital and Industry X.0, business and IT leaders need to bring their A game, as in an Agile mindset to the game. Don't commit $5M and two years; instead, commit $50,000 and three months. Don't seek a wholesale transformation to start with, such as digitization of the entire supply chain. Start with a modest, measurable goal such as implementing a demand forecasting solution and integrating it with your ERP.

'Next, adopt an agile development model, that is, fail fast—if you must fail—and reiterate. Rather than completing your development steps in major, sequential chunks—we call it the waterfall approach—perform them in smaller bits in parallel. Involve your functional teams from business in daily calls with the IT team that clarify the requirements up front and enable the functional people to really get what they want, now. Your business people may traditionally be hesitant to commit time on a daily basis, but if you tell them you'll deliver the functionality—okay, just the first iteration of it—in two weeks, you'll suddenly find they're enthusiastic about committing time.

'In other words, and here's your bullet point #4, Cyril: *commit to an agile mindset in budgeting, formulating, strategizing, tracking and executing your digital agenda.*

'Which brings me to a biggie on the list, culture.

Build the Culture First; The Culture Will Build Your Capability

'In my very first job,' said Dillon, 'I had a boss who had a unique way of dealing with difficult situations with employees or peers. He'd reach out to a third person, who may not even be involved in the situation, and share details of the situation, even ask for help. Management experts call this behaviour "triangulation, a typical dysfunctional pattern of managers who don't have the courage to deal directly with an issue by communicating honestly to diffuse the situation."'[7]

'But are there cultural deficiencies that especially afflict Indian organizations?' asked Dinesh.

'In some Indian companies—I'm stating this at the cost of sounding like I'm generalizing—I have noticed a culture of fear and dictatorships. Subordinates don't speak up; feedback isn't provided to bad managers; dictators are often tolerated for purposes of production quotas. Authoritarian decision-making is common; collaborative leadership is not rewarded.

'Challenges like this will typically erode your profitability and competitiveness. In case of digital, these will likely stifle, or, at worst, kill DTs. Since digital involves the most modern of technologies and practices, it requires a positive, healthy culture of innovation and transparency.'

'Perhaps you can outline a few cultural aspects that you believe are essential to success in running a digital program?'

'First, you need to be proactive,' replied Dillon. 'If digital is important, you can't forget about it while putting together your annual business plan. If you're the CEO, don't delegate digital; have the CDO directly report to you. Don't react to situations; lead proactively. For example, don't keep ignoring a budget request for predictive analytics, only to approve it when an equipment goes down. Or ignore allocating capital for technology while continuing to fund new manufacturing lines and equipment.

'Second, develop a sense of urgency. If the CDO is not getting traction or buy-in from business leaders, you as the CEO make it happen. If your CDO or digital leader is going in circles for months for identifying the scope and requirements for a critical initiative, step in and pave the road for him. If business leaders always prioritize the urgent over the important, subject matter experts quickly size up the situation; they stop accommodating digital projects in their calendars.

'Third, let the expert be the expert. You don't want to bring in a CDO and tell him, in detail, how he or she should do the job. Former Apple Chairman Steve Jobs said, "it doesn't make sense to hire smart people and tell them what to do; we hire smart people so they can tell us what to do".[8] Assume that you don't know digital as well as you need to and listen to the CDO and the experts he or she brings in to talk to you. Don't be afraid to ask common sense questions, but accord due respect. An influential chairman of an Indian conglomerate once said in an internal meeting, "This—digital—is just process automation. It's nothing new. Digital is just a new name. Has been around for years." Comments such as those don't convey a great deal of respect.

'Fourth, establish digital best practices. As I've shared at other forums within this company, ensure organizational buy-in from the top. Develop agility. Think digital first. Be customer-centred. Keep your belief in the process.

'Finally, do the little things right. It's the little things that make the biggest difference.[9] Eschew politics in favour of ideas. Mandate that all meetings support your digital strategy. Celebrate failure as learning opportunities. Cancel status meetings in favour of brief, written updates. Teach employees to let go of old mindsets and practices. Encourage employees to ask the hard questions, the ones they discuss in the hallways after the meeting gets over.'

'Thanks; that's a lot of information,' said Cyril. 'I've made bullet point #5 as: *Incorporate culture as an important priority; build the right culture so that the culture will drive digital. Pay attention to the little things that define culture.*'

'I couldn't have said it better. Thanks, Cyril,' said Dillon.

Learning the Language of Business and Finance

'The next aspect I'm going to talk about probably applies equally around the world. When technologists communicate, business leaders don't take them seriously enough. Why is that?

'Well, it's because technologists speak a different language. For example, you may have an architect or IT or digital leader giving a presentation to a finance manager for additional funding as follows: "We must scale up our instance. The virtualization software would enable us to do that while additionally certifying both the originating host and the destination host and migrating live jobs between the two. If we do this, we can integrate ABC and XYZ seamlessly."

'What do you think the finance manager would say to that?' asked Dillon.

Dinesh chuckled. 'He or she may need to pop in an aspirin tablet to take care of an impending headache.'

'Funny,' said Dillon. 'However, he would certainly be confused about what's being proposed and why it's important. In contrast, however, suppose the IT leader had said: "We want to ensure business continuity and disaster recovery in case of IT issues. Buying virtualization software enables us to improve system uptime and business continuity. In other words, we want to make sure your operations continue free of disruptions 99.99 per cent of the time". Would you now think the finance manager would understand?'

'Of course,' replied Cyril. 'Even I'd understand, although I have no background in technology infrastructure.'

'Precisely,' said Dillon. 'One thing IT leaders—including architects and other senior technical resources—need to keep in mind is to speak the language of business.'

'My guess,' added Dinesh, 'is that tech folks assume everyone knows about virtualization and in-memory and IoT.'

'Right,' said Dillon. 'In order to make digital successful, technologists would do well to follow these two suggestions: first, they need to learn to speak the language of business. Avoid jargon and acronyms. Speak revenue, speak cost, speak business continuity, etc. For example, "Buying this software would allow you to reduce cost by 3 per cent" is better than "We want to migrate live jobs between the two hosts, and integrate ABC and XYZ seamlessly."

'Second, they need to communicate at a high level unless someone asks for the technical details. For example, "We are reducing costs by 30 per cent by performing the upgrade" is better than "ERP's in-memory database needs an upgrade in its production instance, which will employ the workbench and our latest release methodology."'

'Thanks, Dillon,' said Cyril. 'My sixth bullet point here says: *For ensuring a successful* DT, *technology leaders need to ensure that they speak the language of business, for example, cost, revenue and EBITDA.*'

Developing the Quantification Muscle

'Another reason digital may fail is because of a related point,' said Dillon. 'Suppose you're driving digital and have learnt the language of business. So you don't talk "Active Directory" or "redundancy protocols" any more, but profits and FCF. Your finance folks love you. They understand you.

'Except when it comes to the time to approve your budget request. You find your requests are rejected, even when you believe you're clearly describing the benefit. Your digital budget shrinks to 5 per cent of what you envisioned, and the team gets demoralized and moves on someplace else where they'll get a real budget to work with. *What's going on here?* You wonder. *My CFO asked me to make a business case, and I came back with 15 per cent productivity improvement, or 5 per cent higher employee satisfaction numbers. Isn't that good enough?*

'Turns out, it isn't good enough. You see, benefits are direct or indirect. Let me first describe the one that doesn't work very well: *indirect* benefits, for example, productivity enhancement. And why doesn't it work very well? Because you obtained a productivity benefit—so what? Your finance people or production people can run a report in 10 minutes as opposed to in three hours—and therefore....? Does it enable you to eliminate jobs? Or reduce costs in some other way? The answer is no.

'Contrast that with *direct* benefits: cost reduction or revenue increase. A payback in six months or RoI of 15 per cent per year. *That* is the language that'll get your budget request approved.'

'But there's a problem,' said Cyril. 'In many cases, it's hard to come up with a quantifiable benefit. For example, let's suppose the IT team is implementing an ERP. How can you tell exactly how much is the benefit?'

'I agree that you can't *always* quantify the benefit,' conceded Dillon. 'ERP implementations and infrastructure upgrades are examples of the few whose benefits are perhaps hard to quantify. However, often the technology team hides behind these use cases and refuses to develop what I call are *quantification muscles.*'

'What's that?' asked Dinesh.

'That's the process of becoming comfortable with analysing technology requirements and prioritizing those that bring higher direct benefits. Always being able to spot direct benefits. And you know what's cool? Most, if not all, digital initiatives do bring about direct benefits—cost, revenue, etc. Even those that appear as though they don't—say employee experience or safety and environment. Let's take the former. If your employees' experience improves by x per cent, it isn't hard to extrapolate that to a y per cent reduction in turnover, which saves you money in recruitment. And if you improve safety by 5 per cent, or eliminate fatalities, it boosts your stock price and market cap, which is a direct benefit.'

'Got it,' said Cyril. 'My seventh bullet point says: *Develop the ability to spot, and prioritize, business requirements with direct financial benefits.* Is that good enough?'

'Absolutely,' replied Dillon.

One Last Pitfall—You've Got to be Professional!

'Just a time check,' said Cyril. 'We're just about five minutes away from our one-hour mark. And, more importantly, my lone PowerPoint slide is bulging with points.'

'We hear you,' said Dillon, smiling. 'But there's one last pitfall we must cover. It's a culture thing, but it's so important that we should cover it separately. I've observed that this is a big issue in India. Here it is: you must be professional if you want to initiate and sustain digital.'

'Can you elaborate?' asked Dinesh.

'Oh, I mean an "n" number of things that we take for granted in the USA in Europe, but are unaware of in India. For example, start and end meetings on time. Don't make people wait for meetings and if you must, then apologize. Don't speak in a regional language or dialect if there's someone in the room who doesn't understand the language; stick to English. Accept or decline meeting requests; show up for the meetings you accept.'

'All of which are excellent points,' observed Dinesh. 'However, I wonder why these are specific professional considerations for digital alone. Shouldn't these precepts apply to business in general?'

'Of course,' replied Dillon. 'However, these ideas are especially relevant to digital because your high-tech team—which is what the digital team is going to be—is especially vulnerable to talent drain if the level of professionalism is low. In other functions, such as production or maintenance or engineering—the regular functions of business which don't fall under the "high-tech" bucket—while being critical, can nevertheless be staffed by local talent much easier than a digital team can be staffed by local talent. High-tech talent flies away quickly if the environment isn't innovative, fun and, most critically, professional. Digital programs can die out quickly for want of in-house talent.'

'Okay, my eighth and final bullet point is as follows,' said Cyril. *Provide a professional work environment if you want to attract and retain excellent quality digital talent.*

The Anatomy of an Unforgettable Family Outing: Memories Count

'I must say you're a remarkable man!' said Prabhat, the head of projects, the following Tuesday afternoon, while getting his cup of coffee in the break room.

'Thanks, but what prompted this sentiment?' asked Dillon, smiling, while stirring his own cup of green tea.

'Well, your office faces mine, and I couldn't help observing how you appear full of energy and good cheer, tackling one meeting after another and, in general, giving the impression of boundless energy.'

'Oh, I appreciate that, Prabhat, but there's a simple secret,' admitted Dillon.

'What's that?'

'Well, as our friend Srini likes to say, "the person with the constructive off-the-job life nearly always is more successful than the person who lives in dull, dreary home situation".[10] My family and I just received a dose of psychological sunshine last weekend, as we do every single weekend. This was a big dollop of a dose, so that's probably added a bounce to my step this week. I literally feel extremely focused and effective!'

'You must tell me more about it,' said Prabhat.

'Well, we visited Anubala Hills and spent a couple of nights at a resort.'

'Wonderful. My family's been meaning to visit there. Any tips?'

'Well,' replied Dillon, thoughtfully. 'Our biggest goal is always to create memories.'

'How do you do that?'

'Well, we go on hikes, take lots of pictures, explore different types of cuisine and, in general, exercise our "explore and enjoy" muscle. No one is allowed to surf the Internet or watch TV.

'At the end of the day, Prabhat, I've found that success without the backing of a loving family is meaningless. Creating shared memories is your most powerful tool if you wish to strengthen family ties. By that, I mean remembering to take pictures and collect souvenirs from trips. And not forgetting even the intangibles: laughing a lot and being silly, almost like little kids. And, for sure, putting your smartphone away.'

Being Effective Is Important in Personal Life as Well

'I couldn't agree with you more,' said Srini, who walked over near where Prabhat and Dillon were speaking. 'I didn't mean to eavesdrop, but couldn't help overhearing my name being mentioned. What Dillon was saying about creating shared memories is a powerful concept. It literally changed my relationship with my wife as well, a few years ago.'

Dillon shook hands warmly with Srini and said, 'I must say, however, I struggle to prioritize my activities with my family. There are so many things to do, while there is so little time.'

'Why?' asked Srini. 'If you're familiar with Covey's *7 Habits of Highly Effective People,* you probably know that you pick what's important over what's urgent. If you can do that at work, why not at home?'

'Well, in my case, my family activities are all important,' replied Dillon. 'How do I pick one important activity over another?'

'All right, so you'd like to know how to prioritize your activities,' said Srini. 'Here's what I recommend. List your family-related tasks and number them, starting with the most important. Let's suppose you write: 1. Take family out for dinner, 2. play ball with son, 3. help with son's homework. Anytime two activities seek your attention at the same time, simply pick the one that is higher on your list.'

'You're right, it sounds simple if you write it down,' said Dillon.

'Correct,' reiterated Srini. 'If push came to shove and you could only do one thing this day—just one thing—then it was going to be what you had at the top of your list. That would be acceptable to you. Indeed, it may be an exhilarating feeling: it was the best thing you could do on this day!'

'Thanks, Srini,' said Dillon. 'For some reason, it didn't occur to me that I can do that in my personal life which comes naturally to me in my professional life: how to be effective by prioritizing.'

'Remember: Covey's principles on effectiveness are as powerful in family life as they are at work,' said Srini. 'It pays to re-read this classic every year or two.'

References

[1] McKinsey. 2013, September. *70% of Transformation Programs Fail.* Available at https://www.slideshare.net/aipmm/70–26633757 (accessed on 16 April 2019).

[2] Davenport, Thomas H. and George Westerman. 2018, March. 'Why So Many High-Profile Digital Transformations Fail.' *Harvard Business Review.*

[3] Gartner. 2018. 'Digital Dexterity at Work.' *Gartner Executive Guidance Q3 2018 Edition.* Available at https://www.gartner.com/en/executive-guidance/digital-dexterity (accessed on 16 April 2019).

[4] Das, Shyamanuja. 2018, March. 'Decoding Digital Transformation.' *CIO & Leader*. Available at http://www.cioandleader.com/article/2018/03/29/cioleader-march-2018 (accessed on 16 April 2019).

[5] Bendor-Samuel, Peter. 2018, July. 'Where Most Companies Go Wrong in Digital Transformation.' *Forbes*. Available at https://www.forbes.com/sites/peterbendorsamuel/2018/07/18/where-most-companies-go-wrong-in-digital-transformation/#230ca3716884 (accessed on 16 April 2019).

[6] Gupta, Sanjay. 2018, March. 'Digital Transformation is a Long Journey for Most Firms.' *Live Mint*. Available at https://www.livemint.com/Companies/6lC5Fp1Q53o7wUzOJmxFyH/Digital-transformation-is-a-long-journey-for-most-firms-Hic.html (accessed on 16 April 2019).

[7] Schwantes, Marcel. 2017, 6 April. '6 Toxic Work Habits That Will Kill Your Office Culture.' *Inc.* Available at https://www.inc.com/marcel-schwantes/6-toxic-work-habits-that-will-kill-your-office-culture.html (accessed on 16 April 2019).

[8] Rafati, Shahrzad. 2015, June. 'Keeping Your Best Employees.' *Fortune*. Available at http://fortune.com/2015/06/09/shahrzad-rafati-keeping-your-best-employees/ (accessed on 16 April 2019).

[9] Scheibenreif, Don, David Willis, W. Roy Schulte, John-David Lovelock, Elsie Olding, Hank Barnes, Helen Poitevin, Marc Kerremans and Lars Van Dam. 2018, December. 'From Digital Transformation to Continuous Next.' Gartner Research Notes. Available at https://www.gartner.com/doc/3895472/digital-transformation-continuousnext-key-insights (accessed on 16 April 2019).

[10] Schwartz, David J. 1987. 'Manage Your Environment: Go First Class.' In *The Magic of Thinking Big*. New York: Simon & Schuster Inc., page 125.

7

You Must Crawl before You Walk

The Steps

'Can I come in, sir?' asked a young woman, about 24, waiting outside Dillon's office. As a matter of practice, Dillon kept his office door open, except when he needed to hold a private conversation.

'Of course!' replied Dillon. He put his laptop and phone aside so he could focus on the newcomer. It was Dillon's practice to provide his full attention when he was in dialogue with a colleague.

'Please allow me to introduce myself,' said the newcomer. 'I'm Aishwarya, or Ash, a two-year veteran at Dykstrand India. I'm an electronics engineer from IIT, Chennai. Mr Srini is my mentor, and I learnt from him that you're starting to put together a team that'll lead the DT of this company. I'm interested to hear from you more on this topic, and in joining your digital team if you feel my background is good enough.'

Dillon looked intently at her. She was of medium height, a little on the plump side, and spoke sharply. She seemed sincere.

'All right,' said Dillon, processing the information and smiling. He didn't have anyone on his digital team—yet. But he needed to establish that Ash had the competencies needed to get on his team.

'I'm sure you're wondering whether I belong,' said Ash, smiling, as though she could read the expression on the CDO's face. 'I was the digital secretary in my final year at IIT, and my project concerned optimization of machine performance using digital twins.'

'You wrote the code?'

'Yes, using product life-cycle management (PLM) software from Siemens. I configured the IoT platform and performed the process modelling, but my teammates did the front-end visualization bit.'

'Which IoT protocols did you use?'

'Personally I'm familiar with constrained application protocol (CoAP) and message queuing telemetry transport (MQTT).'

'How would you simulate an IoT device's behaviour in the real world?'

'By writing scripts.'

'What challenges do you think an IoT developer or tester faces?'

'I felt getting the hardware and the software to work together was the biggest challenge. IoT is an architecture or integrated system, which requires close coupling among various hardware and software components. Getting the hardware, for example, sensors, communication gateways, etc., to work with the software, in my view, is a challenge. Especially in terms of the transfer of data from the hardware to the software.'

That more or less settles it, thought Dillon. *She's in, and I need more folks like her.*

'That's wonderful,' said Dillon, as he sat back and reclined against the back rest of his comfortable leather chair. 'You're definitely the kind I need on the digital advisory board. Do you have some time on your hands?'

'Absolutely, sir,' replied Ash, pulling a chair towards her and sitting.

Dillon clasped his fingers and smiled. Then he looked down at the desk and pensively played with his phone.

'You appear preoccupied, sir,' said Ash. 'Perhaps you won't mind sharing what's on your mind?'

'Not at all,' Dillon said, as he put his phone away. 'Perhaps a short conversation with you is the perfect outlet for my thoughts.'

'You see, I've just come in to the company,' he said, after a short pause. 'It's been a week, but I can clearly see how much work there's to be done.

And don't get me wrong, that's the way I like it. High expectations and a transformation waiting to be executed, these are the kind of things that get my imagination going. I had a chance to meet with this company's senior management, and I couldn't be more excited about our journey.

'The only thing is to figure out a practical way to get on with the first steps,' he continued. 'Which is why I'm a little thoughtful these days. I didn't mean to ignore you and appear pensive.'

'Sure, sir. What will you do first?' asked Ash.

'As with anything else that's big,' replied Dillon, 'we'll have to start with a mission and a vision. The mission tells us why we exist, and the vision guides us with what we want to become. This step is crucial. A lot of transformation journeys get bogged down after a while because the "why" isn't clear. With anything worthwhile, you must start with the "why."'

'And then?'

'Next is an important step in any digital journey. It's what's known as digital maturity assessment. An immediate next step after figuring out the mission and vision is to assess where we as an organization find stand in the digital journey.

'Like Peter Drucker, the noted management guru, said, "You can't manage what you can't measure". It's important we assess our key capabilities on leadership, technology, culture, people and customer experience. This gives us a quantitative measure on our current state, and, at the same time, enables us to set the North Star on our aspiration, where we want to be.

'Next would be what we call strategy. What is going to be our approach? What's our methodology going to look like? For example, what kind of a team shall we need? Which technical capabilities would we need to bring in? What sort of processes would we need to incorporate? In other words, what do we do next?'

'I do have a question, however,' said Ash. 'Do you figure out these questions—I mean the strategy—on your own, since you're the CDO? Must you collaborate with senior management?'

'Collaborating with senior management is one way of doing it,' replied Dillon. 'In my view, it's better to figure all these out with the help of a digital advisory board (DAB) that consists of two groups of individuals:

- Senior decision-makers (Senior DAB) such as heads of functions, divisions, plants, maintenance and operations, finance, sales and marketing, supply chain logistics and IT.
- Young talent (Young Talent DAB), that is, a group of young and dynamic employees from various verticals such as the ones I mentioned just now.

'A DAB gives the CDO a working team to start making progress even before key positions get hired into the digital organization. In India, due to long "notice periods", it takes months to make new hires and put a new team together.'

'What happens after that?'

'Well, our next task is to compile a list of digital themes and projects, also known as initiatives. Which business results are important, and which are urgent? Which technologies can be leveraged quickly? How do we build a list of capabilities to be implemented now and in the future?'

'Exactly how do you compile such a list?'

'By conducting what we call value discovery workshops. The outcome of the workshop is a list of our business challenges that need intervention from technology.'

'That's exciting!' exclaimed Ash. 'This is really the creation of our digital journey. You were right; this is certainly ground zero of our transformation experience.'

'That's correct,' said Dillon, glad to see the excitement written clearly on the face of the young engineer.

'What I'd like to do,' added Ash, 'is to bring in a few of my colleagues—not all of whom work in my department—who I know are excited about technology, and who want to meet you.'

'Of course! As I said a few minutes ago, one of the first steps we need to perform is the formation of a DAB, whose mandate is to drive the digital program in the company. Before we formally launch the council, however, I'll need some helping hands in order for us to get going, sort of a 'Young Talent DAB.' Perhaps you and a couple of your colleagues would care to join this group?'

'Nothing would make me happier than to help in whatever capacity I can,' said Ash. 'I'll bring in the group to meet with you tomorrow.'

'Perfect, let's say 3:30 in the afternoon?'

Dykstrand India's Digital Mission and Vision

'These are my colleagues who're most excited to meet with you,' said Ash the next day in Dillon's office at the appointed hour.

Seven young engineers streamed into Dillon's office. Since there wasn't enough space, Dillon suggested they walk on over to the conference room in the corner.

After introductions, Dillon jumped right in. 'Welcome, everyone. Consider yourself members of a pretty small and exclusive club, the Young Talent DAB. Over the next several weeks, we'll add the senior members of the council, such as the heads of various functions such as finance, supply chain logistics, operations and maintenance, etc. Whether you stay on or not would, of course, depend on your desire and commitment, not to mention your bandwidth outside of your regular job.

'Let's start with a small exercise. Let's define a working version of our digital mission, and then, the vision. You may think of this as a superfluous exercise, but remember what Peter Drucker, the famous management guru said, "That business purpose and business mission are so rarely given adequate thought is perhaps the most important cause of business frustration and failure."'

Bobby, an intern in the engineering department, spoke up: 'This is probably stupid, but I could never tell the difference between the two—the vision and the mission.' Bobby was lean, tall and sported a stylish goatee.

'You're not alone, Bobby,' replied Dillon. 'Let me explain the two words simply. Mission defines why we exist, or the role that we aspire to fulfil in society. Vision, on the other hand, defines what we want to be in the future.

'The mission statement elaborates how to achieve the company's ambitions with the resources and means at its command, stated around the purpose of its existence.'

'I see,' replied Bobby, thoughtfully. 'Tell you what, I believe quite a few mission statements are void of real substance. For example, a leading soda company's mission is to "refresh the world in mind, body and spirit". A leading airline wants to "embrace the human spirit and let it fly". Microsoft, of all companies, came up with a mission statement that was deemed "vague enough to deserve a place in the pantheon of corporate sweet nothings"[1] when it said, in 2014, that it existed in order to "empower every person and every organization on the planet to achieve more". Are mission statements that are so vague really useful?'

'Perhaps not,' replied Dillon. 'Mission statements are a lot more useful if they're meaningful; for example, Google's mission is "to provide access to the world's information in one click". Generic words such as integrity, respect, etc., are not very effective because *they do not explain the uniqueness of the business*. Values are important too. Ultimately, mission and values must be reiterated frequently and lived daily. Or else, they're no more than just words.

'An example of uniqueness in a vision definition is Hitachi's. They aspire to develop "superior, original technology and products". So their unique proposition is superiority and originality.'

'How about this,' asked Cyril, a short, chubby maintenance engineer. 'Our mission could be "to enable our company to be a leading footwear corporation."'

'Good start, Cyril,' said Dillon. 'But is that why we exist? Even if a leading footwear corporation didn't exist, why would the world care?

In other words, what's special about us—what would not happen if we weren't around?'

'I get you,' replied Cyril. 'How about this: Dykstrand commits to providing affordable luxury to people worldwide while maintaining the highest standards of people practices and social and environmental welfare?'

'Excellent,' opined Dillon. 'Let's park that for now. Now, how about defining a vision? In other words, where do we want to be in, say, 5 or 10 years? I'll tell you something right at the beginning; however, most vision statements are empty muddles that only prompt yawns. Any lasting vision needs two core components: *core ideology* and *envisioned future.*[2] In other words, we not only want to articulate a future but also stay true to our core ideology.

'Going back to the example of Hitachi, their vision includes two interesting phrases: "deliver innovations" and "inspire the world". That is who they want to become in the future.'

'Let me take a crack at this,' said Cyril, a maintenance engineer. 'Our vision could be "we want to increase the company's revenue and reduce its costs."'

'I do have a question,' said Dinesh, a tall HR manager in his early 30s, with a hint of belly fat. 'Do we want to include the word "help", as in "help increase?" Can technology increase revenue on its own? I thought it was always a supporting function.'

'Yes and no, Dinesh,' said Dillon. 'Traditionally, of course, technology is viewed as an enabling function, as in, it helps production to increase output and thereby help increase revenue. However, digital takes it one step further. We can really enable business to make more money from additional sales channels. In that case, we're not helping, but actually *making* more money for the business.'

'Makes sense,' said Dinesh. 'Rather than refer to costs and revenue, can we make a direct reference to our mission and state our vision as follows: "Our vision is to build the technology that makes Dykstrand the footwear of choice."'

'That's a good first draft for our vision,' said Dillon. 'I'll tell you what—let me use tomorrow's management council meeting for the purpose of aligning our mission and vision statements with senior management. I'll update you all in about a week's time.'

Obtaining Senior Management Approval

'We must prioritize the important over the urgent,' said the CEO. It was the monthly management council meeting, and Dillon has just broached the topic of the digital mission and vision statements. Falguni, the CFO, had opined that there were more urgent matters to attend to.

'Let's take a look at what you have,' said Eknath. 'I'd like to especially review the digital vision that we aspire to achieve.'

'Thanks, sir. Before I begin, I'd like to simply say this: the young talent on the DAB already had a crack at this. However, if we can obtain validation from senior management, it'll bolster organizational support; it'll enable us to use the organizational muscle in order to make quick progress on initiatives that matter to us. We also surmised that the CEO would personally like to review the vision and mission of the digital organization. That's why I wish to discuss this topic with all of you today.

'First, here's the provisional mission statement: Dykstrand commits to providing affordable luxury to people worldwide while maintaining the highest standards of people practices and social and environmental welfare.'

'That's good, but shouldn't you include a reference to technology?' asked Om, the COO. 'Or else, how would the digital mission be any different from the organization's? By the way, I like the way your team has framed the organizational mission.'

'That's useful feedback,' said Dillon. 'Anyone else want to take a crack?'

'How about adding a relevant phrase at the end?' asked Punit, the head of engineering, 'such as "It strives to remain a profitable and growing business by the deployment of next-generation technology for efficient and effective ways of working with high-quality products, customer focus and productivity."'

'That's good,' said Dillon. 'How about this for the digital mission statement: *Dykstrand commits to providing affordable luxury to people worldwide while maintaining the highest standards of people practices, and social and environmental welfare. It strives to remain a profitable and growing business by the deployment of next-generation digital technology for efficient and effective ways of working with high-quality products, customer focus and productivity.*'

There were nods. 'OK, let's now take a look at our first draft vision statement: "Our vision is to build the technology that makes Dykstrand the footwear of choice."'

'I like that,' said Falguni. 'The focus of the digital organization is clear and is aligned with the organizational vision.'

'That's a good start,' responded Eknath. 'How about our core ideology that we want to provide people with affordably luxury, etc.?'

Hari, the head of HR, spoke up. 'Shall we say—I'm borrowing what you said in an earlier meeting—"We wish to develop and deploy digital technology that would change the way we do business—the way we think, the way we operate and the way others view us?"'

'That's nice,' said Prabhat, the head of projects. 'But usually, vision statements are smaller and are aligned with the mission. Hence, we should probably say "... providing affordable luxury to the people". That makes a direct reference to our mission.'

'All right,' said Dillon, making notes on his laptop. 'How about this for the digital vision statement: *The vision of the digital organization is to build the technology that makes Dykstrand the footwear of choice, providing affordable luxury to the people of the country where it operates.*'

'Sounds good to me,' said the CEO. 'Thanks, Dillon. I enjoyed this process of making very meaningful definitions that'll guide our digital organization in the coming years. Both the vision and the mission are essential components of an organization's strategy. They enable the company to stay ahead of competitors and provide a coherent message and direction to employees and other stakeholders.'

Digital Maturity Assessment

'How "digitally mature" do you think we are?'

It was the following Tuesday afternoon, when Dillon organized a quick meeting with the Young Talent DAB. The conversation turned to the approved mission and vision statements and then to digital maturity.

'I would say we'd qualify as beginners,' replied Bobby. 'Perhaps not complete novices, but beginners nevertheless. At least that's my guess.'

'We'll see, Bobby,' said Dillon. 'What I propose is that we first review, within this group, how we can figure out our digital maturity. When we carry out the actual study, you may want to be involved.'

'Does this make sense?' Dillon asked. 'Ready to discuss this important topic?'

'Certainly, we're hungry for directions on what to do next in digital,' chimed in Ash.

'Wonderful,' said Dillon cheerfully. 'Let me look in my laptop where I have my.... there it is—the assessment framework.'

He projected the following picture.

Assessment Parameters	Attributes to Assess										
Leadership	Governance	Organization Structure	Vision/ Mission								
Technology	Storage	Computing	Server space, App Hosting	Analytics	Platform	Network	System Integration	Mobility			
Culture	Custom	Respect	Trust	Change Orientation	Results Orientation	Employee Engagement	Learning	Decision Making	Communication	Freedom to Fail	Skill Levels
Process	KPIs	Effectiveness	Efficiency	Productivity	Order to Pay	Record to Report	Manufacturing / Production	Finance	Invoicing / Billing	HR Processes	
Ecosystem Partners	Coverage	Time to delivery									

'We measure the following parameters on a scale of 1 to 5, the higher the better: leadership, technology, culture, process and ecosystems. For each parameter, we analyse a variety of attributes. For example, leadership is rated on the basis of governance, organization structure, vision and mission. Next is technology and so on.

'I have an external partner, Arks Tech, coming in tomorrow, to run a survey at our office of Dykstrand India, in order to determine where we stand on each of these parameters. They'll ask all employees in the organization to fill out the survey, stressing that, in order to be effective, the survey needs to be filled out by 75 per cent or more employees, representing all layers and functions of the business. After the initial survey, the assessment will continue to be performed periodically so as to measure the progress of digital maturity, in the form of Assessment 1, 2 and so on.

'The output of the survey would be shown in the form of a spider chart, such as the example I'm showing on the screen,' said Dillon, as he projected the following picture. 'The direction of skew of the diagram would reveal the areas to work on, even after multiple assessments have been performed.'

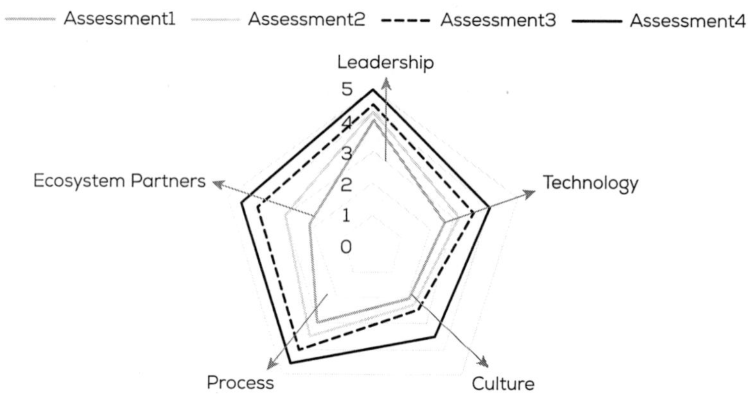

The Digital Strategy

A couple of days later, Dillon had his one-on-one with his boss, the CEO, and narrated what the working DAB had accomplished.

'I'd really look for the digital organization to produce results much sooner than three years down the road,' Eknath said.

'Of course, Eknath,' said Dillon. 'The timeline for the vision statement doesn't means we can't produce results quickly.'

'What's your strategy going to be?' asked the CEO.

'There are a few pieces to it,' replied Dillon. 'To start with,' he said, and then paused. 'It'll be better if I drew this up.'

He walked over to the whiteboard and made a few blocks.

'The first piece is the vision, which we already have. We have considered our top priorities and a path for the digital journey across the enterprise. The company is a "digital novice", but we're on our way to becoming a "digital leader."

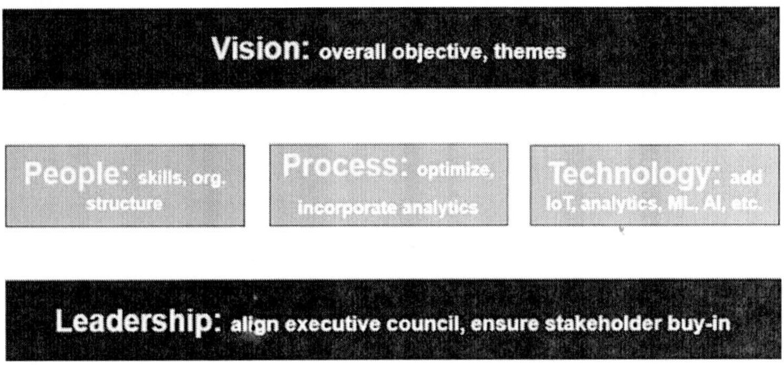

Digital Strategy

'The second piece is the block I have drawn on the bottom, which is leadership. We need to align digital to business goals through leadership alignment and stakeholder buy-in. The CDO needs to be excellent, but the most influential leaders of the organization, that is, the members of the executive council need to rally behind the push for digital.

'The last piece consists of three components which are equally important. First is people, we need to enhance the skills of our employees and put in place the correct digital organizational structure. Second is process, how to work analytics, paperless and other digital technologies into our processes. Finally comes the technology piece itself—how to bring in software and hardware systems based on IoT, analytics, AI, ML and other staple digital technologies.'

'This sounds good, Dillon,' said the CEO. 'But how long does this all take?'

'There are steps we can take right away, like forming a DAB and holding workshops that will let us identify the first digital initiatives we want to take up as a company. But the strategy won't get executed in a month or even a year. Going digital is a long-term journey.'

'Perhaps, but we need results quickly,' said the CEO.

'Sure, Eknath. I'll assure you that every single digital project we take on will have a definite payback—typically a few months—unless we're tackling a compliance or regulatory requirement, or HSE. And, of course, we agree that any dependent investments we make in IT infrastructure will not have a payback, strictly speaking,' said Dillon.

Governance of DT

'Fine,' said the CEO. 'Can you show me, pictorially, how the steps of our digital journey will look like? I get it that there's a strategy and prioritization of goals, but what does a transformation journey look like, from beginning to end?'

'Sure,' replied Dillon. 'Let me show you the template. I'll be glad to answer any questions you may have.'

Dillon projected the following image on the projector.

'All right, this gives me a good perspective on the various steps involved in a transformation journey. How's our governance going to be like?' asked Eknath.

'Governance of digital consists of two components: sharing and coordination,'[3] replied Dillon. '*Sharing* refers to the fact that local business units employ common technology capabilities and resources from a central pool of such capabilities and resources. *Coordination,* on the other hand, refers to a central, or corporate, leadership that sets the

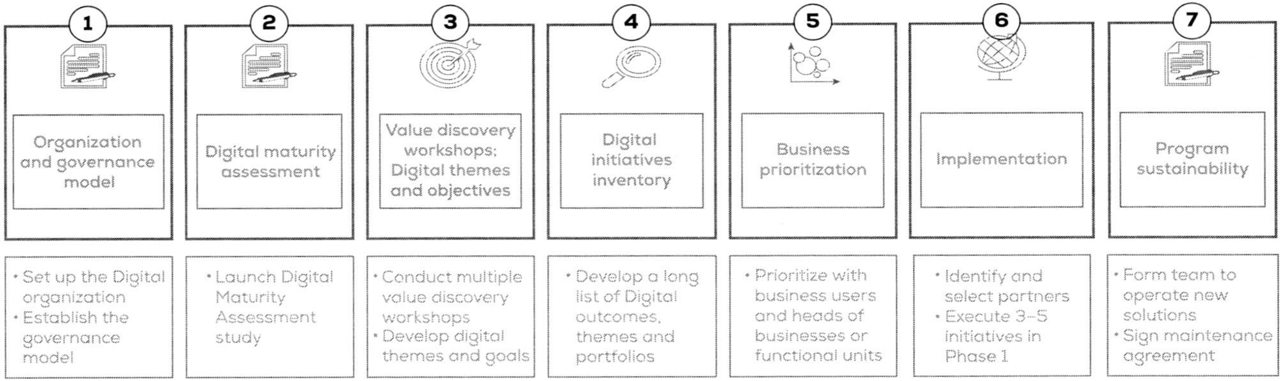
1
Organization and governance model
• Set up the Digital organization
• Establish the governance model
2
Digital maturity assessment
• Launch Digital Maturity Assessment study
3
Value discovery workshops: Digital themes and objectives
• Conduct multiple value discovery workshops
• Develop digital themes and goals
4
Digital initiatives inventory
• Develop a long list of Digital outcomes, themes and portfolios
5
Business prioritization
• Prioritize with business users and heads of businesses or functional units
6
Implementation
• Identify and select partners
• Execute 3–5 initiatives in Phase 1
7
Program sustainability
• Form team to operate new solutions
• Sign maintenance agreement

overall expectations, prioritizes initiatives, tracks progress and ensures that execution compliances with standards and policies.

'In order to perform governance, we need to set up a few committees that will govern DT. First, a Digital Steering Committee (DSC), at the corporate level, performs the coordination function at the corporate level. It can consist of you, the CFO, the CDO and two or three other function leaders that will answer questions such as how we prioritize initiatives, make investment choices, allocate resources and policies we need to ensure regulatory compliance.

'Second, a DAB, again at the corporate level, that provides the CDO the arms and legs to organize and run the digital program when a fully functioning organization has not been set up yet. The members of this committee are functional heads and cross-functional employees who're tech-savvy and wish to participate in the execution of a digital program.

'Finally, there are smaller committees at the local business unit, or plant, which track innovations, prioritize local objectives and ensure alignment with the central policies and procedures. The shared resources that would be performing local initiatives at any point of time may be made members of this committee as well.'

'Makes sense,' said the CEO. 'And how's the digital organization going to look like?'

Starting the Digital Organization

'Sure, I'll go a step back,' said Dillon. 'I'll first explain to you the philosophy of starting a digital organization.

'Yes, sure,' Dillon responded. 'The first person to hire, of course, is the CDO. In general, you're looking for a bright, sharp and multi-talented young professional with a passion for leading, the zeal to do something extraordinary and possessing a sense of curiosity about technology or how things work. If the candidate has experience in manufacturing with a focus on technology, all the better.'

'I guess you fit the bill perfectly,' said Eknath.

'I guess, except the "young" part,' Dillon said, laughing. 'But here's what's even more important. While the description I provide earlier is the profile of the ideal candidate, there are a few more characteristics that're important.'

'First, the CDO must be able to navigate the internal maze of the organization. If you don't know how to figure out a plan to engage with the influencers, you won't make it. Second, he or she must understand the processes of the IT department, especially how IT works with commercial—you know, the product evaluation, ordering, vendor management, etc. If not, you'd get bogged down; you'd slow your team down.

'Third, he or she must be an able translator.'[4]

'Can you explain the translator bit?'

'Well, successful CDOs are a little like software product managers. At the outset of a DT journey—and throughout—translators utilize their domain knowledge to help business leaders identify and prioritize business problems that are the greatest value creators, that is, which will create the highest returns when solved. These may be business problems within a single business unit (e.g., improving operational efficiency in manufacturing) or across separate units such as planning, logistics and finance (e.g., reducing product turnaround time). This is similar to how a software product manager would translate a business problem into the features of an upcoming software product; not everything the user wants can be incorporated, but the ones with the most value will be.

'Fourth, the leader must possess great interpersonal skills. Success in this role has as much to do with persuasion and selling skills as it has to do with technology know-how. Finally, the CDO must be result-oriented. At the end of the day, like every other CxO, the CDO must also answer to the ultimate yardstick of success.'

'That's an impressive list of skills,' remarked the CEO. 'What's the next step?'

'Let me show you the proposed organizational chart, Eknath,' Dillon replied, as he projected the following image.

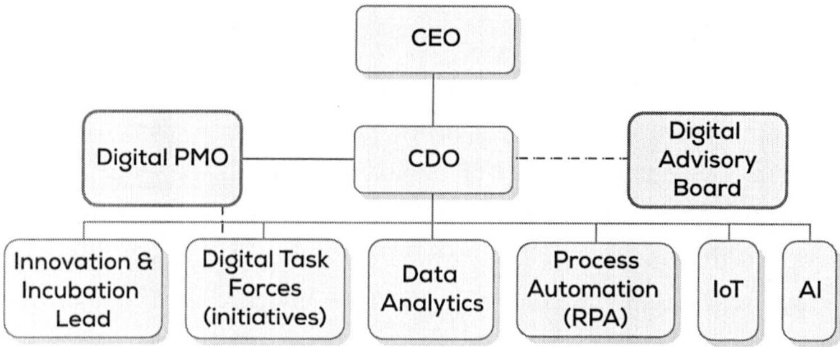

'After the CDO is hired,' Dillon continued, 'there are a few more key positions that need to be filled.

- A project or program manager who helps the CDO with setting up, monitoring and tracking the several initiatives that will form the digital portfolio. Additionally, this person will work closely with the CEO office to drive the CDO's agenda in the organization while a new team, namely digital, is set up.
- An innovation and incubation lead, whose function is to run pilot projects or POCs, in order to test the feasibility of new technologies and evangelize the adoption of such technologies in various business functions.
- A dedicated DAB: One of the main responsibilities of the CDO is to excite existing employees to be a part of this journey. With approval from department heads, bright, young change agents with a love for technology can be deputed part-time to assist in formulating and executing the digital mandate. In addition, this board would contain functional heads such as the heads of finance, supply chain logistics, operations, maintenance and others. This cross-functional group is typically 10–12 strong and does not report to the CDO directly. Rather, it's advisory in nature and has a dotted line relationship to the CDO.

- A digital task force (DTF), one per digital initiatives, consisting of multiple teams of 3–6 employees. Once digital initiatives are identified and prioritized, seek full-time employees who can be deputed full-time from their regular jobs in order to work on digital initiatives. A typical digital project lasts 8–12 weeks, which is sufficient for the employee to learn new skills and for the initiative to be completed successfully. The task force disperses and employees return to their regular work following project implementation. The DTFs roll up into the digital PMO with a dotted line relationship.
- Robotic process automation (RPA), analytics, IoT and AI teams, typically consisting of an architect, and potentially two to three technical members. In the first year of the digital program, architects with key technology capabilities, such as technical architects in analytics, IoT, ML, etc., need to be hired.'

Planning Value Discovery Workshops

'Dillon, what exactly is this workshop you're talking about? I saw your e-mail last night but thought of giving you a quick call this morning!'

It was Hari, the head of HR, who'd placed an early morning call to Dillon the next day.

'Hari, remember our business diagnostic meeting, and our discussion on what we needed to be doing in the technology area, specifically how we needed to build a list of capabilities to be implemented now and in the future?' asked Dillon.

'Yep.'

'Well, how do you compile such a list?'

'I don't know—you tell me, you're the tech guru,' replied Hari, with his signature laughter, hearty and loud.

'Yes, of course, Hari,' said Dillon. 'We obtain a list of our most compelling digital initiatives by conducting what we call value discovery workshops. The outcome of the workshop is a list of our most important business challenges that can use the intervention of technology.'

'That's great!' exclaimed Hari. 'How long would these last?'

'I'd say we run value discovery workshops and technology roadshows for the next three months. That'll be enough to ensure that employees at all levels of this company become engaged with digital. DTs work best when they're all-inclusive so far as employees are concerned and combine a top-down approach of management mandate and bottom-up approach of employee involvement.'

'Wonderful,' said Hari. 'Your single point of contact from now on would be Dinesh, my operations lead.'

'Thanks,' said Dillon. 'I've already had the pleasure of getting acquainted with Dinesh. Based on my initial meetings with employees, I've picked four young and energetic professionals who would be part of my Young Talent DAB: Ash, 24, production engineer, Bobby, 23, engineering intern, Cyril, 23, maintenance engineer and your HR operations lead Dinesh, 35.'

'Fantastic, it looks like you've got your folks all lined up perfectly, Dillon!' said Hari. 'If you need anything from me, give me a buzz.'

Holding Workshops and Technology Roadshows

'Can I come in, Mr Dillon?'

It was Dinesh, the senior HR professional.

'Sure, you couldn't have come in at a better time,' said Dillon. 'I wanted to see if you had time to help me. First, however, you may tell me why you wanted to see me.'

'Well, sir,' said Dinesh. He seemed to be hesitating. 'It so happens that a window of opportunity has opened up for me to learn digital. Hari has assigned me to lead the learning and development component, and I was supposed to take over from Geeta next week. However, Geeta's move has been pushed out by two weeks, which means I am basically jobless for the next two weeks.'

Dillon laughed. 'It's perfect, then. I was about to ask you for help, and you've come in, saying you have time.'

'Let's do this, let's plan for a few events we want to organize in the next 4–6 weeks. I was planning to spend the better part of the next week, with the core members of my DAB, planning two to three value discovery workshops and a technology roadshow. Since you've had some time open up on your calendar, you can be my primary helper, and we'll pull in others as needed.

'Ready to go?'

'Yes, sir,' replied Dinesh.

'First of all, I'd like to organize a value discovery workshop, then a second one after a week. We should also hold a technology roadshow.'

'I'm aware of value discovery workshops,' said Dinesh. 'But what framework would we adopt in scheduling such an event?'

'Well, here are the usual steps,' explained Dillon. 'We want to gather representatives from the major verticals of the business: engineering, maintenance, production, finance, etc. Attendees need to set aside a complete day for this event without worrying about their regular deliverables. What do we do when we get these folks into a room?

Preparing a (Long) List of Themes and Initiatives

'First, we want to list the current environment and landscape: what functions and verticals do we have? Which systems and solutions do we use currently?

'Second, we want to analyse current issues and pain areas. These are the known "problems", the existing challenges. During this stage, some of the issues are resolved on the spot because all the primary stakeholders are in the room. If the issues are not completely resolved, at least a broad resolution approach is identified. We call these "instant wins."'

'Third, we ideate on potential areas for technology intervention. These may or may not be the areas envisaged by senior management. Nevertheless, there's tremendous power in the synergy obtained from multiple stakeholders in the same room. Some of the best ideas I know of emerged from such workshops.

'I'd like to spend a moment here reiterating the first three steps, which, combined, is what we term the ideation phase. We generally adopt a top-down approach: senior leaders provide high-level ideas and detailing comes from employees. Some challenges, such as the need to digitize paper-based processes, would roll easily off the blocks. Some others, such as a need to replace the existing production chain and supply chain by a digital core, would take some deliberation. If onsite workshops fail to provide the necessary spark, we invite employees to offsite ideation sessions and challenge them to think of what could be, if there were no time or budget constraints.

'Fourth, we prioritize the issues and ideas on the basis of parameters such as financial benefit, productivity gain, UX enhancement, operational effectiveness, risk mitigation, etc.

'This is an important step; let's take a step back on the process behind the step. When we brainstormed, we just jotted down all ideas regardless of merit; we didn't evaluate. Clearly, not all ideas were practical or an immediate priority. However, the present step being the one of *comparative evaluation* of ideas, we develop and use a formal structure for evaluating ideas based on the following criteria. Here is one potential way the framework can be structured:

	Evaluation Criteria	Weight	Score (0 to 10)	Weighted Score
1	Strategic fitness			
2	Financial benefit			
3	Aids competitiveness?			
4	Ease of adoption and use			
5	Time taken to realize benefit			
6	Total cost			
7	Degree of stakeholder buy-in			
	Total	100%		

'Fifth and final, we document the findings and recommendations from the workshop, making sure to forward it to senior management and workshop participants. Here's where we begin to uncover the *grouping* or *theming* of ideas: a set of central themes repeated in numerous ideas.

'Groups of ideas, say three to five, get consolidated into an outcome, and groups of outcomes form a theme. For example, ideas such as "No more paper-based forms for new employee on day of joining", "Make it intuitive for employees to request for access to software systems", etc., may be grouped into outcomes such as "Make it easy for employees to get on-boarded". Subsequently, outcomes can be consolidated into a theme, such as "Enhance the employee work experience". Themes such as employee experience, revenue increase, cost reduction, etc., may finally be lumped into what we call our "digital portfolio."

'Here's a pictorial representation':

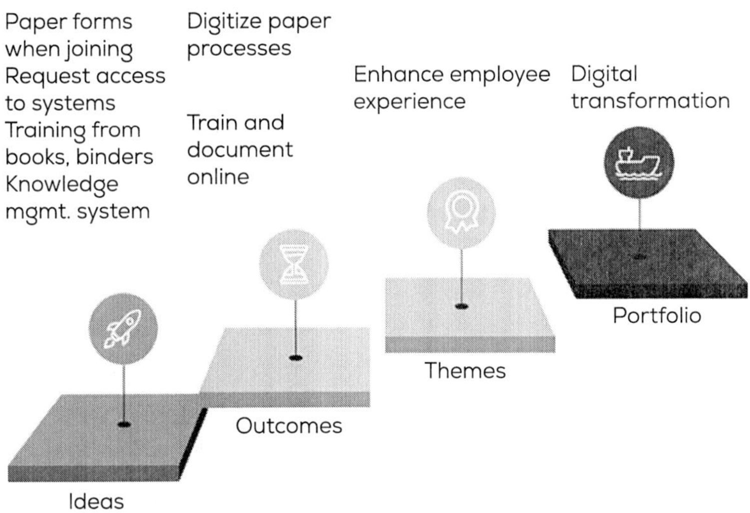

'So far, so good,' said Dinesh, furiously jotting down on his little notepad. 'How about technology roadshows?'

'Those are simpler,' replied Dillon. 'We hold a half-day or full-day events where we give presentations to employees on technology topics and upcoming projects. We also invite partners to demo cutting-edge technology products. The idea is simple: create a buzz, get a sense of excitement going.

'Can I count on you to help organize these events in the next few weeks?' asked Dillon.

'Absolutely,' replied Dinesh.

Family: Even Status Quo Takes Effort

'Something bothering you?' asked Srini of a thoughtful Dillon who was stirring his cup of afternoon coffee.

'Yes and no,' replied Dillon. He paused for a few moments, smiled wryly and added, 'I didn't mean to sound enigmatic, but my work and family lives are up and down. While things have improved substantially after I followed your suggestions, things don't always stay good.'

'What do you mean they don't stay good?' queried Srini. 'Tell me about your work life first.'

'I'm quite fed up with Falguni. Om, too. But with Falguni, mostly. What's she got against me? Am I not likeable enough for her?'

'She's got rough edges, sure,' Srini said after a brief pause. 'But you've got to realize that—and I may have said this before—imperfect people are the only kind of people we have on earth. Falguni had a couple of tough IT deployment experiences early in her career as a CFO. Unfortunately, she generalized it to imply that all tech leaders were incompetent, unaware of business priorities or both.'

'How should I deal with her?'

'Like you'd deal with any business leader. Look for common ground, be professional and don't, I repeat, do *not*, react to what she says. Ignore her tone. Treat her kindly. I'm sure she'll come around soon.'

'Well, I can try,' Dillon sighed. 'I get it that work life would be up and down, since work-related situations are dynamic by definition,' he continued, choosing his words carefully.

'Like that cyberattack, eh?' asked Srini, smiling.

'Yes, that, and other situations,' said Dillon. 'Interviews, high-pressure presentations, fun events with team, etc. However, at home, I expect my relationships to stay stable, more or less. However, my relationships seem to deteriorate within days if we've not had an outing or some other kind of a fun event together.'

'I see,' said Srini. 'Ever had weeds in your grass?'

'Beg your pardon?'

'I'm asking: you must have noticed weed in the grass in your garden while growing up in India or the USA?'

'Sure, but what's that got to do with anything?' asked Dillon, looking perplexed.

'I'm just trying to highlight a metaphor here. Weeds are automatic in gardens—you don't have to make any effort to grow them. If you haven't maintained your garden for a while, you'll notice weed growing automatically. However, it takes effort to grow flowers, doesn't it? Beautiful flowers don't grow automatically, have you noticed?' said Srini.

'Got you,' said Dillon. 'You're saying we have to keep working on our relationships—that beautiful relationships will begin to suffer if we don't work on them, and mental negativity will creep in automatically?'

'Precisely,' replied Srini. 'Spend time regularly with your family, create memories, be unselfish. You'll notice your relationships staying consistently healthy.'

'Great suggestion,' said Dillon. 'I'll keep your advice in mind. I'll admit that most days I still carry work home, and don't make a committed effort to "be there" completely.'

'When you realize the truth, you've won half the battle,' said Srini. 'Remember, in order to maintain a positive status quo in your relationships, you've got to keep working on it. Never take your foot off the gas pedal. Develop consistency.'

'Sure thing,' said Dillon. 'I've been meditating daily, scheduling regular outings with my family, becoming more mindful and working on increasing my effectiveness. Now I'll remember that *consistent, daily effort is essential.*'

Mindfulness and Peace of Mind

'I do have another question, however,' said Dillon, after a few moments. 'You've been very patient with me as I've tried to build up a meditation routine. Being always the one to start with the "why", I must say I still find myself asking these questions regularly. Why meditate? Are its benefits clearly established in science? How long do I meditate in order to maximize its benefit?'

'Good questions, Dillon,' responded Srini. 'I, too, struggled in the beginning. I wasn't convinced. You couldn't get me to sit down quietly at a place, period. If you were asking me to do meditation, hypnotism or some mumbo jumbo like that, I was not doing it. It was hard. It was complex. How exactly did one meditate anyway? How long did I need to sit? My mind has always been super active. Was it even remotely possible to quiet it?

'But, being a man of science, I researched the topic. In a reputable journal I read, "We have been conditioned to believe that life must be hectic and unmanageable, that it's just a dog-eat-dog world and we all have to scramble to survive. Meditation has been shown in a number of peer-reviewed studies to reduce stress and improve health, not to mention focus. It induces a more realistic perception of the world. Learn to remain calm; you'll get to the very basis of problems like depression and anxiety.[5]

'I found the primary objective of meditation was to *still the mind,* which was the key to achieve peace. If you could somehow "still" the mind—remove the agitation and turmoil—spiritual masters make a bold declaration: not only would you be comparatively happier, you'd be happy in the absolute sense.

'I found there are four causes of agitation: anger, fear, greed and likes or dislikes. I can't tell you how much I've put this assertion to the test. Whenever my mind is in turmoil, all I have to do is to pause for a moment and reflect. Invariably, the reason was one of these four.

'I also found your mind can be trained to respond calmly to these causes of agitation. The goal of meditation is to still the mind, to make it thoughtless. This helps you overcome sorrow, kill your ego and achieve peace, according to gurus. It takes months of effort—it isn't achieved overnight. I can say in all humility, but with the conviction of my own experience, that it took me about six months of daily meditation, often for as little as two or three minutes, to start reaping some of these benefits.

'In order to achieve success in any aspect of life, I learnt, concentration was key. My mind used to be full of thoughts—there was a certain restlessness about it. No matter what I thought or did, my mind had to "be somewhere else". This was the fatal flaw of my mind—it was always full of outside thoughts, including negative thoughts about others, and thoughts of material gain and greed. However, meditation helped me increase my concentration. It let me be completely "present" in the moment, giving complete attention to the task on hand or the person I was interacting with. In other words, my mind had learnt to become completely still.'

'I get it,' said Dillon. 'However, I still ask myself from time to time, how often do I really do it? And I remember you telling me meditation as short as a minute can still benefit me, but it's probably going to help me if you reiterate those thoughts one more time.'

'I believe you should only meditate on the days you want to be happy,' replied Srini, smiling. 'So far as the duration is concerned, there is literature to support the notion of benefits from meditation as short as just a few seconds. In my experience, even five minutes will help. It's not how long you do it, just that you achieve a state of calm and "one-pointedness", even if it's for as little as a minute.'

'Thanks,' said Dillon with genuineness. 'I now get it fully—or am at least more aware than before—and I am determined to *meditate regularly*.'

References

[1] Stolzoff, Simone. 2019, 1 February. 'How Do You Turn around the Culture of a 130,000-Person Company? Ask Satya Nadella.' *Quartz at Work*. Available at https://qz.com/work/1539071/how-microsoft-ceo-satya-nadella-rebuilt-the-company-culture/ (accessed on 17 April 2019).

[2] Collins, James C. and Jerry I. Porras. 2011. *Building Your Company's Vision*. Brighton, MA: Harvard Business Review Press.

[3] Bonnet, Didier and Patrick Ferraris. 2017, July. *Governance: A Central Component of Successful Digital Transformation*. Capgemini Consulting and the MIT Center for Digital Business. Available at https://www.capgemini.com/wp-content/uploads/2017/07/Governance__A_Central_Component_of_Successful_Digital_Transformation.pdf (accessed on 17 April 2019).

[4] Henke, Nicolaus, Jordan Levine and Paul McInerney. 2018, February. 'You Don't Have to be a Data Scientist to Fill this Must-Have Analytics Role.' *Harvard Business Review*. Available at https://hbr.org/2018/02/you-dont-have-to-be-a-data-scientist-to-fill-this-must-have-analytics-role (accessed on 10 June 2019).

[5] Dillard-Wright, David. 2011, December. 'Want Peace of Mind?' *Success, page 17*.

8

Execution Journey Starts in Earnest

'In the best companies of the world, it's the ideas that rule, not titles and hierarchies.'

Dillon was at Dykstrand India's central cafeteria, inaugurating the company's maiden value discovery workshop.

The audience applauded. It appeared refreshing to the group that a leader was speaking of the primacy of ideas in the evolution of the company, and not simply issuing orders.

'We're here today to celebrate,' Dillon continued. 'Celebrate the fact that, going forward, the evolution of this company will be based on digital technology. We expect that there'll be quantum leaps. There're no limits to our powers of imagination other than those that we impose on our own. We have one of the most educated workforces in corporate India; we can, and should, feel confident in a future that is based on the quality of technology ideas we can generate.

Value Discovery Workshop

'I'd like to thank Dr Ishani for organizing today's workshop,' Dillon continued. 'Most of you know her as a manager in the R&D department. I know her as a brilliant scientist, the only employee in our organization to hold three patents. Her latest patent, approved two weeks ago, involves a biometric data transmission system. It can transmit users' workout data to a smartphone and provide precise, customizable insights that can help customers stay healthy.

'Dr Ishani, would you like to kick off the session?' asked Dillon.

'Sure,' replied Ishani, smiling, as she took the microphone. She was 30, slim, slightly built, with bright and sensitive eyes. 'Thank you, CDO sir. The reason we're here today is to generate digital ideas that'll take our company to the next level. Ideas are powerful things. To cite an example, a company that didn't even exist 10 years ago is worth almost $100B today, having disrupted the transportation market the world over. Based on a simple idea—that users and taxis can be connected by a system, and a sensor—that can track the physical location of cars using the GPS. Any guesses as to which company I'm talking about?'

'Uber,' went the chorus.

'That's right,' said Ishani. 'To put it simply, the purpose of today's session is to ideate. We have carefully picked employees from all major functions of the business from various levels of seniority. The first half of the session today would be the "ideation phase", which consists of three steps: first, we list the current environment and landscape. Second, we analyse current issues and pain areas. Third, we debate potential areas for technology intervention.

'That'll take us through lunch. In the afternoon, we'll hold what's called the "prioritization phase", which is when we prioritize the issues and ideas we collect in the morning, on the basis of key parameters such as financial benefit and productivity gain.

'Our deliverable, at the end of the day, would be a list of digital themes and initiatives. To help streamline the discussions and ideation, we have seven facilitators, or team leaders, who'll lead parallel meetings in about 10 separate locations in this building. The seven facilitators are: Hiren, engineering manager, Gagan, finance analyst, Dinesh, HR manager, Cyril, maintenance engineer, Bobby, engineering intern, Ash, production engineer, and finally me.

'Any questions?'

'I have one,' asked a middle-aged employee from the front row. 'As we share ideas, can we reject those that are clearly unviable?'

'I'd suggest that you don't,' replied Ishani. 'It's important to note down all ideas when we're brainstorming in the morning ideation session. In the afternoon, when we begin to prioritize, we may discard ideas that are not practical and keep those ideas aside in a separate bucket if they can only be worked on after some time. Any other questions?

'Let's go!' Ishani said, after a pause.

Planning Digital Initiatives

'We can't take a step forward unless we know where we're going!' said Falguni.

It was the CFO's office, the following Monday, where Dillon wished to provide an update on the progress of digital. The business plan finalization was merely weeks away, which meant the digital program needed to be understood and incorporated rather quickly.

After all, as the CFO said, you can't make progress unless you know where you're going, especially, as she was fond of saying, if 'progress' required funding to proceed.

'We agree, Falguni,' said Dillon. 'We're at a crucial phase of our digital journey, where we decide and agree on the initiatives that we're going to work on. I've invited Dr Ishani to take us through the details. Ishani, as you know, is one of our leading scientists.'

'And a female leader from whom I have great expectations,' said Falguni. Ishani smiled.

'One caveat, however,' added Dillon. 'We need urgent and decisive support from your team in order to provide budgetary clearance. Unless we can finalize the list of initiatives in the next 10 days, we'll miss the approval of these initiatives in our business plan for the next financial year.'

'I'm sorry, Dillon,' said the CFO. 'Your lack of planning doesn't automatically constitute an emergency for me.'

'Point conceded,' said the CDO. 'I admit we've been late to the party, due to a variety of reasons, such as me getting onboarded just a few weeks ago. However, we're making haste, and with the level of clarity of our objectives already at a high level, as you'll see, we're hopeful we'll align the senior leadership team in short order. Ishani?'

'Thanks, sir,' said the R&D leader. 'Madam CFO, here was our approach. We started by defining our portfolio, the name of the container under which our digital program will run. We came up with "DT Phase 1". We wanted to ensure that all stakeholders were aligned that this was part of our transformation program.'

'And that it was Phase 1,' added Dillon, 'since transformation is generally handled in three to four phases.'

Falguni nodded.

'Then we had to come up with the objectives serviced by the portfolio, and, in fact, by portfolios which are going to come in the future,' said Ishani.

'Since the objectives are big enough to take a few years to complete,' added Dillon.

'That's correct,' said Ishani. 'We outlined the following objectives. These were identified by senior management as the most critical of the company's objectives.

- Revenue up by 50 per cent in 3 years.
- Cost down by 25 per cent in 2 years.
- Improve HSE by 30 per cent in 2 years.'

'Question,' said Falguni. 'While I like our objectives around cost and revenue, don't we also want to tackle employee and consumer experience? Because employee experience improves employee engagement and productivity—"take care of employees and they'll take care of customers"—and because consumer experience ultimately differentiates our footwear and creates additional sales channels?'

'Because both of these measures would increase our sales,' said Dillon. 'So we've included them in the first objective. A number of measures would enhance our revenue. For example, operational efficiency, employee productivity and consumer experience would all contribute to increased sales. We need to be able to distinguish between those for reasons of clarity. We do that in the themes, which define the broad groups of digital initiatives.'

'All right,' said the CFO.

'Moving right along,' said Ishani, 'themes are the groups of initiatives that lead to the same objective, such as the three themes CDO sir just shared. Operational efficiency, employee productivity and consumer experience would all be part of the objective "increased sales". It is important to define 3–5 themes, in order to ensure that DT occurs in a broad, cross-functional manner.'

'The more of the company we involve in the journey, the higher our likelihood of success. When everyone buys in, everyone ties in, to our goals,' added Dillon.

'We defined the following themes:

- Connected plant, connected operations
- Smart, agile supply chain
- Digital employee and consumer experience
- Intelligent sales and marketing'

'This is excellent, but you'll need to excuse me,' said the CFO. 'I'm going in for a meeting with the CEO. Would you be able to join us in about 20 minutes? What you're sharing is important, perhaps you'd also like to show it to the CEO?'

DT Phase 1

About half an hour later, Dillon and Dr Ishani found themselves in the CEO's office. Dillon provided the context first, and Ishani continued from where she'd left off.

'Sir,' she began, 'our themes allowed us to pick the following initiatives for the first phase of our DT journey. We defined an initiative as a project, staffed by a cross-functional team of 6–10 employees, which takes between one and three months to complete.'

'Before we get into the digital initiatives, I have a question,' said Eknath. 'On what basis did you prioritize the ideas or issues that came from your ideation session?'

'Eknath, we employed an evaluation framework,' replied Dillon. 'Here it is.' He projected onto the screen the following image.

	Evaluation Criteria	Weight	Score (0 to 10)	Weighted Score
1	Strategic fitness			
2	Financial benefit			
3	Aids competitiveness?			
4	Ease of adoption and use			
5	Time taken to realize benefit			
6	Total cost			
7	Degree of stakeholder buy-in			
	Total	100%		

'All right,' said the CEO. 'Please proceed.'

'Before Ishani takes over,' interjected Dillon, 'I'd like to say that we compiled a list of about 75 ideas from the employee ideation session. By eliminating duplicate or similar ideas, and consolidating some others, we compressed the list to 20. Now, in Phase 1 of our DT, we need to focus on the top 3 to 6 ideas. Therefore, by the use of the evaluation criteria we indicated a moment ago, we pruned the list of 20 to the top handful of ideas.'

'I presume you restricted the number of initiatives to a small number, say between three and six, so that the small digital organization can manage the workload,' said the CEO.

'Yes,' replied Dillon, 'and also because we could establish the digital function by virtue of a handful of quick wins. A few self-contained successes need to occur before long-term successes can, because the latter need broader alignments between business functions and bigger budgets.'

A few moments of pause ensued. Ishani spoke up, 'Here is the set of objectives comprising Phase 1.'

She projected on the screen a simple table as follows:

Serial No.	Business Challenge	Initiative	Key Performance Indicators
1	Predict the failure of machines much before it actually occurs. This can substantially reduce unplanned downtime, maintenance cost and cost of spare parts.	Reduction of costs through predictive asset maintenance.	Reduction by 25%, or more, of maintenance cost, mean time to repair (MTTR), mean time between failures (MTBF).
2	Optimize inventory levels of products. Currently, too much cash is locked up in maintaining a 30-day inventory.	Reduction of inventory levels to an optimal level through the use of analytics.	Reduce inventory levels from 30 to 20 days.
3	production is hampered due to process inefficiencies and ineffective root cause analysis.	Increase production by the use of process modelling, IoT and digital twins.	Increase production by 5% or more.

'What's a digital twin?' asked the CEO.

'It's the "virtual model of a process, product or service",'[1] said Dillon. 'It combines the physical and virtual model of whatever it is that we're modelling. It takes engineering to be able to build a digital twin. Once built, the digital twin can enable us to predict and optimize the performance of a device, for example, if something is wrong with a device, the digital twin can tell us what's wrong and prescribe a way to fix the problem.'

'All right,' said Eknath. 'I understand analytics, which is the systematic analysis of data in order to derive insights. Can you explain Initiative #3?'

'Sure,' replied Dillon. 'It's an excellent scenario for us, obviously because it addresses an important area of need for us, namely production. Also it's a dream use case for the technology team, because it combines four different types of digital technologies.

'First is the use of IoT that allows manufacturing equipment and computing devices to be connected. When we connect equipment, we can monitor and optimize the performance of processes.

'Second is digital twin. As I described a few moments ago, digital twins provide for extremely accurate models of processes and machines, which means we can monitor and optimize production—or throughput to be accurate.

'Third is analytics. There are lots of data in the PLCs and SCADAs, which are the electronic controllers of industrial equipment. In addition, there are historical data in the data historians, which are software programs that store process and production data over time. By carefully analysing these data, we can predict, and therefore prevent, machine downtime.

'Finally, there's the ML or AI. We can train the software system to learn over time based on the machine performance data that accrue over time, as well as maintenance history and past breakdown information. By the use of sophisticated algorithms that improve over time, we can troubleshoot production issues and determine the root cause very accurately.'

Business Plan: How the Digital Journey May Get Scuttled

'OK, that's a good list,' said Falguni, when Dillon had finished. 'Thanks to both of you, Dr Ishani and Dillon. Now you'll have to excuse me; I need to run into another meeting.' Soon afterwards, the CEO adjourned the meeting.

Two weeks later, as Dillon emerged from his office after a long call with a vendor selling its capabilities, he ran straight into Srini and Falguni, who were both exiting the CFO's office.

'We were talking about you,' said Srini. 'Mostly good things,' he added, smiling. 'But I do have a concern.'

'What's that?' asked Dillon.

'You have put in your digital budget request into the business plan, haven't you?'

'No, I haven't yet!' replied Dillon. 'The last two weeks were a blur. I was working with my barebones DAB to prepare the necessary artefacts and engage with vendors. Have we missed the bus?'

Srini looked at the CFO. 'Almost,' said Falguni. 'I realize you have to work through quite a few bureaucratic processes and artefacts, but unless you engage with the relevant business leaders and get their buy-in on the three initiatives you shared with us the other day, your budget request doesn't have a chance of making it.'

'Can you explain the process one more time, Falguni?' asked Dillon earnestly. 'I want to make sure I have the money when I need it.'

'You have computed the potential benefits from your proposed initiatives, right?'

'Yes, we have calculated the payback and RoI for all three.'

'Now, these benefits aren't your department's, right?' continued Falguni. 'In each case, a business function or functional leader will reap the benefit, won't they?'

'Correct,' said Dillon. 'Let me see. For Initiative #1, asset performance optimization, it'll be the head of engineering. For #2, inventory reduction, it'll be the COO and for #3, production increase, it'll be the head of production.'

'Now, if these leaders will benefit from the projects,' said Falguni, 'they will need to put in a request in their respective budget requests. Afterwards, our overall business plan will consolidate the capital and operating expenses (OpExs) from all functions!'

'Gosh, you're right,' exclaimed Dillon. 'We'll have to fast-track some of our artefacts and make sure to get the buy-in from these leaders. However, since the benefits are clear, I have no doubt that getting these leaders' buy-in is a mere formality.'

'If I were you, I won't be so sure,' said Srini. 'I was discussing the first initiative with Punit, the head of engineering. He had some concerns. Why don't you have a quick talk with him?'

Dillon walked over to Punit's office right after lunch. He had to wait for some time before Punit got done with his meeting. Presently the leaders shook hands, and Dillon explained the purpose of his visit.

'You are making assumptions about unplanned production downtimes, Dillon,' said Punit. 'I have a challenge when you say the downtime is 12 per cent.'

'But that's what my team obtained from the data historians,' said Dillon.

'That may very well be,' said Punit, 'but we don't believe or use those numbers. We keep track of uptime manually. And we show an uptime of 92 per cent, so far, for the year. So when you show in your initiative that we'll get an additional uptime of 10 per cent, I can't accept that; the math doesn't add up.'

'So the engineering team is being less than forthcoming about its equipment downtime, is it?' asked Srini, later that afternoon, as Dillon shared his story. 'This is going to blow up your plans.'

'Not so fast,' said Dillon. 'My team will sit with Punit's leaders, and come to an agreement on the target uptime numbers. Once I obtain their buy-in, I'll ensure that Punit includes the relevant budget ask in his departmental business plan.'

'You see how this step is crucial in ensuring you get the budget your team needs?,' asked Srini.

'Absolutely,' concurred Dillon. 'I'm certainly glad I bumped into you today! I am slowly realizing that success in DT is much about influence and bringing others along as it is about the technology.'

Resourcing and Staffing

'Can you please drop by at my office?' It was the CEO, early on a Friday morning. Dillon walked over, wondering what it was going to be about. *Budget—covered. Initiatives—finalized. Scope documents—being worked on. Anything else—have my laptop handy.*

'I'm discussing with the head of HR our hiring plans for the upcoming quarter,' said Eknath. 'I thought you showed me your proposed organization when we spoke last. Can you please share that with us?'

'Sure, here it is,' Dillon said, projecting the following image.

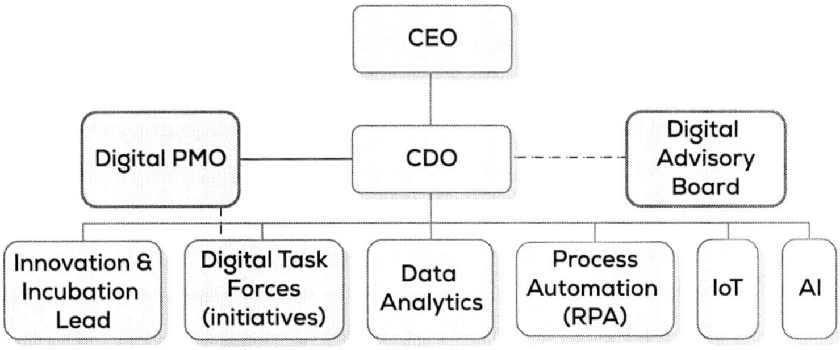

'I'm sorry, but you'll have to briefly explain the roles,' said Hari. 'I understand you already did so to the CEO.'

Dillon explained in brief.

'Thanks,' said the head of HR. 'Pardon my ignorance, but why should this be any different from your IT organization, which is heavily outsourced?'

'There's one fundamental difference between IT and digital, especially analytics, IoT, AI and RPA,' responded Dillon. 'While IT support is based on products, which means once you pick the technology, your IT support is like a plug-and-play strategy involving commoditized technologies.

'Digital, on the other hand, involves fluid technologies.[2] So we need direct access to front-line workers.'

'So you'd in-source most of the roles?' asked Hari.

'Well, I promise I'll answer your question,' replied Dillon, 'but first, let me take a step back. In general, I'm a fan of outsourcing because of a number of powerful reasons. First, technologies are fluid, which makes it hard to make long-term permanent hires. Second, the competencies are less commoditized than IT, which means I have to look hard, and spend lots, to find the right talent. Third, hiring just takes too long in India, due to the long notice periods.

'For all these reasons,' Dillon continued, 'I'd lean towards outsourcing some—or even, most—of my digital team. Having said that, however, I'd insist that the resources work on-site with my team, at least three days of the week.'

'All right,' said the HR Head. 'So which roles must we in-source?'

'Well, the digital PMO and innovation and incubation lead—I'd in-source them since they'd need to spend lots of face time with internal stakeholders and influence the strategy greatly. DABs and task forces are mostly picked from the existing employee base, so there's nothing to look there.

'In my actual technical areas, I'd mostly outsource the implementation roles, except for a few key positions.'

'We need to understand the order of magnitude of the numbers, Dillon,' said Hari.

'It depends on the company's needs, of course, but, in general, digital teams are small and focused, because of the essential need that they be nimble and agile. For a company of our size, my entire digital team may comprise between 10 and 20 FTEs (full-time equivalents), including in-house and outsourced teams.

'In each of the technology areas such as analytics, IoT, etc., I'd like to hire an architect in-house, full-time, but outsource the execution piece; however, there is one specific need. There is a great need to hire someone, in-house, who'll write the *algorithms*—the rules that will guide my digital systems. This is typically someone who knows computer science and mathematics or statistics.'

'All right,' said the head of HR. 'Can you please have someone on your team write the job descriptions of all the roles and send them to Sucheta, my talent acquisition lead?'

'Yes. I need another bit of help with identifying the outsourcing partner. While my team will perform a competency check and shortlist a few firms, HR will have to help us with the terms and conditions of the contract.'

The Need for Artefacts: Request for Proposal, Expense Approval Note, Statement of Work

'Thanks, Dillon. It appears that you're clear in your mind on the roles we need,' said the CEO. 'Just make sure you're ready with your artefacts, or else your projects will never see the light of the day!'

Hari and Dillon walked out of the CEO's office shortly afterwards.

'Hari, let me make sure I align properly with you on this one,' said Dillon, 'because in my experience, this one step is the graveyard of many a fine idea.'

'I hear you,' said Hari. 'The world certainly needs brilliant ideas, but it needs something even more urgently: ideas that are implemented, even if they're middling sort of ideas.'

'Precisely. You know why ideas don't get implemented?' asked Dillon rhetorically. 'Because a step gets left out from the process that's followed at a company. Before you know it, people are fighting over little things, and in the melee, the budget approval doesn't occur, and the brilliant idea never sees the light of the day.

'During my stint as a consultant in the USA,' continued Dillon, 'an expense approval note (EAN) didn't have the cost–benefit analysis in the normal format. It took the CIO a month to prepare the numbers in the new format because a key subject matter expert was away. The approval window had passed; the CIO eventually had to shelve the project.

'And you know what's interesting? A few months later, this company, which specialized in the manufacture of power-related equipment, got acquired at a valuation of $1.2B, and the private equity firm said the valuation would have been upwards of $2B, had the company's suppliers been part of a single electronic platform.

'Remember the project that got shelved because the CIO didn't get the document right? You guessed it—a platform to get all the suppliers on one system. It would have cost the company $8M and taken a year to do it, but they didn't do it, and lost $800M because of it.'

'That's fascinating,' said Hari. 'At Dykstrand India, we have a standard suite of artefacts that are required to approve budget requests.'

'All right, let me list it out the list of steps for you,' said Dillon. 'Please stop me when you need any clarification.

- RFP or RFQ: As we know well, the RFP or RFQ lists the problem statement, broad scope, inclusions and exclusions, and the technical architecture. The document is then shared with a group of partners, with a typical timeline of about a month for the partners to respond. The document is signed off by the CIO or CDO.

- EAN, or more commonly called just the "Note", which contains the capital outlay and the value proposition of the project. First, how much money do we need to spend? What part of it is capital expense (CapEx), and how much of it is OpEx? Second, what is the benefit? What type of benefit is it—financial, operating efficiency, safety? If it's going to cause a financial benefit, how long would it take? We list either the payback period in terms of how many months or years it would take for us to recoup our investment, or the RoI, which means the benefit in terms of multiples of the investment. Typically, this document is signed off by the heads of the relevant business functions, the CFO, CIO or CDO and the CEO.
- The SOW, which is a response from the company to the proposals submitted by partners. It contains the description of the proposed solution at a fairly detailed and technical level and describes the new "system" in relation to the existing systems and the integrations that would be required to be developed. It lists either the number of resources or the size of the work package that would need to be performed. Naturally, exclusions are listed. This document is signed off by the technical leader and the CIO or the CDO.

'Did I miss out anything?' asked Dillon.

'No, you did fine,' replied Hari. 'The only thing I'd have to add is that as the leader, you'll need to keep the ball rolling. One document, then the next and finally, the last one. Approvals take time and many one-on-ones. As the overall technical leader, it would be upon your shoulder to ensure that the process completes. This is one of those things you may not want to delegate!'

'Agree, Hari,' responded Dillon. 'Do you have a few more minutes? I'd like to go over the essentials of these documents.'

'Absolutely,' said Hari. 'I'll grab a cup of tea in the meantime.'

Dillon looked over the collection of documents on his laptop and brought up a few documents by the time Hari reappeared.

'I started his career as a consultant and worked in several industries,' said Dillon, 'which means I have seen about 50 different versions of these documents. However, I'll spare you the gory details, and just go over the essential aspects, covering those that *must* go into the document.

'First, the RFP or RFQ. Here are the sections that must go into the document at a minimum:

- Purpose: Explain what the objective of the project is, for example, "This RFQ has been prepared to enable (company name) to execute DT Phase 1. The underlying basis for the digital framework will be the company's existing IT landscape, supporting applications and the associated infrastructure".
- Coverage: Which locations or plants of the company are covered? How many phases are there to the work? What is the approximate time frame?
- Scope: Suppose you pick three initiatives to be part of the project. Here you describe the initiatives in some detail, say between 200 and 500 words. You may want to preface the section with a clear statement on intellectual property (IP), for example, "Important: Please note that the IP output from this project is the sole property of (company name)".
- Timeline: Here you provide details on the timeline on (a) date of acceptance of commercials, (b) date of commencement and (c) date of delivery.
- Deliverables: What shall constitute the deliverables? For example, reports, systems, dashboards, features, solutions, etc. If you wish, you can also include technical architecture, process flows, flow charts, risks, mitigation plans, tools and test cases.
- Project and program management: What would be the approach and the methodology? What would the project plan contain? What infrastructure and resources would be used? How would execution be tracked, monitored and managed? How would the project be governed (e.g., steering committees)?

- Annexure: Here you include any detailed information, for example, descriptions of the initiatives or the technical architecture. This is optional, because this information goes more commonly in the SOW.

'Next comes the EAN. This document has three broad sections.

- Project background: This includes the context, background, objectives, scope and features. This section is not as detailed as the RFP, RFQ or the SOW, which I'll discuss in a minute. Remember that the management team will read this, so the objectives and background need to be explained at a level which is accurate but not too technical. Any acronyms, if used, need to be explained clearly. Write this section succinctly and clearly. Write this as though you were selling the project to the senior management team, because you are. You're answering the question: why should we bother to fund this project?
- Financials: Devote an entire subsection to project benefits, that is, additional revenue, reduction of costs, avoidance of losses, avoidance of procurement (or any supply chain) errors, improved productivity, improved customer satisfaction, compliance and regulatory.

  Two suggestions here: first, provide annualized benefit numbers, clearly mentioning the source (e.g., \$0.5M reduction of costs due to 2% lower inventory). Second, keep the benefits direct, that is, revenue increase or cost reduction. Anything else is indirect, for example, increase of employee productivity. Senior managers will ask you: so what if we increase the productivity? Can we reduce our headcount? If not, this is only an indirect benefit.

  Write the next subsection to cover project costs. Divide the costs into two: CapEx, which includes hardware, software platforms, program management and execution costs, and OpEx, which includes annual maintenance, ongoing licence or subscription fees and costs for any annual activities such as audit or evaluation.
- Acceptance and approvals: In this section, you should provide a space where signatures can be provided by including a list of all the

"accepters", who are typically your IT and digital leaders and business heads of the departments which will benefit from the initiatives, and the "approvers", who are the management council members such as the CDO, CMO, COO, CFO and the CEO. I must say you need to explore ways to obtain these approvals digitally, that is, turn the paper-based document workflow into a digital one.'

'I have a question here,' said Hari. 'Should you put all your digital initiatives into one EAN document, or would you recommend that we separate it all into separate documents, that is, into one EAN per initiative?'

'In my experience, Hari, it's better to prepare one EAN per initiative,' replied Dillon. 'There are several reasons for it. First of all, the accepters are typically different for separate initiatives. For example, the head of engineering and maintenance are typically two different leaders. Second, the timelines may be different for the individual initiatives, for various reasons, so it doesn't make sense to accept and approve an initiative that'll be executed after 6 months; you lose the immediacy of the decision. Third, and this is a psychological reason—it's easier to obtain management approval when the amounts are small, which is what happens when you prepare separate EANs.'

'All right,' said Hari. 'How about the SOW?'

'Of course,' replied Dillon, 'I'm not going to forget the one document that, above all, determines whether the initiative would be a success.'

'Are you referring to the detail that must be included and the accuracy of that detail that, in turn, would drive precise execution?'

'Exactly,' replied Dillon. 'Naturally, the SOW should be succinct—no one has the time to read a tome—but it has to provide the required information in precise detail. Scope inclusion and exclusion lists are both equally important. I've seen numerous projects fail because the executing partner takes exception at a request that was in neither of those lists. Here are the sections of the document.

- Background—including the introduction, business opportunity and the specific objectives. I've noticed the tendency to make this section either too verbose—which is useless—or too succinct, which leads to confusion on the aspect of scope. Include just enough details here. What is the broad function, what are the terms and phrases essential to the project, and what are the high-level processes?

- Description of the work—that outlines the existing condition, proposed solution at a high level and the scope of work, including the list of included and excluded items. In this section, you describe the business problem or opportunity in significant detail. In the process description, you must include all the relevant parameters and the mathematical function or formula that describes the output, if appropriate. Include pictures and flow charts as needed. What does the proposed "system" do? Assume the system is a black box, and describe all that you want it to perform.
- Technical detail—this includes the TA, integration and bill of materials (BOM). What is the existing architecture? How would the new system be integrated with the existing set-up? What are the testing and verification conditions?
- Governance—including project team, execution plan, project timeline and assumptions. In this section, you'd describe the structure of the steering committees, the make-up of the execution team that would typically consist of a program or project manager and subject matter experts from both our side and the partner's. Also detail the timeline, the milestones of the project and the assumptions that we make about how the proposed solution may look like.

'That just about covers it,' concluded Dillon.

Where There's Love, There're Fights

It had already been a tough day even before the fender bender occurred. After eight back-to-back meetings with employees and would-be partners, Dillon felt completely spent. *Why am I the only one to give, give and then give some more?*

He was surprised to find a stretch of bad traffic on his short ride home this Friday afternoon. *These morons, will they ever learn to drive properly?* While overtaking a particularly slow three-wheeler, his car accelerated and bumped into the back of a taxi cab that braked suddenly in order to avoid hitting a two-wheeler.

The cab stopped, and Dillon stopped a little ahead. The cab driver got ready to shout before noticing there was hardly a dent on his car's rear bumper; he got back into his car in order to drive away. Dillon, relieved, now noticed his own car's front bumper, which had received a healthy dent.

Sighing, and his mood darkening, he pulled into his own apartment complex.

'Hey Sweetie, hey Aaron!' he called out mechanically, without any feeling, as he turned the key in the door. The house was empty. Dillon wondered where everyone was.

He washed up and sat down to check his e-mails, when the door opened, and in walked Kavya and Aaron.

'You didn't show up!' said a sullen Kavya.

'Show up where?' Dillon said, looking honestly perplexed.

'Dad, did you forget? You were supposed to meet my table tennis teacher today at 6!' said Aaron.

Damn, Dillon thought. *Every day I'm home at 5:45, and I had to be late today, of all days, when I'd promised to meet the teacher at 6?*

'Sorry, Aaron. You won't believe the kind of day I had!' Dillon said, trying to avert Kavya's gaze.

'Excuses, excuses,' she muttered under her breath.

'What do you mean?' Dillon retorted, his cheeks getting a shade of crimson. 'First of all, I don't give excuses. Second, I hit some traffic on the way and bumped into a taxi. You can check the dent on the front of the car, if you don't believe me.'

'Aaron, can you please go into your room?' Dillon said. Aaron shrugged, as if to say, 'There you go again, you two.'

Turning to Kavya, Dillon said, his voice rising, 'Can I never get a little slack? Can't you see I may be having a bad day once in a while?'

Kavya began sobbing. 'All your love is so superficial. There's nothing but anger, lurking just beneath the surface. You always shout, when you know I'm right and you're wrong! That's just men's way of reminding the women who's the boss.'

'Don't make this into a man-versus-woman narrative!' Dillon hissed, taking a step towards his wife. 'You *never* try to understand my perspective!'

'As if you do mine,' she said.

'And I have no desire to! Just leave me alone,' Dillon almost shouted. He marched into the bedroom and slammed the door behind him.

'You may be wondering if you can ever make it work,' said Srini the next afternoon, over a cup of coffee in Dillon's office.

'Not really. Strangely enough, despite what happened yesterday, I'm encouraged by our progress overall,' Dillon replied. 'Earlier, we'd not speak for days when we fought. Last night, barely an hour after our fight, we were speaking and laughing about it all. The dinner was quite pleasant.'

'I'm glad to hear that,' said Srini. 'That means you're progressing in terms of repairing the relationship, although the road may appear rocky once in a while.

'During my 25+ years of marriage, and 10+ years of counselling that I've provided to young couples and men on relationships, I've discovered a three-step process to end fights. Would it interest you if I outline my approach?'

'By all means,' said Dillon, as he pulled his chair closer to Srini's.

'As a couple, you seem to be doing the first step right: Communication. No matter how severe the fight, keep the channel of communication open. Never, ever burn the bridge. Your natural response to fights is to stop talking. You must fight your natural instincts, and reach out to your partner. And if your partner reaches out, embrace the opportunity.'

'In other words, sulking doesn't work very well, as I found out in the initial years of my marriage,' said Dillon, smiling.

'Or shouting,' remarked Srini. 'You know why we shout when arguing? Because we think the other person is not able to hear what we're saying. Because, emotionally, there is just a big gap.'

'That's remarkable,' quipped Dillon. 'I never thought about it that way.'

'Right,' said Srini. 'The second step is to speak your spouse's love language.[3] There are five ways in which a person experiences love: receiving gifts, quality time, words of affirmation, acts of service and physical touch. For example, my wife's love language is acts of service. During the week, I perform little acts of service around the house, for example, cleaning out the desk, doing laundry or making tea for us. My love language is words of affirmation. My wife makes it a point to praise me and bolster my self-esteem from time to time. This can be quite challenging.'

'Sounds straightforward to me,' said Dillon. 'Why do you say it's hard? It's as simple as understanding what your partner appreciates, and giving it to her!'

'No, it's not that elementary,' said Srini. 'What happens is, a partner naturally tends to express love in the way that he prefers to receive love. For example, if I love being affirmed, it's natural and easy for me to provide self-affirmations to my wife. The fact is, I have to make an effort to remember my wife's language, which would demonstrate to my wife that I care enough about her to communicate in the love language she understands.

'Does this make sense?' Srini asked as he paused. Dillon nodded. 'Yep.'

'The last step is to practice non-retaliation. In my case, I can trace most of my personal struggles in relationships—both personal and professional—to how I reacted to an adverse situation, what I said on the spur of the moment. You may say I was retaliating.

'For example, I would be upset with something my wife said or did. I'd say or do something stupid. She'd counter, and I'd fight back with something more potent. In time, all we'd be left with was just the hurtful things we'd said to each other while we were retaliating. Years later, I learnt that this was simply a conditioning—a *reflex,* a behaviour. It could be changed.

'I found the solution in ancient scriptures: *ahimsa*—literally "doing no harm", "non-violence" or "non-retaliation". You can respond to a hurtful word or gesture with peace.

'Whenever I retaliated, a sort of mental poison suffused my mind. I'd see the worst in people; I'd assign them ulterior motives. When I responded kindly, however, my mind became peaceful. I didn't damage relationships at times of stress. Even if there was reason for me to snap back, the other party noticed that I responded with gentleness; that I refused to raise my voice or get angry. Relationships became strong. A sense of well-being took hold.'

'This has been extremely helpful, Srini,' said Dillon, his voice betraying his emotions from a surge of accumulated, painful memories. 'I didn't know what I didn't know. I'm always going to remember your three-step plan to end all fights.'

References

[1] Marr, Bernard. 2017, March. 'What Is Digital Twin Technology—And Why Is It So Important.' *Forbes*. Available at https://www.forbes.com/sites/bernardmarr/2017/03/06/what-is-digital-twin-technology-and-why-is-it-so-important/ (accessed on 17 April 2019).

[2] Corsair's Business. 2017, June. *Whether to Outsource or Insource Your Analytics Team*. Available at https://corsairs-business.corsairs.network/whether-to-outsource-or-insource-your-analytics-team-a56009228bda (accessed on 17 April 2019).

[3] Chapman, Gary. 2015. *The Five Love Languages*. Chicago, IL: Northfield Publishers.

9

Safe Sailing towards Success

'Haven't seen you in ages; we certainly need to catch up,' said Prabhat, the head of projects.

'Oh yeah, we do,' remarked Dillon with a feeling of fulfilment and wonder. *Days are flying by,* he thought. *But in a fun way. It's fun being busy when you're going somewhere.*

'It's been extremely busy, these last three weeks,' he continued. 'The team's in the execution mode.'

What Ought to Be the Execution Model?

'What's your execution model like, by the way?' asked Prabhat. 'In projects, we contract out our work using the engineering, procurement and construction (EPC) model. But I've been curious to understand how *you'd* execute a project in your world.'

'In the mysterious world of technology?' replied Dillon, smiling. 'Well, it is different. I call it the *6-step Solution Co-Creation Model.* Here are the steps:

- Business problem: This is the starting point. We state the exact problem we're solving. We state the objectives.
- Empathy map: Here, we capture what the customer thinks, feels and says. Why? Because if we understand where the customer is coming from, which may be gleaned from his or her thoughts, feelings and words, we can design a better solution for him or her. Empathy, after all, is the "experience of understanding another

person's condition from their perspective. You place yourself in their shoes and feel what they are feeling."'[1] Empathy is known to increase "prosocial", or helpful, behaviours.

- Pains and gains: What exactly are the benefits of the proposed solution? Or what pains is it going to eradicate? We list the key performance indicators (KPIs) that'll measure the success, or the lack of it, of the initiative. What you can't measure, you can't change.
- Features: Here, we view the proposed solution from the perspective of a product manager. What features does the system need to have? In other words, if you do X and Y, the system is going to give you Z. We can describe the features on the form of a use case or business scenario, which is probably the most effective way to do it. Why? Because we don't want features; rather, we want our pains to disappear, or gains to appear, and the business scenario would describe both.
- Prioritization: I tell business leaders if they're going to give me one or two things they need from us, they'll probably get them, but if they tell us 10 things they want, we may not be able to deliver any. Why? We can only focus on a few things at any time. Similarly, users may wish the proposed solution to have 10 features, but it'll need to be prioritized, so we can focus on the features users must have, or else the project would be considered a failure.
- MVP: Once we have the prioritized list of features the solution will deliver, we then proceed to work using an Agile model. The hallmark of this approach is that we don't take a dump of all the knowledge from business users and disappear into a cave to emerge six months later with the product in our hands. Instead, we provide users with the initial iteration of the solution in two weeks, working closely with them on a daily basis to collaborate on requirement discussion, test and validate. At the end of three or four such iterations, we may have what we call an MVP, which is the solution in a form that yields a basic level of benefit to the

user. Of course, MVP 1 can be followed by MVPs 2 and 3, and so on.'

'How do you convey the approach to senior management or the project sponsor?' asked Prabhat. 'Certainly, your people can't babble or use techno-jargons.'

'Of course,' responded Dillon. 'We encompass all the information earlier into neat little "four blockers" or 2×2 slides that provide the relevant information from the steps mentioned earlier. I'll shortly show you an example of what I'm talking about.'

'Thanks, but I have two more questions,' said Prabhat. 'First, how long do these six steps take? Second, you discussed something called an MVP. Is that the same thing as a PoC?'

'Good questions,' replied Dillon. 'First, the six steps I mentioned earlier are supposed to take a few weeks, not months. I'd say, typically, eight weeks. Multiyear projects are passé.

'Second, I don't like the word PoC in relation to digital projects, because they communicate a degree of uncertainty regarding the outcome. When we say PoC, it communicates a sense of our trying to prove a technology, as in, *is this technology viable?* Instead, I recommend we call the first iteration as MVP 1, which indicates the high level of confidence we have in the technology. The reason this is a smart approach is because most digital technologies aren't required to be proved anymore. They're already *proven*.'

Reducing the DT Initiatives Into 2×2s or Four Blockers

'You mentioned project charter,' said Prabhat. 'I understand it in the EPC context, but I never heard of it in the software context. Can you elaborate?'

'Sure,' responded Dillon. 'The 6-step solution co-creation model really works. However, it's too cumbersome to explain. The idea behind a so-called project charter, or project four blocker, is to communicate the central idea behind the project in a succinct, effective way. It's the quickest answer to the senior management question, "So, what's this project all about?"

'Here is an example of how the four blocker looks like,' Dillon said as he projected an image on the screen.

Project Charter 2x2 for Predictive Asset Management

Project Description	Benefits
The machines in Dykstrand shoe manufacturing unit in the 'Pattern Making & Cutting' line operate at an OEE of 56-58%. The project objective is productivity improvement: to utilize the equipment more effectively and predict the failure of parts. Substantially reduce unplanned downtime, maintenance costs, productivity losses and cost of spare parts.	Benefits: • Auto capture of equipment start time, down time and other data for process operations and maintenance KPIs: • OEE → Increase +3% • Mean time between failures MTBF → Increase by 50% • Mean time to repair MTTR → Reduce by 20% • Unplanned downtime → Reduce by 30%
Team	**Technologies Employed**
Project Sponsor: Plant Head (Vikas Sengupta) Project Lead: Operations and Maintenance Head (Rudra Narain) Project Manager: Sambit Prasad Team Members (Cross Functional) • Arihant • Sonali • Samuel • Shona	• PLC/ SCADA data, integrated with ERP • Data storage, computing • Visualization • System integration • Additional sensor deployment

'OK, let me see,' said Prabhat and paused. 'So this is for improving our OEE. The numbers are that low, are they? Fifties is not good enough. So what you've said here is you want to increase equipment effectiveness and reduce machine breakdown.'

'Correct, and our objectives are listed in the KPIs in the upper right block,' said Dillon.

'All right. Now, when your team puts up a slide like this, then which steps of the 6-step solution model, in your estimate, are covered in the slide? The reason I ask is because I'm assuming the more of it you're able to cover, the better off you are.'

'That's right. Now, let me see,' replied Dillon. 'The first step in all this is the formation of the *team*. The better the team, the more effective the solution. As you can see on the slide, we have defined a sponsor, a project manager and cross-functional subject matter experts.

'The team has to be so structured that empathy maps can be formulated easily. In this example, I can see that an HR Manager, Shona, and a Strategy Leader, Sonali, comprise what I call the emotional quotient (EQ) team, or the leaders of the team in terms of the EQ. Diversity improves the empathy mapping process.

'The business problem has been defined, as captured by the upper left block. Empathy mapping is done, or the pains and gains wouldn't be known. Features haven't been described here due to lack of space. However, prioritization of the features has been finished, or else you won't see a small list of KPIs. MVP is not something you show on the four blocker, since it's the schedule that guides the release of the functionality and, as such, isn't of interest to leaders or employees who're not part of the technology function.

'In summary, you can expect the four blocker to cover all the steps in the 6-step model, except features and MVP,' concluded Dillon.

'And you'll have one of these for each initiative?'

'That's right,' replied Dillon. 'In DT Phase 1, we've included three initiatives, which means we have three four blockers in total.'

What Not to Delegate?

'That's not always a good thing,' said the CEO thoughtfully. It was the afternoon of the Friday of that week, and Dillon had just finished providing an update to Eknath on the progress of Dykstrand India's DT.

'How're you dealing with the demands of the job?' the CEO had asked, to which Dillon had simply responded with, 'I'm a master delegator; I first empower my people; then I delegate whatever I can!'

'I'll never argue with you on the matter of empowering people,' asserted the CEO. 'And when it comes to delegation, of course you should delegate common activities, but not those that are your most important tasks.'

'You're right, Eknath,' said Dillon, thinking. 'I would consider "Agile" and "culture" to be the most important tasks on my plate. Agile, because that's the way to maximize the team's effectiveness, and culture, because having the right culture, to me, trumps everything else when it comes to ensuring success.'

'I like to say you need to have a direct report handle tasks that are important to you,' said the CEO. 'In your case, you can probably have a manager on your team be responsible for Agile, and another one take charge of culture. If so, you'd have effectively delegated the two activities, won't you?'

'Yes,' replied Dillon, wondering what the CEO was trying to convey.

'But what I was asking is, what is that you may not wish to delegate?' asked Eknath.

'I'd never delegate defining the vision, the why, Eknath,' replied Dillon. 'I agree with Steve Jobs when he said, "The biggest responsibility of a leader is to define a vision and articulate it". I believe it's my primary job to find the problems to solve, not to solve them. Also, businesses "rarely understand the problems they have until you show them a better way."'[2]

'Well said,' responded Eknath. 'Here's what I consider your most important, *un-delegatable* tasks for your team. First, you must be the chief meaning officer of your team.[3] Clearly explain where you are, where you're going, and, most importantly, what's in it for them to get there with you. You must articulate what's in it for them to commit to change with you. For example, do they want more money? More flexibility? Growth?

'Second, you must be the empowerer-in-chief for your team. I think you already alluded to this, but what I mean is, not only hire smart people but also empower people you trust by removing their roadblocks.

'Third, and most important, be the chief celebration officer for your organization. Be extremely generous and unselfish. You can't have a jealousy bone in your body. Be glad for people when they get promoted. Be thrilled to give raises and bonuses. Get excited for them! Promote "having fun" as a culture in your team. Do whatever it takes to make work fun. Your team needs to have fun. Constantly be on the lookout for small victories; celebrate every one of them. It doesn't have to be anything fancy, but just cut a cake!'

'This is indeed extremely helpful,' said Dillon, making notes on his phone. 'In order for leaders to move up to the next level, these are invaluable suggestions. Thank you!'

Survival Kit for the World of Agile

'Do you just accept Agile, or really *embrace* it?'

Suresh, a 'top-5' management consulting company manager, had dropped by at Dillon's office. They'd been old colleagues in the US; when Suresh had told Dillon he'd be visiting, Dillon had gladly said yes. Although Dillon avoided salespeople, Suresh, by virtue of his friendship, had earned the right to demand a slice of Dillon's time.

When being told that digital execution was on in full earnest, Suresh had popped this question to the CDO, in terms of embracing Agile.

'You may be surprised at my response,' replied Dillon, after a longish pause. 'As the chief proponent of technology in this company, I'm probably expected to enthusiastically support Agile. After all, it is the way development and operations, or DevOps as we know them, are supposed to run in the 21st century. It's the antidote to the typical projects that run for months at a time. It is supposed to lead to "adaptive planning, evolutionary development, early delivery, and continual improvement, and it encourages rapid and flexible response to change".[4] Which technology leader won't like that?

'But I'll tell you where I have a problem. When it comes to the development and delivery of self-contained objects, such as analytics and the like, I believe Agile does have a place. However, when we talk about complex, tightly integrated systems such as ERPs, I have my doubts as to how effectively an Agile approach will fit into the scheme of things.'

'Fair point,' said Suresh. 'I'd highly recommend that you attend our Agile workshop in Chennai the Monday after next, where we've invited 20 of the top manufacturing and technology executives in South India, to show them how Agile can give them a step up in executing their digital strategies.

'I'll be facilitating that workshop. It may be the best investment of four hours of your time. No, seriously,' Suresh added when he observed Dillon smiling. 'You may think I've put my sales hat on, but I really believe you'll reap tremendous benefits. My colleague and I'll go into how Agile renders your execution journey highly effective.

'In a nutshell, however, I'll say this. There are two things that are absolutely essential if you want quicker results from digital. Notice that I didn't say "faster execution". Your overall execution time may stay the same, but your business teams will start seeing results sooner.

'As I was saying,' Suresh continued, 'you'll need to do the two things in your role as the chief empowerer. First, persuade senior management and obtain buy-in from functional leads for daily calls. That is a primary requisite to make Agile work, and takes some effort, so you'd do well to get started right away. You understand what I'm trying to say?'

'I guess so,' replied Dillon. 'Since Agile will require daily reviews between functional and technology teams, it's essential that the functional leads free up their time on a daily basis, so they can validate the work that's been done in the last day, and provide their feedback.'

'Precisely,' said Suresh. 'And the second thing you may want to see to is that your program management office, or PMO, ensures that detailed project plans have been made and projects executed following the Agile methodology in Sprints. If your program manager doesn't actively drive Agile, it won't happen.'

'I guess I will have to attend your session on Agile,' said Dillon, smiling. 'I have many basic questions on Sprints, Scrums and the various roles and responsibilities. I need to get going for a meeting with the CFO, but Suresh, my friend, it's great seeing you again, and I'll see you in Chennai in less than two weeks!'

How to Keep DT Execution on Track?

'Dillon, can you come to my office right away?'

Dillon sensed urgency in the CEO's voice. *What could it be?* He thought. *No security attack. Check. ERP systems up. Check. No one died. Check.*

'Dillon, let me introduce you to KV, the senior-most member of our board. He said he'd like a quick update on our progress in digital. KV, this is Dillon, our CIO and CDO,' said Eknath, by way of introductions.

KV? Dillon's mind raced. *The influential board member who could make or break careers with a word or a look?*

'Pleased to meet you, KV,' said Dillon, extending his hand. 'It's a privilege that you're visiting us.'

'Cut out the pleasantries, young man,' said the older man, almost snarling. He was a tall, imposing man. Except for a shock of white hair betrayed his age, which, Dillon estimated, must be in the mid-70s, the man exuded the energy and confidence of someone decades younger than him. 'The largest companies in India are struggling to make progress on their digital programs. What makes you believe we can do it?'

'Sir, we have the right team and the right strategy in place,' said Dillon, even surprising himself with the sense of calm confidence that he exuded.

'And what may you mean by that?' asked KV, his voice sounding a little more reassured, probably because the young man wasn't backing down from a fight. 'I've heard the word strategy so commonly bandied about that I must ask you to be more specific.'

'KV, first of all, we have a specialized program management role, and a project manager, both part of the PMO, that works closely with the CEO's office to monitor and report the progress of the digital program to functional heads, project sponsors and the CEO.

'The program manager reports to the CDO and ensures that detail project plans have been made and projects executed following the Agile methodology in what we call "Sprints". The goal is to give to func-tional users something called the MVP, which means success or failure can be determined in a matter of weeks, not months,' Dillon said.

'And so far, are we succeeding, or failing?' asked the old leader.

'Out of our three initiatives, we've started work on two. We got the first MVP of the first initiative out last week. On Friday, we get the first MVP of our second initiative out the door. Based on what I've seen, that'll make it two out of two, in the win column,' said Dillon.

'That's fine, but who assigns responsibilities and tracks the progress? Obviously we're highly matrixed and all the folks responsible for execution can't be reporting to you or the PMO, can they?' asked KV, still combative.

Assigning Responsibilities and Tracking Progress

'No, they can't,' admitted Dillon. 'But we guarantee success by *building in the reporting* to the teams.'

'What do you mean?'

'Sir, in each project team, the business head is the project sponsor. The line head, or line manager, is the project leader. The project manager is a senior professional from the business team. The team members are cross-functional, including finance, HR, IT, engineering, quality and maintenance, and other functions.

'In effect, the project team is working for the project manager, the leader and the sponsor, who're all from the function where the initiative is going to be delivered. So we're positioning the team for success by ensuring that accountability and reporting are built in,' Dillon concluded.

'OK, fine,' said the old warrior, becalmed by the confidence projected by the young CDO. 'But I need to see it to believe it. Can you show me a picture, a representation, *something*?'

'Sure, KV, here you go. Here's how our project structure looks like, for our "predictive asset management" initiative,' said Dillon, as he projected an image on the screen.

'But…' continued the old leader, as he appeared to look for a weapon, 'how about the meeting cadences? How do you *guarantee* things are progressing?'

'Here's what we do,' responded Dillon. 'The project team meets daily with the project manager. Project leads review the progress once every two weeks. Project sponsor reviews the progress every one or two weeks, depending on their preference. Meeting minutes are circulated,

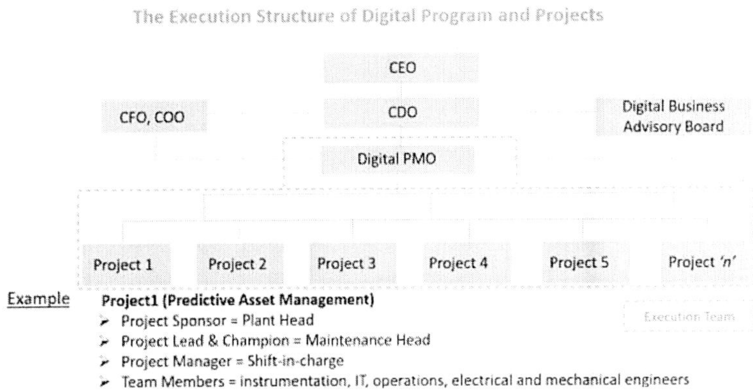

along with action items. Items which do not get resolved after two reminders get flagged for escalation to the next level.'

'There's one other factor I consider the most important function of the PMO,' said KV. 'But I won't like to spell it out. Instead, let me ask you: what's the most important determinant of your success?'

'I'd say it's culture,' replied Dillon, after a careful moment's pause.

'That's darned right,' said the old leader. 'I expect your program manager to proactively drive culture. How does he or she accomplish that objective?'

'Here's how my program manager does it,' replied Dillon. 'He has three major responsibilities relating to culture.[5] First, he ensures that best practices are consistently practised, from among all the initiatives running at different departments or plants. Next, he makes sure that, rather than purely guess-based estimates, teams provide data-driven estimation, for example, one based on similar projects executed at other companies of comparable size. Finally, he ensures that we are in control of our initiatives, rather than always living in "firefighting mode."'

'Congrats, young man,' said KV, after a pause. 'Looks like you've got a good handle on this thing.' Then turning to the CEO, he winked and said, 'You've got a good one!' as he strode out of the office. The CEO grinned broadly.

How Work Relationships Influence Success

'I can never understand people,' said Narain, fuming, 'although I'm at an age where I should. Can you believe it? The productions head just cancelled his meeting with me, for the third time in a week!'

Narain was Dillon's first major hire—head of digital applications—an experienced leader with nearly 20 years of experience in ERP, analytics and software delivery management. Bald, slim and bespectacled, he projected the aura of a professor of the fine arts, until he delved into the nitty gritty of technology, where his expertise was considerable.

'What happened?' asked Dillon.

'He's been accepting my meeting requests,' replied Narain, 'but cancelling them at the last minute. It happened for the third time today. I've been around the blocks enough times to understand this does happen; nevertheless, the lack of professionalism and respect does bother me.'

'I know how you feel,' said Dillon. 'However, if my experience teaches me something, it is that work relationships matter, and matter a whole lot more than they perhaps should. *Forbes* tells us, "Most naively assume that the key to their success is hard work, dedication, and long hours in the business. In reality, their effectiveness is usually more related to how well they develop their work relationships with peers and business leaders."'[5]

'I guess you're right,' said Narain, shrugging his shoulders. 'I don't mind saying this, but you're better than me in building and maintaining relationships although you're a full decade younger than me. Would you mind sharing some suggestions on how I, too, can improve?'

'Are you sure I can tell you something you don't know?' asked Dillon, smiling.

'Sure, you're better than me at this, and I'm not saying that just because you're my boss,' said Narain, smiling back.

'The first lesson I've learnt is: *always be working on your EQ*,' said Dillon. 'You can't be settling personal scores at work. You have to understand your own emotions, and those of others. Attend some EQ and EI training. Observe how your inner dialogues help or hurt your relationships. Be more concerned about listening to what others have to say than sharing your own thoughts. Care. Love. Forgive.

'The second lesson I can share is: you need to *understand the working styles of your key stakeholders and senior decision-makers*. If a CFO or CEO likes printouts and not PowerPoint slides, don't e-mail them a big PPT file. If the COO expects the meeting minutes after the steering committee meeting, send it! Align yourself to others' styles. If the productions head hates formal meetings, drop by informally. If a leader is moody and makes decisions impulsively, watch out. Learn how to catch him in the right frame of mind, say, early in the morning.

'The third and most important lesson is while you're going to align yourself with others' styles and stay flexible, *don't forget to be assertive when there's a need*. Sometimes, as a leader, you'll need to impose your thoughts and be decisive. You'll need to be bold and courageous, if you're convinced you're on the right track. If you feel your position is going to be questioned, obtain a "committee buy-in"; it'd help your cause when you present it as a group decision rather than saying it's your personal thought.'

'What you're saying makes sense, logically, but honestly, I wonder if I'm too old to learn these tricks,' said Narain, with the look of someone who'd much rather talk about the latest technology than what makes people tick and what ticks them off.

'Narain, you can *certainly* learn this skill. I'll tell you what, why don't you grab a copy of Alan Loy McGinnis' fabulous book, *Bringing Out the Best in People*, and let me know when you've read the first couple of chapters?'

'All right,' said Narain. 'Which brings me to the question, what do I do with the productions head?'

'I already shared my suggestion,' replied Dillon. 'Here's a hint—it's in the second lesson.'

Is Work–Life Balance a Myth?

'Yes, I realize it was our 30th wedding anniversary, but we believe we're just getting started,' said Srini. The previous evening his family had hosted a simple meal for family, close friends and colleagues. Dillon made a mention of the remarkable number—30—the next day to Srini.

'You know why we always believed we'd get to 30, 40 and even 50 years of our marriage—God willing, assuming good health of course?' Srini asked. 'Because we were determined and always balanced our work and personal lives.'

'I get the part about determination, but come now, frankly, is there such a thing as a balanced life anymore?' asked Dillon. 'In my view, work–life balance is a myth. You define what's more important and devote most of your time to it.'

'Not only is it not a myth but also it's very achievable,' said Srini. 'You can do it if you wish to. The key, you see, is to make "balance" important, a priority. What's your purpose?'

'I guess it's to be the most transformational and effective CDO I can be,' replied Dillon.

'No, your life's purpose!'

'Oh, let me see—achieving a loving and close-knit family, achieving financial independence, becoming spiritually grounded, etc. Why do you ask?'

'Because knowing your purpose is the first, critical, step,' replied Srini. 'There is something here which, in my opinion, most of us overlook. My "purpose" is simply not the one mission of my life, the one thing that consumes me. Let's say that my passion is to grow at work. Does that mean I focus solely on work to the exclusion of my other roles and duties? For example, I can't tell my wife, "For the next five years, I'll pursue my purpose of becoming a top executive of my company. I'll need to take a break from my responsibilities as a husband and dad". Of course not! I still must work on being a good husband, a son, a dad, etc.

'A certain type of *balance* is required among the various roles. According to Glenn Bland, one of America's most successful sales executives, balance is a foundation of success.' "Success is the progressive realization of worthwhile goals, stabilized with balance".[6] He talks about a balance between spirituality and finances, and between education and recreation, etc. The point here is that "your purpose" doesn't refer to one simple mission—it's the combination of various roles and responsibilities of life.'

'I get it,' said Dillon. 'I can, and really should, define balance as a key purpose in life.'

'And then, just go and make the daily decisions that'll make it happen for you,' said Srini. 'Most of which you're already doing, such as setting aside time for the family on a daily basis, planning and executing trips and creating memories, etc.

'It starts by *setting boundaries at work*. For example, if you need to leave for home at 5 p.m. every day, so be it. You should clarify expectations with your team, boss and peers.'

'Well, what if I'm viewed as a less-than-stellar professional?' asked Dillon.

'This one is certainly a myth,' replied Srini. 'Who says longer hours equals higher productivity? Stanford University has published a study on how overwork sharply reduces total output.[7] Companies like KPMG and Toyota are telling employees to reduce their work hours.[8] According to studies cited by *Inc.* magazine,[9] working for more than 40 hours a week is a big health hazard that can actually kill people, and it reduces productivity.

'Next, *stick to your hours, unless there's an emergency at work*. Your people should see you value your family time. Your actions speak louder than words; your team will do what you do, not what you say.

'Finally, *build a culture where work–life balance is not only accepted; it's also embraced*. Reward outstanding efforts by gifts that the employee's entire family can enjoy, such as a dinner coupon at a popular local restaurant. Tell your employees explicitly why you value such rewards. What you focus on, grows. Your team's behaviour will change to reflect your priorities.'

The Kid's School Event and a Breakthrough

'And the breakthrough performer of the year award goes to…' Mrs Anu, the teacher making the announcement, stopped and looked around the sprawling auditorium in Siruseri. One of the largest in South India, this theatre could seat 2,500 guests at a time. The occasion was the annual graduation ceremony of SK International School, the largest in Siruseri, and one of India's largest boarding schools.

Parents took pictures. School kids jostled for space next to the cavernous stage. Crying babies added to the din. The extravaganza, a 'production' planned for over four months and executed flawlessly by the kids, was over, and a dozen prizes were given out. There was just one last award, and parents and children waited with bated breath.

At 9:30 p.m., finally, it was time for the giving away of the biggest prize of the evening, the breakthrough performer award, traditionally given to the most improved student of the academic year.

'…. award goes to,' continued Mrs Anu, 'Aaron D'Souza, for inspiring his class, for transcending past performances and circumstances in order to record a remarkable turnaround during the school year. With a jump in academic, sport and musical results, Aaron has inspired each one of his classmates to expect more of themselves, and go ahead and deliver. Please give it up for Aaron!'

Beaming with pride, Aaron ran up the steps and accepted the award from the teacher. Soon afterwards, Dillon and Kavya joined their son on stage. While Dillon tried to record the moment on his phone, Kavya wiped a tear away from her cheek. The auditorium stood up as one and delivered a standing ovation for two minutes.

When Dillon narrated this to Srini the following afternoon, Srini, too, felt for his friend. 'You've gone through a lot,' he said. 'I'm very glad for

Kavya and you, and, of course, for Aaron. But tell me more. How did this award come about?'

'It goes back six months,' replied Dillon. 'One night I was putting Aaron to sleep, and after the usual kisses and wishes, began to leave his room when I thought I heard him sobbing. Puzzled, I walked over and hugged him.

'What happened, honey?' I asked. 'Dad,' he replied, 'when I'm not being a good boy, you scold me. But when I do the things I'm supposed to do, I never hear a good word from you. The last three days I focused on my studies. I put my things away properly and kept my room clean. I also put my dishes away after dinner and packed my breakfast in the mornings. Don't you think I've been a *pretty good boy*?'

'The words pierced my heart like a hot knife through butter. Why did I point out my kid's shortcomings but neglect to appreciate it when he did right?

'I pledged to myself that I'd be a better dad from then on. That I was going to reform. I finally got it that everyone needed encouragement, not only if they conformed to our expectations. That unconditional love was key. That it applied to family, and also to my team.

'That unconditional love and encouragement may have played a role in Aaron's felicitation last night in that huge auditorium, but there's no way for me to know. Kavya got it from the day Aaron was born, that love was the key, but I was slow to realize the fact. That public recognition of Aaron's came after much private suffering; but such is life,' concluded Dillon.

'You nailed it,' said Srini. 'What is worthwhile takes commitment, discipline and focused effort, backed by the love of someone who believes in you.'

References

[1] Coppola, German. 2017, November. 'What Is an Empathy Map, and Why Is It Valuable for Your Business?' *Medium.com*. Available at https://medium.com/swlh/what-is-an-empathy-map-and-why-is-it-valuable-for-your-business-14236be4fdf4 (accessed on 18 April 2019).

[2] Fowler, Jim. 2016, September. GE internal meeting, attended by one of the authors.

[3] Acharya, Nish. 2015, May. 'Jack Welch—Be the "Chief Meaning Officer."' *Forbes*. Available at https://www.forbes.com/sites/nishacharya/2015/05/19/jack-welch-be-the-chief-meaning-officer/#6e9514ba3441 (accessed on 18 April 2019).

[4] Agile Alliance. 2013, 8 June. *What is Agile Software Development?* Available at https://www.agilealliance.org/agile101/ (accessed on 18 April 2019).

[5] Zwilling, Marin. 2016, January. 'Your Success at Work Depends on Peer Relationships.' *Forbes*. Available at https://www.forbes.com/sites/martinzwilling/2016/01/07/your-success-at-work-depends-on-peer-relationships/#cf1a3dc25aa4 (accessed on 18 April 2019).

[6] Bland, Glenn. 1972. *Success, the Glenn Bland Method: How to Set Goals and Really Make Them Work*. Dolton, IL: Living Books.

[7] Roberts, E. *The Relationship between Hours Worked and Productivity*. Stanford University Department of Computer Science. Available at https://cs.stanford.edu/people/eroberts/cs201/projects/crunchmode/econ-hours-productivity.html (accessed on 18 April 2019).

[8] Chan, Jonathan. 2018, January. '3 Scientifically Backed Reasons Why Working Less Leads to More Productivity.' *Huffington Post*. Available at https://www.huffingtonpost.com/jonathan-chan/3-scientifically-backed-r_b_14509568.html (accessed on 18 April 2019).

[9] James, Geoffrey. 2018, November. 'Elon Musk Is Wrong, You Can Definitely Change the World on 40 Hours a Week.' *Inc.* Available at https://www.inc.com/geoffrey-james/elon-musk-is-wrong-you-can-definitely-change-world-on-40-hours-a-week.html (accessed on 18 April 2019).

10

The Agile Philosophy of Delivery

'Quite frankly, your execution plans are going nowhere because you're bringing in old-school techniques to execute new-school technology!'

It was two weeks later, in Chennai, that Dillon found himself with a roomful of CIOs and CDOs, attending a session on using Agile in the world of digital.

Suresh—Dillon's ex-colleague who'd visited Dillon in Siruseri a couple of weeks ago—was the facilitator and main speaker.

The Agile Mindset: A Way to Deliver Quickly and Effectively

One of the CIOs raised his hands. 'Are you suggesting that Agile is the magic ingredient that'll work for each and every one of our projects?'

'No,' replied Suresh. 'Lest we should start forming assumptions and ill-advised conclusions in our mind, let me take a step back and briefly explain the basic concepts relating to Agile.

'When you have a few moments, you'd do well to review the 12 principles of Agile software development.[1] For your benefit, I'll reduce the 12 to the "Chief Four", as I call them:

- Ensure customer satisfaction by early and continuous delivery
- Welcome changing requirements
- Deliver working software frequently
- Carry out close, even daily, cooperation between business people and developers

'It's been shown that Agile development methods deliver quicker, are receptive to change and produce high-quality software.[2] The reason Agile is especially important for executing digital programs is because technologies such as analytics, AI or IoT don't involve monolithic, complex and tightly integrated software components that would take months to plan, analyse and develop.

'Essentially, rather than a team of developers, or a product manager, collecting requirements from business people, only to reveal a year later a software product that "doesn't work," according to the users, in Agile you have business people and developers working in a close-knit model, interacting daily to develop the software together. You will need to hire a software partner who's dedicated to this mode of delivery and work out the terms and conditions in a way that is win-win for both the parties.

'Most of your digital programs would be delivered in the form of pilots, or PoCs, which means you'd always have the pressure of quick execution upon you. Agile is, therefore, an excellent fit for you, in terms of a model of execution. The key to Agile is in the iterative model of software development, which supports a *product* rather than a *project* mindset.'[1]

'Question: my developers don't understand the language of business people. If I let them all loose, won't it lead to chaos?' asked a senior lady sitting in the first row.

'On the contrary,' replied Suresh, 'if you let them loose like you're saying, pretty soon you'll find the developers and the business people speaking one another's language. Or all hell could break loose. That's a possibility, but based on my experience, a remote one.'

'All right,' asked another, 'but shouldn't my developers have the peace they need to spend a few weeks on their own, rather be disturbed every day and given changing requirements?'

'Fair ask,' replied Suresh. 'But let me ask you this: would your development teams rather have the peace to work without obstructions to churn out something after nine months that is of no use, or be given input daily—even if conflicting requirements occasionally—so the business people get their hands on what they actually want?'

Quite a few in the audience nodded.

'Another question,' said Dillon. 'What if the development team has little or no experience in using Agile? What if leadership doesn't understand the broad organizational change required to enable digital, or that the cultural philosophy is at odds?'

'Excellent questions,' responded Suresh. 'These concerns are normally alleviated using a combination of mentorship or coaching, reduced management control and high customer availability.[2] You can educate your senior management, add experienced professionals to the team or hire an Agile Coach.'

The Definitions of Agile

'Tell me something,' said a leader from the back, 'is there a standard definition of the various terms thrown around? For example, what's the difference between Scrum and Sprints? What's a backlog? And so on.'

'Sure, I can answer that one,' replied Suresh. 'However, rather than simply providing you with a few definitions, I'd like to list the various roles and mention the *functions*, that is, what task this person really performs to progress your project.

'I'll start by quoting that immortal sage, Scott Adams,' said Suresh, smiling. 'Boss says, "We're going to try something called Agile programming. That means no more planning and no more documentation. Just start writing code and complaining."' Laughter ensued.

'In another instance,' continued Suresh, 'Dilbert walks up to boss and says, "We need ten more programmers". Boss says, "Use three more programmers", to which Dilbert responds, "Agile programming doesn't just mean doing more work with fewer people", to which pointy haired boss responds, "Find me some words that *do* mean that and ask again."

'Some of you may be thinking, "That's not far from how my organization operates!" Jokes aside, here are the basic definitions:

'Scrum is an Agile software development framework, designed for teams of three to nine members performing actions that can be completed in time-bound iterations. *Why the limit on the number of members?* Because the bigger the team, the more exponentially complex the communication and the lower the effectiveness.

'Sprint is the time frame in which the iteration mentioned earlier is performed, commonly two or four weeks. *Why two or four weeks? Why not three months?* Because Agile iterations need short in order to effectively spit out chunks of work that can be independently delivered.

'Stand-up meetings are daily, 15-minute "standing only" meetings where Scrum teams track progress and plan their work. *What happens if the meetings are planned to be of 30 minutes' duration?* There's no hard restriction, but we want people to be succinct, to the point, and be gone. You need 15–30 minutes just to discuss impediments—everyone either says they're fine or mention their impediment. The operations person can also raise production issues resulting from a new Scrum release.

'Backlogs refer to an ordered list of product requirements that a Scrum team maintains for a product.[3] *Why backlogs?* Because—remember we said product and not project? A requirement backlog is essential for products because it ensures visibility of the product's development road map to customers.

'Product owner is an individual who identifies product features or requirements, prioritizes them and continuously reviews the product backlog. *Why is this necessary?* We need it in order to ensure that the product meets customer requirements.

'Scrum master ensures that the Scrum process is followed, "ceremonies" are performed and project members are not interfered with by external parties. *Isn't that the role of the project manager?* Well, a Scrum master is a coach and facilitator, while a project manager manages the scope, timeline and resources.

'An Agile Coach assists teams in adopting Agile methods and practices. A coach performs mentorship of software developers in conforming to Agile methodologies. *Why do you need a coach?* Because most developers think they're doing Agile if they're following just one or two

Agile practices, such as a stand-up meeting. In reality, Agile is a whole lot more, which the Agile Coach would monitor and ensure.

'It's probably easier to grasp the concepts if we show you a picture,' said Suresh, as he projected the following image. 'Product backlog, or requirements, get filtered and prioritized into a Sprint backlog, which then get developed during the Sprint.

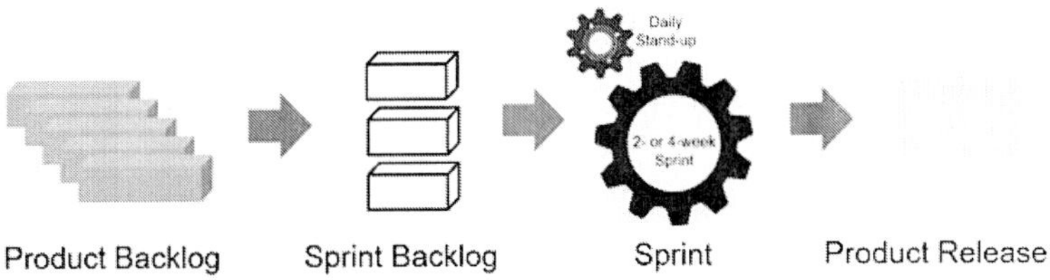

'Those interested in more details can of course look it up.[1], [2] I don't want to spend any more time on this topic than necessary, but want you to understand the basic concept that Agile is essential if you want your teams to execute faster, and, more importantly, deliver what the customer really needs. Make sure you get a handle on Agile, because it's an essential prerequisite for another important concept, commonly referred to as CI/CD.

The Case for CI and CD

'What is CI/CD? Why is it relevant to digital?

'Well, think of it this way,' Suresh said by way of answering his own question. 'Digital has to do with the automation of tasks that are repetitive and error-prone. These tasks, however, are not limited to industrial functions alone; they even include high-tech processes, such as software development and deployment, which are complex and mostly manual.

'How does CI/CD work? Well, normally, the software development landscape consists of development, quality assurance (QA) and production instances or systems. Your programmers would develop the product or solution on the development box, which goes by DEV in technology lingo. The code would then be moved into a system built especially for testing, known as QA or quality. Finally, the code would move to PROD after it was determined that the software was functioning as expected.

'The software in the PROD system is what is used by business users. In non-CI/CD software development processes, code is deployed into the PROD system once a month, quarter or even six months. With the CI/CD approach, however, code is deployed potentially every day, or even instantly, as it's written and tested. In other words, the movement of code from DEV to QA and then onto PROD is continuous.

'In development parlance, you'd "check in transports" regularly, that is, as soon as a Sprint finishes, you check in the software. That way, you'll know if it works, and users can provide feedback on the same day.

'Here's a pictorial representation,' said Suresh, as he projected the following image.

'Why did you write daily and monthly below the arrows?' asked someone from the back. 'Didn't you just say that code is moved to PROD continuously in CI/CD?'

'I meant to convey that, in some situations, the deployment of code into PROD is not automatically performed. It's *not daily* although it's continuous; it may be weekly or monthly, or even quarterly.

'Why, you may ask. In certain systems, it's too risky to release code into the PROD system daily. Especially in highly integrated and complex systems such as your ERP—such as SAP or Oracle. In such cases, it's safer to perform rigorous testing and then release the code less frequently, because "production down" in such cases would mean loss of millions of dollars of business. However, in most digital systems such as analytics, IoT or AI applications, it's quite safe to release code daily if the code is not used to support manufacturing processes.'

'What am I getting out of CI/CD?' asked an older executive sitting in the front row.

'Some serious benefits,' replied Suresh. 'For example, your *product development time will reduce.* In other words, accelerated time to market would allow you to provide the solution to your business users earlier than otherwise possible.

'Additionally, your business customers would be able to *provide feedback quickly,* which would allow your digital team to incorporate the feedback and course correct much sooner than if it didn't employ CI/CD. As a result of this, *customer satisfaction would improve.* Your business users, not having to wait for months for a product or solution, would be much happier with your team.

'Finally, *product quality would improve.* That's because enhancements, corrections and fixes would be incorporated quickly into the product.'

'I've heard two terms represented by CD, namely continuous delivery and continuous deployment,' said Dillon. 'What's the difference between the two?'

'Continuous deployment is automated deployment,' replied Suresh. 'Continuous delivery is manual deployment. In case of ERP, I'd suggest continuous delivery as the preferred technique because of the ability to control the release process. For non-manufacturing systems, continuous deployment is all right.'

'If I don't have an automated testing system, can I still use CI and CD?' asked a young lady sitting in a middle row.

'You may not be very effective if you did,' replied Suresh. 'A chief obstacle to CI/CD is the lack of test automation. If it takes your team weeks or months to test the software, by definition you won't be able to perform CI and CD. Test automation is a necessary, and highly recommended, prerequisite to CI and CD.

'In other words, you'd look to use *automated regression testing* that runs on a nightly basis, and a script would run that would e-mail the developer a status update, for example, "build is successful, we passed testing", or "build unsuccessful". You can also employ *automated code review*—nightly—where your developers would know which incremental software caused the problem, if any.

'A final word, relating to architecture,' concluded Suresh. 'The preferred architecture for incorporating CI and CD is "microservices". If your software features are simple, reusable and independent—in other words, the architecture is a microservices type of architecture—CI and CD are easy to implement, as contrasted with complex, integrated, monolithic architectures.'

Demonstrating Business Value in Weeks, Not Months

The class then moved on to the second phase, group discussion. The group was broken up into six teams of four members each, for purposes of brainstorming. Dillon found himself in a group with Abhay, the CIO of an FMCG major, Bhasker, the CDO of a mining company and Manisha, an IT architect.

'Our topic is "rapid realization of business value",' started Dillon. 'We understand, at an intuitive level, that Agile aids in the expedited delivery of software, so it's a preferred execution approach for digital. The questions are: how to determine business value? And what specific benefits are delivered by the Agile methodology?'

'Let me take a stab at this,' said Bhasker. 'For determining and demonstrating business value, I first like to understand the total cost of ownership (TCO) since costs go beyond what we know as pure IT costs, such as the cost of IT staff and user productivity. In fact, studies have shown that the bulk of the three-or five-year "total IT costs" comes from two critical, if unexpected, areas: staffing costs and user downtime.[4] Almost 75 per cent of total costs come from these two areas.'

'That's interesting; thanks,' said Dillon. 'Any other thoughts on business value?'

'I guess I'd include all the other usual suspects, such as increase in revenue, increased customer satisfaction, manpower reduction from increased productivity, etc.,' replied Abhay.

'That's right,' said Bhasker. 'We essentially need to translate cost to value with an analysis of RoI that leads to all of the factors Abhay mentioned. Such an analysis needs to employ the usual techniques such as net present value, or NPV, internal rate of return, or IRR, and payback.'

'Which brings us to the second point,' said Dillon, 'in terms of how the use of Agile software development techniques in digital helps us *accelerate the demonstration of business value.*'

'In my view,' said Manisha, 'Agile enables the acceleration in the following ways. First, the *increased speed of deployment.* By getting a product to business users faster, Agile speeds up the delivery of value—be it increased revenue or reduced cost.

'Second, *faster user acceptance and adoption.* I've noticed that, during Agile development, when we pull in business users to our daily Sprints, at first they're reluctant to join because of a number of reasons. However, when they do participate a few times, they're amazed to observe the speed at which their feedback is incorporated into product development. It's almost daily. Subsequently, users buy into the product much more easily than if they were shown the product after months of development.

'Third, *increased team collaboration and destruction of silos.* Since your development teams will be spending the time to break down big requirements into user stories with user emotions, over time the collaboration between business and IT increases substantially. Which means silos get busted and everyone lives happily ever after. Well, probably not, but I've seen Agile impact culture positively.

'I believe that, due to these three important reasons, development teams can demonstrate value to business users in a matter of weeks, not months,' concluded Manisha.

'What challenges, in your view, can derail the rapid development and deployment of software that Agile promises?' asked Dillon.

'In my experience,' replied Abhay, 'vendor delays, management funding cuts, technology incompatibilities and dependencies on other projects are the four major risks.'

'That's right,' said Bhasker. 'There are other challenges, but those are the major ones. For each of the risks, digital leaders can develop mitigation strategies. For example, vendor delays can be alleviated by detailed project management, and funding cuts can be precluded by continuing to align with senior management on the benefits of the proposed initiative.'

'Which means,' said Dillon, 'that risks can be mitigated and, at the end of the day, *Agile can enable digital to demonstrate value rapidly to users and senior management.*'

Scrum Teams and the Agile Coach

'We still have 15 minutes left in our group discussion slot,' Abhay pointed out. 'Can we discuss a question that's been on my mind these past few weeks?'

'Sure,' replied Dillon. 'Let's make the best use of our remaining time. First of all, let me answer a question that went unanswered in our session: who's on a Scrum team? The answer: product developers, product manager, tester, QA and an operations person, for a total of between 5 and 7 people.'

'Thanks, but my question is different,' said Abhay. 'You may even say it's a concern. I have a 100-member digital team working for me, part of the IT organization which is about 280 strong. Last year, the digital team transitioned to an Agile development model. I felt that the digital team, working on the latest technologies, would adopt Agile quickly because it's full of younger professionals who haven't had much experience working in the waterfall model of software development. They won't have much to unlearn, I thought.

'So far, however, the team's productivity has hardly changed. I decided to do a little bit of digging myself. What I discovered was that while the team performs some of the ceremonies of Agile, the thinking is still not fully Agile. The team leads still perform like project managers. Alignment with business users is still not uniform or effective. In my view, the team thinks it's Agile while it's not.

'I'm thinking of bringing in an Agile Coach. Does anyone else have any experience with such a role? What would be the ideal background for such a person, and what would he or she do? What would the reporting look like?'

'Good questions, Mr Abhay,' said Bhasker. 'I can take this one, because two years ago I was going through similar thoughts. At the time, I was the CIO of a large MNC's India arm, with a 250-strong organization. The MNC had just hired a global Agile transformation leader, a highly acclaimed female leader based out of the USA. Together with her, I defined a new role of Agile Coach, aligned the local leadership with the idea, hired the person and, in a little under nine months, watched the productivity of the organization shoot up substantially.

'Here's how we did it,' continued Bhasker. 'The person we hired had a total of 17 years of technology experience; had been a programmer for seven years, a project manager for three years, a Scrum master for five years and then an Agile Coach for just over two years. His primary objectives were to mentor Scrum masters, train members in Agile methodologies and techniques, hold weekly Scrum of Scrums and work with senior management to monitor and enhance the effectiveness of Agile. The approach worked!'

'That's an excellent step,' remarked Dillon. 'In my experience, an Agile Coach helps individuals and teams adopt Agile methods and practices.[5] In my prior role, the Agile Coach reported directly to me, since I wished to drive Agile adoption myself. How about in your case, Mr Bhaskar?'

'I did it the same way,' replied Bhasker. 'Since the role is meant to impact all development teams simultaneously, you can't have this person report to the digital head or ERP, infrastructure or applications leader.'

'Was Agile adoption uniform on your teams, Bhasker?' asked Abhay. 'Was there resistance?'

'Well, the adoption was not uniform, and yes, there was resistance,' replied Bhasker. 'The ERP teams, especially, had a hard time of it in the beginning. The analytics and IoT teams picked it up quickly and moved on. But the ERP teams told us their products were too integrated, complex and critical, for them to fully implement Agile.

'The Agile Coach brought a measured, middle-of-the-road thought process to resolve the ERP teams' quandary. He suggested that they adopt Agile and adopt 4-week long Sprints, except in one aspect; they won't have to release the code from QA to PROD daily. That would ensure that there'd be no outages in the ERP systems, impacting goods movement, production planning, finance and such.

'We engaged closely with the ERP leaders, continuing to hammer the benefits of Agile. Eventually, they bought in, and now, the entire team is more or less aligned with the Agile approach,' concluded Bhasker.

'Thanks, everyone,' said Dillon. 'This interesting discussion brings us to the stroke of lunch. My conclusion is that *the role of an Agile Coach is essential to the success of Agile adoption in a technology organization which, in turn, is crucial to the ability of the digital team to deliver quick results.*'

Using Feedback Loops to Turbocharge Agile Development

'*Move fast and break things* is more than just a slogan, it's part of Silicon Valley's culture and partly the reason why Google, Apple, Tesla and Facebook are who they are,' said Suresh, when the participants reassembled after the group discussion sessions and lunch.

'There's even a book out by this name, although it's not complimentary about the culture at these companies.[6] The point, however, is this: the iterative approach of development that is afforded by the Agile methodology to developers, enables programmers to move fast, discover what doesn't work based on feedback from users, fix things and keep moving forward.

'The critical element in all this, in my view, is the concept of the *feedback loop*. It is the secret ingredient in the recipe that enables your Scrum framework to turn out features and functionality at lightning speed and high quality,' Suresh concluded.

'What exactly is a feedback loop?' came the question from a gentleman sitting in the back.

'It refers to the receiving of positive and negative feedback about the product, and the incorporation of the feedback into the development process. Who gives the feedback? Business users primarily, but it could be developers, product owner, Scrum master or any other member of the Scrum team. Who is the feedback meant for? The developers and architects developing the product.

'Here's a picture, to make it easy for you to see what I'm describing,' said Suresh, pointing to the following picture. 'The feedback loop operates throughout the Sprint, allowing users to test, developers to correct and the whole process to repeat.'

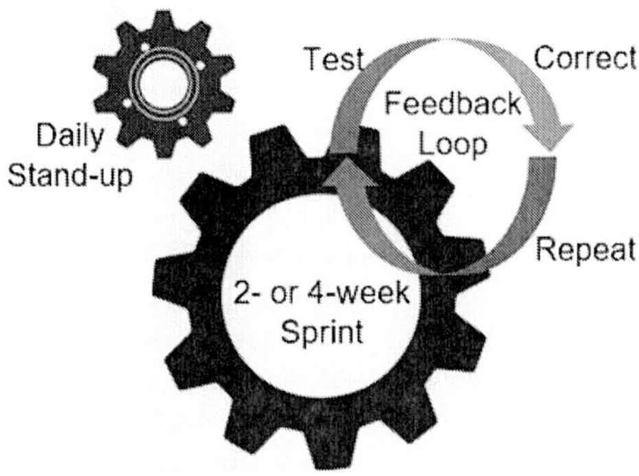

Sprint

'How is the feedback shared?' asked Dillon. 'I guess what I'm asking is, is the feedback only to be shared at the Scrum or stand-up meeting, or is it an ongoing process?'

'In my experience, it's best to create an open environment,' replied Suresh, 'where feedback can be shared using whatever tool or forum available—over chat, e-mail, phone and, of course, the stand-up meeting. In fact, avoid organized meetings to seek feedback, because such meetings can suck a lot of time from everyone's calendar. Agility, after all, is the core reason behind going for Agile in the first place!

'Here are some forums in which feedback can be generated,' continued Suresh. 'Daily Scrum meetings, meetings with product owners and business users, code profiling and tracing[7] and code reviews.'

'Whose responsibility is it to generate feedback?' asked a young lady sitting in the front. 'Should users and others take it upon themselves to provide feedback?'

'Good question,' responded Suresh. 'In my view, it's best that developers and architects *proactively seek out feedback.* I also advise business users to proactively provide feedback. I figured if I asked the two primary stakeholder groups to be proactive, at least one of them will be,' Suresh said, smiling.

He paused for questions and when they were none, he continued, 'At the end of the day, the logic behind a feedback loop is simple. *It's a way for a developer and a business person to sit together, bounce ideas off each other, design, build and fix an application in real time.* It's the innovation sans the technical detail.'[8]

What Holds It All Together? Product Backlog

'I do have a fundamental question,' said an older gentleman sitting in the first row. 'Agile depends, in an elementary sort of way, on fast execution and delivery. Which, of course, means, the developers need to always have the next thing to do, or the next requirement. They can't be done with a Sprint and not have anything to do, which would not only break the momentum but also render the team unproductive. What do you do to ensure that doesn't occur?'

'Thanks,' replied Suresh. 'This is indeed an essential concept in Agile development. What is the construct, or framework, that holds the Agile methodology together? It's the "backlog". Earlier today, we defined the backlog as an ordered list of product requirements that a Scrum team maintains for a product.

'Expanding on the definition a little, the product backlog is an "ordered list of everything that is known to be needed in the product".[9] Based on conversations with business users, senior managers and architects, a list emerges of requirements both high level or broad, and low level or detailed. For example, a senior manager may say, "I need my sales force effectiveness product enhanced with customer relationship management capabilities". This is a broad requirement that will likely result in the need to incorporate dozens of new features. On the other hand, an end user may say, "I need my customer address to appear just below the map, not in a separate window", which would likely require a simple change to an existing feature.'

'Who is responsible for building and maintaining the backlog?' asked a middle-aged female leader from the back.

'The product owner is responsible for the backlog, including the list of contents, release schedule and order,' replied Suresh. 'Which is not to say that he or she is accountable for every single item. Typically, the collection, prioritization and delivery of the features requires the collaboration of a number of parties. Having said that, the product owner is the single point of contact.'

'When does the backlog get exhausted?' asked a young CIO from the front of the room.

'Technically, never,' replied Suresh. 'A backlog is never complete, because so long as a product lives, there are always new requirements. However, it's true that the backlog evolves and reaches a high level of maturity in the first few months or a year. That's because the initially known and best understood requirements are developed right out of the gate. Afterwards, the requirements are likely to be incremental in nature. Also, depending on how the usage of the product evolves, the backlog matures. The backlog is dynamic; it's constantly evolving in order to reflect the reality that the product needs to meet the needs of the organization—competitive or regulatory—while staying simple and appropriate.'

'How often does the backlog need to be maintained or updated?' asked Dillon.

'Often enough for it to have a name,' replied Suresh, 'which is product backlog refinement,[9] which refers to the actions of addition, modification and detailing of the requirements. The refinement also includes the process of ordering, or changing the existing order of, the requirement list. This continuing process is owned by the product owner and members of the development team, typically in a weekly rhythm.

'To conclude,' said Suresh, '*the product backlog is the construct that keeps Scrum going, and keeps the product alive, relevant and useful.*'

Can You Be Too Agile for Your Own Good?

After a quick coffee break, the group reassembled in the training room for the final session of the day. Some of Suresh's colleagues had spoken, and now Suresh was back to wrap up the day's proceedings. During the break, Dillon complimented Suresh on a job well done, upon which Suresh urged Dillon to ask as many questions as he wanted. 'Keep me honest,' he told Dillon.

'I have a question,' said Dillon on resumption, 'that may be on everyone's mind. Can you ever be too agile? Agile is so much in fashion these days that professionals are even using the approach to clean their house.[10] Kidding aside, can Agile break some of your projects if you're not careful?'

'In my experience,' replied Suresh, 'there's no clear black and white boundary between Agile and Waterfall—the traditional way of software development where stages, each lasting a few weeks or months, follow one another in a sequential manner.

'I would probably rephrase your question. *What types of projects, if any, are less suited to the Agile methodology?* Ah—now we have a more relevant question. Here's how I view this matter, based on my nearly 15 years of consulting with some of the world's largest companies who wish to use Agile.

'Agile is extremely well suited for projects with a high level of uncertainty or unpredictability. For example, an AI project to detect anomalous behaviour from senior management, where innovation and creativity are more important to the successful completion of a project than are control, planning and predictability.

'On the other hand, Agile is somewhat less well suited for projects with a high level of predictability or even certainty—for illustration, an ERP upgrade or deployment—where control, planning and predictability are more important than creativity and innovation.[11] One rule of thumb for me, personally, is *the more complex and chaotic the environment, the more suitable Agile is.*

'Bottom line: if you have analytics, IoT, AI and ERP projects taking place concurrently, you may consider Agile for all the projects other than the ERP project. Why? Because ERP needs to be predictable; it is essential to manufacturing, logistics, finance and operations of the company. ERP deployments and upgrades, these days, aren't considered complex or unpredictable.'

'Can I summarize your point by saying this,' asked Dillon. '*Don't adapt Agile mechanically into every one of your projects; if the technology project is predictable or needs to be controlled and planned closely, use non-Agile methodologies?*'

'That's quite accurate,' said Suresh. 'In other words, I won't recommend that you use Agile to clean your house or assemble the furniture you purchased at the superstore. However, understand the mindset and definitions or Agile closely, and use the expedited business value realization potential of Agile in order to drive fast and effective digital projects. Hire an Agile Coach if appropriate. Develop a healthy product backlog. And, most of all, drive a culture where the feedback loop is embraced.

'You'll notice multiple benefits flowing in, including better ability to collaborate with stakeholders, higher trust and goodwill from global stakeholders, and better UX because you put individuals and experiences over processes.'

The Romantic Getaway

'You look positively jazzed,' remarked Srini about 10 days later on a Monday morning. 'You've *got to* tell me what happened.'

'Well, it *was* great,' replied Dillon, laughing and blushing slightly. 'Kavya and I just made a short trip to Malavli Hills, leaving Aaron behind with close family friends. It was our first romantic weekend after Aaron was born; it had been *that* long. It was almost… therapeutic. I feel charged up, as though I can plough through about a week's worth of work in just one day.'

'I'm glad to hear it, old fella,' said Srini with the comfortable air of a pal. It had only been six months, but Dillon, the tall, young Indian–American and Srini, the toothy, friendly and mature middle-aged Indian leader, had begun to bond over the common scars of everyday life.

'It's important that you know that what happened isn't even remotely as important as *why* it happened. Nearly two months ago,' continued Dillon, 'An event occurred that impelled me to change. As a result, I consciously began to work on my anger and selfishness. It didn't take long for my behaviour to bear fruit. At first, Kavya viewed my changed nature suspiciously. In a few weeks, however, she could tell the changes were real. She picked up the vibrations and responded. My wife had now rediscovered the old flame. It all led to our first romantic getaway in over a decade.'

'What was the event that precipitated all this?'

'Here's what happened, over the silly little matter of TV watching. Now, I'm not much of a TV watcher. In my 20s, I could watch two or even three NFL games in a day. By my mid-30s, my TV watching had dwindled to perhaps one movie per week. When Aaron was born, we decided not to watch the TV anymore because I simply didn't have time anymore. However, there was still one slot in the week when I simply *had* to watch a movie: Saturday night.

'On this particular Saturday evening two months ago, we'd had a very full day; I was tired after a long week, and I really was looking forward to catching a quick movie with Kavya at 10 p.m. However, Kavya took really long to appear in the bedroom after tucking Aaron into bed; it was nearly 10:45. Inside, I was boiling, and my annoyance didn't subside when she explained, 'Sorry I was delayed. I warmed the food too much, and it took me time to cool it down.

'I was peeved, but then it hit me suddenly: "What's the purpose of my life, anyway? Is it to watch a movie? It's so trivial! Instead, if I'm kind to

Kavya, and treat her lovingly, I will have done the right thing in the context of progressing a little in my spiritual journey. How meaningless is my anger!"

'Instead of judging Kavya, I made a few kind and loving statements, and when she went to bed about 30 minutes later, I believe she felt a little more loved than judged. This is a little incident, but life is made of such moments, and I can say that I passed this little test because I was able to overcome the loss of pleasure with some equanimity.

'This marked a turning point in our relationship. I was a changed man, and, as I said earlier, Kavya picked up the cues and responded in due time.'

'I couldn't be prouder of you, Dillon,' said Srini, with genuine feeling. 'Life's little victories are sometimes private and hard-earned, but are the precursors to bigger, public victory.'

The Kid Grows Up Fast

'Mom is seriously unwell, Dad. Can you hurry back?' It was Aaron. He didn't sound like he was panicking, but there was a clear and present sense of urgency in his voice.

The day had started uneventfully for Dillon at the Asia-Pacific Leadership Meet in Singapore. Having taken a red-eye flight from Chennai, Dillon had checked into the hotel at 6:30 a.m. local time. Thankfully the meeting was taking place at that very hotel. Still somewhat groggy at 9:00 a.m., he'd settled in at the meeting with a cup of hot coffee when the phone had rung.

'What do you mean, Aaron?' asked Dillon, as he hurried out of the conference room.

'Mom is extremely dizzy. She's unable to get up from bed. I didn't go to school. Here, speak to her,' Aaron said in clipped speech as he passed the phone along.

'Oh hi,' said Kavya, in a soft voice. 'Sorry to be a bother, but I'm ... I really need you back home.'

'Of course, I'll be on my way just as soon as possible,' said Dillon, trying to think. *Got to go, but how about this meeting? ... All group CEOs here... earliest flight may leave three hours later... what should I tell my boss?*

'I've asked Saroja to take care of Aaron,' continued Kavya. 'And she's already brought some breakfast for the two of us, but I'm not sure she can take me to the hospital.'

'OK, perhaps you shouldn't speak too much,' said Dillon. 'Just give the phone to Aaron.'

'Dad?'

'Aaron, listen carefully,' said Dillon softly. 'Talk to Saroja Auntie. If she can't drive Mom to hospital, ask Deepak Uncle or the father of your friend Yohan. I'm going to fly back starting now, but it may be nearly 10 hours before I reach home. You need to get someone to drive Mom to the hospital. Call me from there, but if I'm flying you may not be able to reach me.'

'I love you, Aaron, and I believe in you,' Dillon added, speaking clearly and conveying a sense of confidence to the 10-year-old. 'Take care of Mom.'

The next hour was a blur. Dillon informed his boss, booked a ticket on his phone, took a taxi to the hotel to pick up his suitcase and then to the airport. Questions assailed his mind. *Could it be blood pressure? My wife is in her 30s, damn it! Could it be some form of heart problem?*

Dillon reached home 10 and a half hours later. On the way from the airport, he'd tried a few times to reach his wife, but the phone had just rung. Dillon's worst fears were beginning to take hold of his mind as he finally reached his house. He turned the key in the door and raced into his house.

Saroja, the next-door neighbour, sat in the drawing room. 'She's ok,' Saroja said. Dillon dashed into the bedroom to find Kavya resting and Aaron sitting near him. Dillon hugged his wife and kid. Kavya didn't respond, other than opening her eyes for a second. She was clearly sedated.

Aaron held his dad's hand and led him outside into the drawing room. Saroja got up. She came near Dillon and softly narrated what had occurred.

'Kavya was diagnosed with a severe form of vertigo,' she said. 'The doctor wasn't sure of the cause, but it could be due to any strenuous physical activity Kavya may have performed recently. There's no immediate cause for alarm. She'll get better in two or three days.'

Dillon exhaled. 'I was scared, I don't mind admitting,' he said.

'There's nothing to fear. Well, I've got to leave, now that you're here. But before I leave, I just want you to know I'm proud of your little boy,' Saroja continued. 'Since I can't drive, I asked my husband, Deepak, to take Kavya to the hospital. I went with them. In the hospital, despite the presence of two other adults who were willing and able to assist, it was Aaron who took charge. He spoke to the doctors, made sure Kavya was taken care of in the emergency room. He asked the doctors precise questions and ensured they were aware of Kavya's medical history and her current, unrelated medication.'

'Aaron took charge so well that after some 30 minutes or so, Deepak was able to leave for his office. I stayed back, but as I observed Aaron, I couldn't help being impressed with his calm demeanour, crisp communication with the doctors and lack of any fear whatsoever.'

'Thanks, Saroja,' said Dillon genuinely. 'I appreciate your comments. Kavya and I have tried our best to spend substantial time, thoughtfully and deliberately, with Aaron. Perhaps that's beginning to show. We realize kids spell love as T-I-M-E.'

'Amen,' said Saroja.

'And I can't thank you enough, Saroja,' said Dillon. 'We'll forever be grateful for your assistance.'

Saroja waved him off, as though she felt that she'd merely done what *anyone* would've done. 'All the encouragement and positive reinforcement that Kavya and you have consciously worked on providing have probably borne fruit,' she remarked as she began to walk out.

After she left, Dillon hugged his boy tightly. 'Mom will be ok, Aaron,' he said. 'Thanks for being the man of the house!'

'Dad, you always said life revealed character, didn't you?' said Aaron, tears starting to form in his eyes. 'I always knew I was unafraid of adversity, but I guess Mom and you never realized it before today.'

'Let's get inside and be with Mom,' said Dillon. *My son's grown up,* Dillon thought.

References

[1] Agile Alliance. 2010, June. *Principles behind the Agile Manifesto*. Beck, Martin & Co. Available at http://agilemanifesto.org/ (accessed on 10 June 2019).

[2] Miller, Gloria J. 2013. 'Agile Problems, Challenges & Failures.' Paper presented at PMI® Global Congress—North America, New Orleans, LA. Newtown Square, PA: Project Management Institute. Available at https://www.pmi.org/learning/library/agile-problems-challenges-failures-5869 (accessed on 18 April 2019).

[3] Sedano, Todd, Paul Ralph and Cecile Peraire. 2019. *The Product Backlog*. IEEE. Available at https://www.researchgate.net/publication/330823863_The_Product_Backlog (accessed on 18 April 2019).

[4] Perry, Randy. 2007, April. 'Demonstrating Business Value.' IDC White Paper. IDC and Microsoft. Available at https://www.platformmodernization.org/microsoft/Lists/ResearchPapers/Attachments/10/IDC_Whitepaper_Demonstrating_Business_Value.pdf (accessed on 18 April 2019).

[5] Kelly, Allan. 2009, November. 'The Role of the Agile Coach.' Agile Connection. Available at https://www.agileconnection.com/article/role-agile-coach (accessed on 18 April 2019).

[6] Taplin, Jonathan. 2017, April. 'Move Fast and Break Things, How Facebook, Google and Amazon Cornered Culture and Undermined Democracy.' Boston, MA: Little, Brown and Company.

[7] Watson, Matt. 2017, June. 'How to Use Fast Feedback Loops.' Axosoft Blog. Available at https://blog.axosoft.com/feedback-loops-agile-development/ (accessed on 18 April 2019).

[8] Goodman, Danielle. 2018, April. 'Agile Process: Why You Need Feedback Loops during & after Sprints.' DZone. Available at https://dzone.com/

articles/agile-process-why-you-need-feedback-loops-during-a (accessed on 18 April 2019).

[9] Scrum.org. 2018, November. 'What is a Product Backlog?' Available at https://www.scrum.org/resources/what-is-a-product-backlog?gclid=CjwKCAiA0ajgBRA4EiwA9gFOR_nrPIdmjt_ZvNYMh5q5M3Pff160_ung5OvmCMrHO5sf_cncOUKCqhoCuwAQAvD_BwE (accessed on 18 April 2019).

[10] Buckley, Paul. 2017, May. 'Can You Ever Be Too Agile?' CodeBurst. Available at https://codeburst.io/can-you-ever-be-too-agile-cf1623747d4b (accessed on 18 April 2019).

[11] Quora. 2017. 'What Type of Projects Are Not Suitable for Agile Methodology?' Quora discussion answered by Chuck Cobb. Available at https://www.quora.com/What-type-of-projects-are-not-suitable-for-agile-methodology (accessed on 18 April 2019).

11

Getting Down and Dirty

'Can I come in?' It was Punit, the head of Engineering. 'Of course, please do come in,' replied Dillon. 'To what do I owe this unexpected, but welcome, visit?' he asked, smiling.

'I certainly hope you're being truthful about the welcome bit,' said Punit, laughing. The last meeting, when he'd argued with Dillon about equipment downtime numbers was still fresh on his mind.

'No, really,' said Dillon, 'I mean it.'

Why TA Matters

'In your predictive asset management initiative, your team is making what I believe to be big assumptions about system integration,' said Punit. 'For example, I have three data historians already on my PLCs and SCADAs on the pattern making and cutting line. However, the technical discussions your team had with my people clearly indicated that the new system you're proposing to deploy contains two new data historians.

'To me, it appears that the planning—the system-level view and design—seems to be missing,' Punit continued. 'First, I don't want to pay for systems I don't need. And second, if your team is unaware of the system-level knowledge, I must say I don't have a whole lot of confidence in their capability.'

'Are you suggesting that the technology architecture isn't optimal?' asked Dillon.

'What on earth is technology arch…. architecture?' stammered Punit.

'Sorry to trip you up with techie jargon, Punit,' said Dillon. 'What I meant by TA is how software systems in an enterprise work with one another, how data flow occurs and how system integrations have been conducted. To define formally, TA is a set of components, their relationships and the principles by which the system operates.[1]

'The reason I am defining this term for you, Punit,' continued Dillon, 'is because I want to clarify your question on the data historians. The new historians that we're proposing to acquire are to satisfy additional requirements, and your investment in the older ones isn't going bust because we need those as well. In other words, our TA is fine.'

'All right,' remarked Punit. 'I get the definition. Can you explain the concept in some detail?'

'Sure,' agreed Dillon. 'We deal with it all the time, and it's good if you're aware of it, and if every other important stakeholder of mine is, as well. TA is the framework on the basis of which we define our technology strategy and road map. We don't proceed with a project unless we first have alignment with the TA. Let me take a few moments to explain why.

'First, *you don't want to break anything*. The first rule of IT is "do no harm". How do we know if we're doing any harm or not, unless we have a picture of the existing system—the components and how they work with one another—and then figure out how the proposed software solution would fit in?

'Second, *we've got to be aligned with a long-term vision*. When we define our TA, what we're saying, in effect, is that "this is the vision we're committing to. We won't change this architecture unless there's a great incentive to."

'Finally, *our system has to be efficient and non-redundant*. Unless you have the TA defined, you'll likely have redundancies in your system; for example, multiple document management systems that all do the same thing differently.'

'Thanks, Dillon,' said Punit. 'But isn't it IT's job—you guys—to ensure that nothing gets broken, and that no redundant systems exist?'

'Yes, it is, but there's something called weak IT leadership,' said Dillon. 'Sorry, I take that back. It's just weak leadership, period. There are instances when multiple function heads or plant heads want a certain system based on their OEM and software preferences. And they have the budget. And so what we refer to as "shadow IT" occurs. A weak IT leader, typically one who doesn't have a firm grasp on the TA, may try to appease the leaders. A strong leader, on the other hand, would push back to ensure that only one common system is based on the best fit with requirements—and one that is aligned with the TA.

'Here's a typical TA,' said Dillon, as he pointed to a picture. 'Specifically, the application stack. It shows the components, systems and integrations in order for the applications to work.

'Here's why TA matters,' concluded Dillon. 'Identifying the interventions and business pain points will be relatively easy if the TA is sorted out at the very beginning of the digital program. Each and every initiative will have an IT need in terms of hardware, software, networking, visualization, etc. The platforms and the solutions need to be defined, and long-term technology landscape cleared with budgetary and TCO considerations.

Unnecessary Pieces: Consolidating the Architecture

'Which brings us to the question: how do we avoid situations where we end up with multiple systems doing the same thing?' asked Dillon, rhetorically. 'You remember, the "redundant systems" point we discussed a few minutes back?'

'Yeah, I remember,' agreed Punit. 'Go ahead.'

'Well, in some businesses, plant heads and functional heads make short-term, impulsive product and OEM decisions that leave the TA encumbered with redundancy. I know of at least three plants in our group that are running competing products for laboratory automation. And four more that use comparable document management systems from different OEMs.'

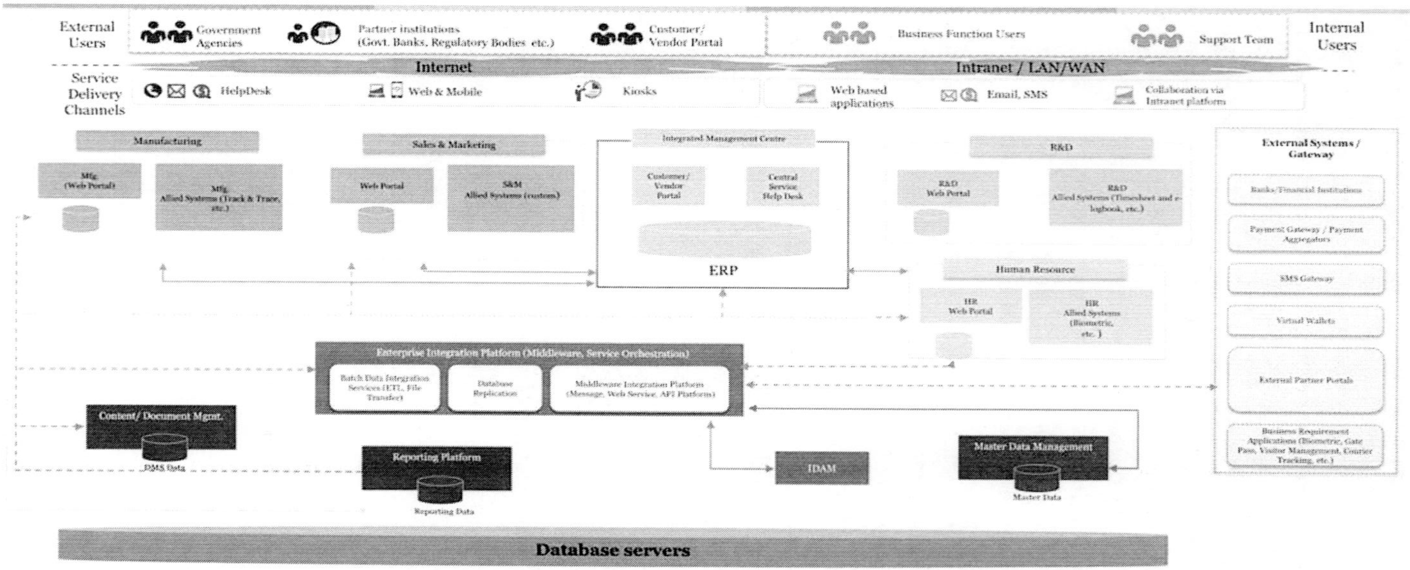
External Users
Government Agencies
Partner institutions (Govt. Banks, Regulatory Bodies etc.)
Customer/ Vendor Portal
Business Function Users
Support Team
Internal Users
Internet
Intranet / LAN/WAN
Service Delivery Channels
HelpDesk
Web & Mobile
Kiosks
Web based applications
Email, SMS
Collaboration via Intranet platform
Manufacturing
Mfg. (Web Portal)
Mfg. Allied Systems (Track & Trace, etc.)
Sales & Marketing
Web Portal
S&M Allied Systems (custom)
Integrated Management Centre
Customer/ Vendor Portal
Central Service Help Desk
ERP
R&D
R&D Web Portal
R&D Allied Systems (Timesheet and e-logbook, etc.)
Human Resource
HR Web Portal
HR Allied Systems (Biometric, etc.)
External Systems / Gateway
Banks/Financial Institutions
Payment Gateway / Payment Aggregators
SMS Gateway
Virtual Wallets
External Partner Portals
Business Requirement Applications (Biometric, Gate Pass, Visitor Management, Courier Tracking, etc.)
Enterprise Integration Platform (Middleware, Service Orchestration)
Batch Data Integration Services (ETL, File Transfer)
Database Replication
Middleware Integration Platform (Message, Web Service, API Platform)
Content/ Document Mgmt.
DMS Data
Reporting Platform
Reporting Data
IDAM
Master Data Management
Master Data
Database servers

'You mean we have duplicate and redundant systems?' Punit asked.

'Can I join the party?' said Hari, the HR head, peeking inside Dillon's office. He had a broad smile on his face, and Punit and Dillon welcomed him in enthusiastically.

'You won't believe what we've been able to accomplish,' Hari declared, as he proceeded to seat himself. A tall, broad-shouldered ex-Army man, Hari exuded confidence and, at the moment, joy. 'We've decided to acquire a new HR system!'

'Then congratulations are in order, Hari!' said Dillon. 'However, I must say business functions—including HR—need to partner with IT in order to ensure we make impactful IT purchasing decisions.'

'What do you mean?' asked Hari, the smile fading from his face.

'Well, if the IT team had been consulted, we'd have told you we already use a major HR module from our existing ERP,' explained Dillon.

'Oh, *that*? That one's too expensive, and it doesn't have the process automation features, especially RPA that we want,' explained Hari. 'Most importantly, it doesn't contain the talent management features we must have.'

'OK, then what happens to our current ERP's HR talent management module?' persisted Dillon. 'What's our plan of getting rid of one of the two systems?'

'I don't know,' replied Hari, pondering the question seriously, as though for the first time. 'We could terminate the current HR module if the ERP provider agrees, or consider swapping the existing licenses for a different product. However, I admit, in the short term, we'll have two competing products coexist!

'I know it sounds bad,' continued Hari, 'but we can't always pick one product that meets all our requirements. We sometimes end up with redundant systems. By the way, what were Punit and you discussing when I barged in?'

'We were talking how to avoid duplicate and redundant systems, Hari,' said Dillon, trying hard to suppress a smile.

Hari laughed heartily. 'All right, then,' he said when he'd recovered his composure. 'I'm the villain around whom you can weave your story. On a serious note, however, what's your recommendation?'

'Well, let's start by agreeing about something,' stated Dillon. 'The root cause of all this is that we never had a central strategy and direction. So, over time, multiple systems, multiple vendors and multiple annual maintenance contracts (AMCs) entered into our TA, causing us to bleed money and manpower. Here's how we can hope to stem the bloodletting and improve our technology health in the future.

'First, *we need to define one vision and one road map for our* TA. Which major pieces do we need, for example, ERP, middleware, analytics, etc. How do they work with each other? How are they integrated?

'Second, *we make deliberate product and OEM decisions.* We take our time, and after performing due diligence, select the products and OEMs that are aligned to our vision and road map. For example, how do they scale up? How flexible are they with pricing? We're brutal in our culling process and avoid adding unnecessary pieces to our architecture at all costs.

'Third, *we craft and implement a strategy for "sunsetting" redundant applications* after careful application rationalization. So that, even if in the interim we have to live with redundant systems, at least we'd have an efficient end state after a defined interval, say, 18–24 months.

'Any questions?' queried Dillon.

'No, but I feel enlightened,' said the HR head. 'I understand application standardization will lead to cost optimization in IT systems. I promise I'll reform. I commit not to buy that new HR system until I've had a word with your technology architects.'

'That'll be great,' said Dillon. 'Speaking of architects, I still don't have any.'

'We'll fix that,' assured Hari, as he got up. He then shook hands with Dillon, and left the latter's office.

How Do You Go There from Here?

'That was quite insightful, Dillon,' exclaimed Punit. 'However, while I can see why the TA is very useful, I'm still unable to see the approach you'd use in order to go from Point "A" to Point "B", that is, from the "as is" to the "to be" architecture.'

'You mean the technical approach, or the philosophy?'

'What I meant was,' elaborated Punit, 'you have an "as is" architecture. You then define your vision and road map, which I assume would come with a "to be" architecture that may include an analytics platform, a middleware layer or an IoT solution. You'd strategize how to sunset the redundant applications. What I was asking was, what's the guiding philosophy behind your team's execution?'

'Perhaps chuck everything out, wipe the slate clean and then start all over again?' said Dillon, smiling.

'Just kidding,' he resumed after a pause. 'It would be hugely disruptive to do that, of course. Our TA is the electronic backbone of our company's operations, from demand planning to manufacturing to sales. *You can't just chuck everything out.* You have to keep the lights on. For example, you may have an SAP or Oracle ERP system to plan your enterprise resources. Deploying such systems costs a huge amount of money and takes time and effort. Once the system is deployed, you can't simply dump it—even it wasn't disruptive to do so—and move to a different system without significant heartburn.

'The second thing to keep in mind is that we'd need to *define the interim and the end states* clearly. Just because you can't chuck everything out, it doesn't mean you can't chuck certain pieces out! For example, you may need to sunset redundant HR, document management or laboratory systems. Or an obsolete software. However, during the time that it takes for the team to clean up your architecture, users do have to live with the mess. What makes it easier for them to accept this situation temporarily is if you explain clearly that it's an interim state; that the end state is much nicer and cleaner. This is where your change management, or user adoption, team needs to take charge and evangelize the process of transformation.

'The third and final step, in my view, is *make sure to get the most out of what you have.* Let me explain. Suppose your users have to live, in the interim state, with a piece of software that you can't legally exit without penalty. For example, you may have plans for migrating to a cloud-based, inexpensive HR automation software, but in the interim, are stuck with an expensive ERP HR module. How do you make the most out of the situation? Well, you can negotiate with your ERP vendor to swap the unused software licenses with those for a new module that your users *would* like to use. Most ERP vendors would be open to doing that, if they can get you to try their newer digital product offerings, such as analytics or IoT. Question?'

'I guess you may file this one under the "dumb questions" bucket,' started Punit, 'but when you talk about getting the most out of what you have, should we also look into how to get more out of our existing investments in ERP and analytics systems, among others?'

'Absolutely, Punit,' said Dillon. 'We must look for ways to maximize our existing investments for sure. For example, we probably only use 30 per cent of our ERP and 20 per cent of our existing analytics solution. These numbers are based on recent discussions with the business users, who informed me we don't use costing and production planning features in our ERP, and warehousing and reporting in our analytics tool. What a waste of money! We must maximize our current systems in the interim state as move forward to the end state.'

The Case for Hiring a Consultant (or Two)

Punit took Dillon's leave for a pre-scheduled meeting, just as Dillon received a call.

'Yes, Sucheta? Morning and good to talk with you, too,' said Dillon. It was the talent acquisition lead. 'Do I have any urgent recruitment needs? In fact, I do. You'll be here at 12? Fantastic. No, thank *you.*'

Dillon jotted down his immediate hiring needs. *Digital program manager and data architect—I need urgently,* he thought. *The first one, because I need to help running the digital initiatives in Phase 1, and the data and analytics architect, since we already have the data—in fact, we're drowning in it—but don't have a way to gain insights from it.*

Sucheta showed up on time. About 30, short, stocky, but bubbling over with enthusiasm. The 'action lady,' as described by her boss, Hari.

'Hari told me last week your team would prepare the initial list of job descriptions and send them to me,' she said rapidly, like the rat-a-tat-tat of a machine gun.

'Correct. However, at the moment, my team is pretty much just me,' said Dillon, with a smile. 'Which is why I haven't been able to get the JDs out. I *will* need quick help. Additional heads, and arms and legs. However, out of all the open roles, there are two I'd put in the "urgent" category, if for no other reason than because, once hired, they'd provide me with the bandwidth to think clearly and complete the rest of the hiring process.'

'Sure, shoot away,' said Sucheta, as she brought out her notepad and pen. 'Just describe for me, broadly, the roles. I'll formulate the JDs on my own and run them past you in a day or two.'

'Excellent,' responded Dillon. 'First, I need a program manager. You may be aware that we'd need a PMO in order to prioritize, execute and monitor the digital initiatives. The leader of this team is the digital program manager. This person should have 5+ years of experience in program or project management—in complex projects, preferably in our industry—and a total of 12 or more years of technology experience. It helps if this person is from an engineering background with an MBA degree. I need a tech professional with excellent communication skills.'

'Noted. What's the second urgent role you need?'

'The second urgent role,' resumed Dillon, 'is a solution architect in the data and analytics domain, or analytics architect or BI architect, as they may be known. This person should possess direct experience in the scripting, warehousing and visualization fields, with a total IT experience of 10 years or so.'

Sucheta looked thoughtful. 'And these are permanent roles within your organization?'

'That's the idea,' replied Dillon. 'Why do you ask?'

'Are you open to hiring consultants?' Sucheta asked, nibbling on her pen. 'You know, the reason I'm asking is because hiring takes time... lots of time. Resignation-related "notice periods" are long—several weeks long. Also, onboarding and ramping them up will take an additional couple of months. On the other hand, consultants with a perfect fit can be found rather quickly, from top consulting firms or niche partner organizations.'

'I'm with you,' said Dillon pensively. 'There is actually a large number of partners in the digital space. It's a buyer's market if you're looking for consulting talent.'

'Exactly,' added Sucheta. 'What I've seen is that external consultants' perspective, especially of those with plenty of domain experience, is crucial. Your "permanent" employees would be attuned to your ways within months and lose that fresh outside perspective that's a critical need if you wish to bring about innovation. On the other hand, consultants would always view your strategy through the lens of their external perspective.'

'Agree. What timeline do you think we can work with, so far as bringing in a couple of consultants is concerned, for the two roles I described?'

'Give me three weeks to bring your consultants on board, assuming you'll make yourself available for interviewing,' Sucheta said. 'As opposed to three months, if you were to fill the roles with full-time employees.'

'I like the three weeks much better,' said Dillon, smiling. 'Do we have a deal?'

'All right, Dillon, we have a deal,' said Sucheta, smiling. 'I'll shortlist a few profiles for you to take a look within, say, a week. You'll hear from me!'

Choosing the Right Platform: IoT and Middleware

'The most important question? No, it's not which initiatives; it's which platforms we're going to commit to.'

It was four weeks later, in Dillon's office. Dillon's first "major hire", Uttam, had joined at the beginning of the week in the consulting role of digital program manager. At about 40 years of age, mostly bald with patches of greying hair, and with more than 16 years of experience in consulting and strategy in two of the world's largest consulting companies, Uttam represented a successful culmination of an intense, two-week search for a consultant who could take on the contract-to-hire role of the program manager.

On his second day of his tenure, at the end of an exciting conversation with Dillon, Uttam had asked for Dillon's guidance on what was the most urgent question that had to be answered.'

'Well,' began Dillon. 'We have a fairly good handle on our "as is" TA, which represents all the software systems we currently have. Most of which we do use and some which we don't. Now, the question is, where do we want to go? In order to answer that question, we have to answer the critical query: which platforms are we going to commit to?'

'Which platforms do we have in mind?'

'I'd start with middleware and IoT,' replied Dillon. 'And analytics. I have my analytics architect joining the team next week, so that'll be a discussion for next week. For this week, I'd like you to focus on evaluating and selecting a middleware and an IoT platform.'

'Taking a step back and rephrasing your ask,' said Uttam, after a brief pause, 'you want to nail down the big components of the end-state TA, so that we can build the new systems around them. Now, just to make sure we're speaking the same language, when you say middleware, you're referring to the "software glue" that makes it easier for software systems to talk to one another exchange input and output data, correct? Pictorially, this is how I visualize the middleware,' he said as he pointed to his laptop screen.[2]

'With no middleware, as in the picture to the left, there are nine integrations to be built. With a middleware, there are six integrations. Naturally, as the number of software systems rises, the benefit of a middleware increases. An example of a middleware is that between an ERP and an e-commerce system or that between the ERP and an analytics system. The more the integration points, the more the effort and the complexity.

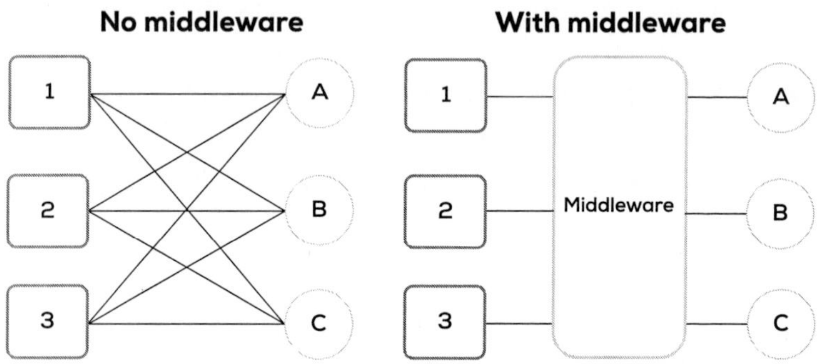

'And when we say IoT platform,' Uttam continued, 'we're referring to the system that enables machines and equipment to be connected to the Internet. It may consist of three components. First, a digital twin, which is the detailed physical and engineering model of the equipment, such as GE's aircraft engine digital twin. Second, a process model that enables us to model a process with input and output parameters, such as ABB's Asset Vista. And finally, an analytics and visualization layer such as Siemens' MindSphere.

'The technology for digital twin is complex and proprietary since it involves deep engineering and physical modelling. So, a GE or a Siemens or a Honeywell won't make it available as an off-the-shelf software package. On the other hand, the process model, commonly known also as the IoT platform, is built using the likes of Java or Go on top of a common cloud platform such as Azure or AWS.'

'Agree. Now, how about the UI? And mobile apps?' asked Dillon. 'I'm unfamiliar with this part.'

'We have multiple options for UI,' replied Uttam, 'such as Polymer, AngularJS or Bootstrap. Mobile app development uses products such as Apache Cordova. The underlying database could be SAP HANA, or Oracle or PostgreS.'

'OK,' said Dillon, having been educated now on his options. It was good to talk to a technical expert who was familiar with common products and platforms. 'Can you run a quick evaluation of the leading products from top three or four OEMs and submit a verbal report to me within a week or so? I need specific product and OEM recommendations that will work with our vision of the TA.'

'All right,' replied Uttam. 'I already have a point of view on this topic, as a senior consultant. However, now that I'm an employee, I'll interview the would-be OEMs formally, with Dykstrand's perspective guiding my discussions.'

And Most Importantly, the Analytics Platform

A week later, Uttam updated Dillon on the middleware and IoT options.

'Good,' said Dillon. He appeared pleased. 'The one remaining piece we have to figure out is the analytics framework. My analytics architect was to join Monday, but he's been delayed by a couple of weeks. Let's quickly discuss the thought process around this topic, so that when you have the bandwidth, you may be able to make some progress with it.

'Regardless of which initiatives we've picked for delivery in Phase 1, analytics will be certainly in the mix. Why? Because as the CEO and CFO said, we already have a tonne of usable data from a number of rich sources of data, such as the ERP and our custom software systems such as the customer portal and the invoicing system. What we don't possess is *actionable insights derived from the data.*

'Insights such as which is our most profitable product line in Europe? In which region in India do we get the most returns? Which product SKU, under which sales director, has witnessed the sharpest drop in sales in the current quarter? And so on. Currently, if the CxO needs a certain report, someone on the team takes the next three days to collect and summarize the data and present it in the form of a pie chart. What we need is real-time, up-to-the-minute dashboards that enable the leader to bring up any report he or she wishes.

'What components of the analytics platform *must* we have? What are some of the typical options we may want to consider?'

'At the lowest level,' replied Uttam, 'we need a data modelling layer, commonly available as a component of the database system such as SAP HANA, Oracle or IBM Db2. Essentially, this software helps us form what's called the data model that's required for the report we need or the query we're answering. For example, we may have a data model called "returned product", which contains product details and information on the return transaction such as date, reason and price. The data modelling layer returns a "view", which contains consolidated information derived from various sources.

'The next layer,' continued Uttam, is "scripting". This layer provides developers with SQL-like programs that perform certain functions, such as the derivation of data using complex formulae from a number of tables from the ERP and other systems. Why is this layer necessary? Because the data model or the views from our data modelling layer must be manipulated in order to derive results which aren't simplistic or straightforward. Examples of scripting languages and systems include R, Python, JavaScript and Apache Spark.

'The top layer that completely determines the UX is visualization. Examples of this include Tableau, Lumira, Crystal Reports and Business Objects. The software analyses the data spewed out by the scripting function, filters the data based on user requirements and presents the data in a format designed to maximize UX and enable instant and simple reformatting of data based on the needs of the user, as in, "now that I saw the sales data per zone, I want to drill down to the sales data at SKU level",' concluded Uttam.

'Thanks,' said Dillon. 'This gives me a basic understanding of the various software layers we'd need to deploy and use.

'Now, only if AI were so simple!' he said.

Should We Start Our AI Journey?

'Why do you say that?,' enquired Falguni, the CFO, of Dillon when the two ran into each other at the conclusion of an executive council meeting. Dillon said in passing that, although the rest of the digital agenda was identified and ready for execution, AI was behind, and that Dykstrand India was perhaps not ready yet for AI. Falguni asked why.

'I think the world of AI,' said Dillon, carefully choosing his words, 'but the concept is widely misunderstood, and, in my view, we should deliberately make the decision whether to tread into the field.'

Falguni chuckled. 'It's funny you should say that,' she said. 'Normally the CDO should be pushing for technology and the CFO should be the one pushing back!'

Dillon laughed. 'I guess I have learnt the language of business leaders too well!' he continued. 'On a serious note, however, most of what passes for AI today doesn't contain any element of real AI. Pardon me for saying "real artificial."'

'Why do you say most of what passes for AI today isn't really AI?'

'People mistake smart systems for AI-powered systems. For example, if my HR system is voice-enabled and responds to my questions and requests, employees and HR professionals alike hail the "AI technology." In reality, the system just uses smart technology; in this case, a chat robot. AI, by definition, has to include the element of learning. Over time, the system has to become smarter. For example, Google Maps is all about AI. Over a period of three years, it's learnt the geographical mapping of the part of the world where we live.'

'All right. So how do you suggest we proceed with AI?' Falguni persisted.

'I'd suggest a three-pronged approach,' Dillon responded. 'First, *ask if we really need AI*. In many cases, an extension of an existing system such as the ERP would be just as adequate to meet our goals.

'Second, *start with RPA*. AI is a journey, of which RPA is a good first step. Use RPA to automate your HR processes such as reimbursement processing, or finance processes such as payroll processing and taxation. This technology primarily uses so-called "chatbots", or simply "bots" that automatically perform manual, repetitive tasks.

'Third, *think small to start with; facilitate pilot projects and PoCs*. One of the beauties of digital is that the philosophy of PoCs and pilots is built in; business people and partners understand equally well that the outcome, or part of it, needs to come before the investment. A percentage of the pricing, in most cases, is linked to the outcome.'

'Understood,' said Falguni. 'What are the software and OEM options we need to start looking at?'

'We need to consider an AI platform which includes functionalities in reasoning, learning, natural language processing and perception,' replied Dillon. 'But there are plenty of options. Almost every major software OEM offers a proprietary AI platform. For example, Amazon's ML, Microsoft's Azure Learning Studio, IBM's Watson, SAP's Leonardo, Google's Cloud Prediction API and many others.'

'Should we make a commitment to a "big" AI platform such as the ones you just mentioned?'

'I used to think that that was the way to go, that we should bet on a "big" AI platform, and drive the rest of our AI strategy off that. What I found was, it made a lot more sense to make software and OEM decisions based on the end-state architecture, rather than on the size of the OEM or the popularity of the product.

'I won't recommend buying a completely unknown brand, but I'm a believer in open-source software. I would just want that our decision takes into account that we don't want the software to require a lot of integration, and we don't end up breaking our TA. Open-source AI platforms have become mature and provide viable options, such as TensorFlow, Keras and Theano.'

'All right,' said Falguni. 'Need to head into a quick meeting with the CEO. It was great running into you. Thanks for patiently answering my questions!'

The Secret Ingredient: Start-Ups

'I just don't think we can work with start-ups!' said Om, the COO. 'We're too big for them. I don't want us to waste our time and money trying some unproven technology provided by a no-name company.'

It was a Friday afternoon. The founder and CEO of a tech start-up, Avi Borade, who'd met the COO at a conference, had been visiting. When he's expressed the desire to meet with the CDO, Om had called Dillon, but mentioned his strong reservations.

'Actually I think it's very worthwhile,' said Dillon on the phone. 'One person? The founder? Send him over. Sure, I will. Thanks, Om!'

An hour and half later, Dillon emerged from his office, along with the start-up founder. He showed the visitor out, and as he got himself a coffee afterwards and walked to the far corner of the building, his mood was buoyant and he had a spring in his step.

'Been having a great day at work?' It was Hari, the HR head. 'I noticed you had a big smile on your face, which is not uncommon, but you were also humming a tune, which indicated to me a state of the mind that was out of the ordinary.'

'I was so off-tune, was I?' asked Dillon with mock dismay.

'No, but do share what caused you to start singing in the first place.'

'I just saw the founder of a start-up. Turned out, they have a perfect solution, using AI, for our challenge of reducing the cycle time for new product launches. This can absolutely be the game changer that we talk about, if it works.'

'It's interesting that you say that. The previous CIO wasn't too tolerant of start-ups.'

'I guess I'm different,' asserted Dillon, 'and to be honest, today's CIOs and CDOs can't have a narrow mindset about engaging with start-ups. Remember that some of today's biggest corporations were start-ups at one time. Someone gave them a chance. Here's how I tackle start-ups.

'First, we may want to *engage proactively with the start-up ecosystem* in our city and at the national level. We should visit these companies, learn from them and encourage them—even if they can't immediately partner with us. Why? Because technological innovation is all about ideas, and large corporations don't have a monopoly on ideas.

'Second, we may want to *hold a hackathon and invite start-ups to the party*. The innovation that'd bring, the excitement it would create and the ideas they'd help spawn in the minds of our employees would make it an endeavour with a fantastic RoI. I can't tell you how many times such an event has provided just the right spark to resolve a long-standing technical challenge.

'Third and last, *give them a chance*. The Googles and Amazons of this world were once tiny start-ups. Of course, only one in a million goes to achieve that kind of success, but the hunger, drive and ambition these entrepreneurs usually display can rub off on us and bring massive, if indirect, benefits. It's good *Karma*—and a win-win all around, even if we decide not to work with them.'

'Thanks, Dillon,' said Hari. 'I'll probably have a smile on my face and a spring in my step the rest of the day!'

'Don't forget to sing!' shouted Dillon as Hari walked away.

Building on the Relationship with Kids

'I'm not sure I completely get through to Aaron every time,' said Dillon. 'But I've come a long way in the last five months.'

Srini and his wife, Nita, had been visiting Dillon's household. While Nita had been in the kitchen with Kavya, Srini and Dillon were discussing kids, and the conversation had turned to how to get through to one's kids—how to be *heard*. Dillon expressed his thoughts simply and honestly to Srini, his trusted mentor and guide.

'Well, let's start with the basics,' said Srini, after some thought. 'You know what's the most fundamental need of kids? Time. The accepted wisdom is that kids spell love T-I-M-E.[3] That's right, they need our time.

'With our busy schedules as executives, it may be a challenge to create blocks of time when we can be with our kids,' continued Srini. 'What my wife, Nita, and I discovered was this: *one of us absolutely needed to spend a lot of time with the kids, and the other partner would try his or her best to spend time to the extent possible.* For the first three years of our younger daughter's life, while Nita completed her PhD, I reduced my work commitment. It was hard, but we realized it was temporary.'

'With us,' chimed in Dillon, 'it's Kavya who's fully committed to spending chunks of time with Aaron, while I make an effort to make the time to the extent possible.'

'That's great,' said Srini. 'Now, when you do spend the time, make an effort to *listen*.' Then he paused.

'What do you mean?' enquired Dillon, puzzled. 'Of course, we listen!'

'I'm not sure,' said Srini, smiling. 'We hear all right, but do we listen? Do we process what we hear, and ask clarifying questions? You'll find that, most of the time, we're simply preparing to respond, not really listening. What I've found is *it pays to listen intently and ask questions.*

'I'll give you an example. Our older daughter, nine at the time, returned from school one day to announce that she won't be participating in after-school sports any more.

'I was somewhat upset. She was good in athletics and in basketball. She was sincere at practice, did well at school events and was growing well as a result of spending three afternoons at school in sporting activities.

'"You're going to continue", I announced. "I don't like kids who give up if the going's tough". At this, my daughter got up and retired into her room. Nita turned to me and asked, "Why do you assume she's not willing to work hard? It may be something else. Let me talk to her."

'After a few minutes, she emerged from my daughter's room with a smile. "It's sorted out", she said. Naturally, I was very curious to learn what was discussed between mother and daughter. It turned out that Nita had listened intently and asked a few questions in a non-judgemental way. And what emerged was this.

'Since our daughter was good at athletics and basketball, both the relevant teachers were pushing her to commit solely to the respective sport. What she'd begun doing was to spend half of her time in both, with the result that she wasn't able to commit to either. Having to choose one sport was draining her mentally. When she reached the point when she couldn't take it anymore, she announced to us that she was quitting after-school sports. And I, not making the effort to listen, had judged her.'

'I see it now,' said Dillon, after a long pause. 'Perhaps I, too, have been judgemental in my short conversations with Aaron. I need to commit to spending more time when I can and listen better and ask questions.'

'I'm glad. Time is the gift that keeps on giving, Dillon,' said Srini.

The New Approach Works Its Magic

In the meantime, Kavya was having a meaningful conversation with Nita in the kitchen. 'I feel blessed,' said Nita, 'that we've been married for over 20 years. It's taken a lot of work, but anything worthwhile in life takes effort.'

'A few months ago,' said Kavya while preparing the salad, 'I can honestly say I didn't even *wish* to be married for 20 years. Now, things are different.'

'I'm very glad to hear that. What happened?'

'I don't know what changes Dillon made, but his outlook towards Aaron and me changed. At first, I was on my guard. Love and trust, once broken, take long to return. However, I decided to forgive him once I sensed that he was making a *sincere* effort. I was determined to extend my hand and cooperate; I wasn't going to hold a grudge.'

'I'm proud of you. Too many spouses hang on to past hurts and just won't let go.'

'Perhaps I was like that when I was 28. But now, being in my mid-30s, I told myself I'd watch for signs of improvement and cooperate.'

'What were the first signs of change? What are some of the changes you noticed in his behaviour?'

'I love hearing words of appreciation. I noticed how Dillon was making an effort to consistently appreciate my efforts in the little things, for example, in the way I prepared dinner or cared for Aaron.

'Second, Dillon's anger went down. Our fights became less frequent, and when they did occur, Dillon quit his habit of shouting. He'd speak softly even if we were fighting, and if he couldn't take it anymore, he'd just leave the room. The angry tantrums subsided.

'Third, he forgave easily. Earlier, if we fought, it'd take Dillon days to get back to normal. Now, we're on speaking terms within minutes. In other words, he doesn't linger on it.'

The two women exchanged a knowing glance. 'It seems as though Dillon's made a number of changes, and you've cooperated and extended your hand of support,' said Nita, finally.

At this time, Srini and Dillon entered the dining area. 'Should I call the kids for dinner?' asked Dillon.

'Just a couple of minutes,' said Kavya. 'Srini, I'd just like to say thanks to you, for having turned around our marriage. Dillon speaks very highly of you and the guidance and mentorship you've provided have doubtless helped him change his own attitude, and in turn, our marriage.'

'Thank you, Kavya,' said Srini with a big smile. 'I wish I could take the credit, but here's the reality. I've rarely seen a man with a greater sense of resilience, of determination, than your husband. He's made some adjustments based on my suggestions, sure, but it's all worked because of Dillon's own *self-talk*, or self-affirmations.'

'Can you explain?' asked Kavya, stopping her work on the fried rice.

'Whatever changes Dillon's had to make,' replied Srini slowly, 'he's first programmed his subconscious mind on it. With your permission, Dillon, I'd like to share a little bit.' Dillon nodded.

'If Dillon's felt intimidated by an obstacle,' continued Srini, 'he's told himself: "I can do it! I've done it in the past, and I can do it again!" If he sensed you didn't trust him, he told himself: "I am trust-worthy! My wife trusts me unconditionally!" Even if you initially viewed him with suspicion, Dillon shrugged it off; he let a feeling of self-worth, from deep inside, deflect the distrust like a duck shakes off water from its back.

'Self-talk is life-changing. By becoming aware of, and then taking control of, your inner dialogue, you can change your life. What do you say to yourself, that is, what self-talk do you use? What's your internal conversation like? How do you respond emotionally to life's situations? What are the guiding values of your life? Dillon's pondered these questions, and by employing the power of self-talk, he's changed how he thinks and, in turn, how he loves Aaron and you.'

Kavya looked at Dillon, who smiled back.

'Let's call the kids in. It's time for dinner, everyone!' declared Kavya.

References

[1] The Open Group. 2018, December. *The TOGAF Standard.* Available at https://pubs.opengroup.org/architecture/togaf9-doc/arch/chap02.html (accessed on 22 April 2019).

[2] Onion, Bill. 2015, January. 'What is Middleware and Why Should You Care?' Briteskies. Available at http://blog.briteskies.com/blog/what-is-middleware-and-why-should-you-care (accessed on 22 April 2019).

[3] iMom. 2011. *Love: Children Spell Love T-I-M-E.* Available at https://www.imom.com/love-children-spell-love-t-i-m-e/#.XBzq6GgzY2w (accessed on 22 April 2019).

12

Transformation Isn't Enough ... for the Long Haul

'That's a sure-fire way for DT to fail,' said Dillon. He had a little hint of red in his cheeks, which meant he was excited. Falguni had challenged him—which had happened often enough—but now she'd intruded upon digital strategy, "sacred territory" so far as Dillon was concerned.

With Digital, Terrible Advice Comes Easily

It was the monthly digital review in the board room. Most of the senior leaders were in attendance. Dillon had shared a brief status update, just two slides long. He didn't believe in long presentations; he'd much rather scribble on the whiteboards.

'So far as I'm concerned,' said the CFO, 'once our year-long DT is complete, I guess we should just look to outsource the whole program. Just lift and shift. Dillon can of course lead the program, and perhaps a couple of senior folks on his team can stay on, but I don't see a reason why we should be burdened with an in-house digital organization for the long haul. Outsourcing completely would allow us to optimize our costs and ramp up our resourcing—or down—as required.'

'Here are two pieces of advice that I've heard all the time,' said Dillon, his cheeks still red, 'that can assure failure for us. First: outsource the whole darned program. Second: focus on demonstrating outcomes.

'Let me explain. Both of these suggestions, while seemingly focused on value and, therefore, sound, don't address one critical area of need:

they don't talk to the underlying capabilities that would accomplish new outcomes and sustain digital for the long term. That makes these suggestions short-sighted and likely to fail.'[1]

'I don't get it,' said Om. 'As the COO, here's how I view the current situation. Your team has done a good job with the inventory reduction initiative, having reduced inventory levels from 30 to 23 days. While we still haven't achieved our desired outcome—20 days—I see a troubling trend. The inventory levels did touch 21 days, but the number crept up to 22 days last month, and 23 this month. The transformation efforts are wrapping up, and my attention—and your team's—is being drawn to other more pressing challenges. Are we reverting to our old ways? If so, isn't it better that we offload the program to an outsourced team who can keep the focus on a small number of specific outcomes?'

'I understand where you're coming from,' said Dillon, 'but it would be prudent to take a step back before we move forward. What's the purpose here? What're we trying to accomplish? *Transformation isn't enough. It isn't even the goal. Continued value creation is our goal,* which means any short-sighted decisions we make is going to come back to haunt us, although they may improve our quarterly results by reducing costs.

'There are three critical elements we need to focus on. *First: define clearly a robust set of competencies that can sustain digital in this company for the long term.*[2] *Second: define a concrete strategy for developing those competencies. Third: build a digital leadership and governance structure.*[3]

'Why is this important? Because, sometimes, the outcomes of digital aren't really the outcomes we should be after. For example, an outcome we're evaluating currently is a supplier portal, where all of our suppliers can register and engage with us. However, if we take a step back, our real focus should be building a fully digital supply chain, where our internal functions, such as production, sales, finance, logistics and others can all collaborate seamlessly on one master data management (MDM) system.

'Broader scopes and perspectives such as this can only emerge if we retain an internal team that engages with stakeholders on a continuing basis. In other words, outsource, but understand you can't offload the entire program to a vendor. Second, most digital initiatives—at least the transformational ones—take several quarters, sometimes a year or two. Digital is a journey. By focusing too narrowly on transformation outcomes, we stunt the very journey on whose back we could potentially grow our profitability exponentially. In other words, focus on building digital capabilities and not on immediate outcomes.'

Competencies, Tools and Governance

'I guess it would help,' chimed in the CEO, 'if you could explain to us what you mean by digital capability. Does the phrase refer to specific technical skills? Or is it a broad description of an organizational structure?'

'Sure, Eknath,' started Dillon. 'First of all, by "capability", we normally refer to the long-term development of competencies, tools and governance. What we're saying is, in order to build long-term digital capabilities, we have to move the needle on all the three of these aspects.

'By "competencies", we mean the complete skill set of employees, consisting of knowledge, experience, technology skills and belief system. When we say, "tools", we mean the technology components—both hardware and software—that it would take to execute an initiative successfully. Finally, by "governance", we mean reporting frameworks, management guidelines, responsibilities and accountabilities, and the monitoring of those.[1]

'It's probably best if I provide a concrete example,' continued Dillon. 'Take our production enhancement initiative, for example. If you recall, our problem statement was that production was hampered due to process inefficiencies and ineffective root cause analysis. What does our initiative propose that we do? That we increase production by 5 per cent or more through the use of process modelling, IoT and digital twins.

'Now, we may view this as a short-term initiative or long-term digital capability. If it's a one-time effort, perhaps an outsourced team of a dozen or so individuals can get it done. However, as I explained earlier today, there're numerous benefits to be obtained from building a long-term digital capability instead. Why? Because production enhancement is not a one-time deal. It's not as though we can raise the number to a certain level and will never have to lift a finger to maintain the number at that level. That's not realistic. Production numbers go up or down, depending on a number of parameters. Accordingly, the technology solution that would be required at a certain point of time, in order to enhance production, cannot be anticipated today.

'If we possess the digital capability, we can address this problem at any point in the future, or even on an ongoing basis. That's why developing the capability is important. Now, what exactly would be the required capability for this specific initiative?

'Let's first consider the *competencies*. The technology skills are the easiest piece to figure out; they include analytics, cloud, robotics, ML, AI, RPA and digital twin technologies. Next comes the experience; we need professionals who possess execution or consulting experience, preferably of more than three years. Finally comes the belief system; we need leaders and professionals who believe in the technology and in the present mission and the viability of the initiative. This is especially important; a technology professional who doesn't believe in himself or herself, or in the technology, would prove detrimental to our digital capability.

'Next, let's discuss the *tools*. We'll need systems—also called platforms—for the development of analytics, cloud, AI, robotics and ML. For example, reporting the production numbers and patterns, we'll need an analytics platform. For ensuring that reports and dashboards are available on the corporate networks or over the Internet, we'll need a cloud platform. We may also need digital twin software for process or engineering modelling of machines and equipment, and so on. All these tools require budgetary support in terms of licensing, development and maintenance, which means the earlier we have clarity on what we need, the easier it will be to ensure that there's an appropriate level of budget set aside for what we need.

'Last, but most important, is the *governance*. We need to make sure the task force reports to the program manager, who reports to the CDO, for the duration of the project. For a long-term capability to exist within the company, many iterations of the project would occur. We need to make sure that a small team of architects and programmers is available over the long term to ensure that the solution is enhanced as required by users over the course of time. We need to spell out who owns the technology deliverable and who owns the delivery of the solution. We need to consider the frequency of the reporting on the progress of the initiative. For example, management may ask for weekly updates for the first iteration, but only require a quarterly summary of the progress once the product is stable.

'Take a look at the summary of the "digital capability" we need for this specific initiative,' concluded Dillon as he projected the following table.

Digital Capability for Production Enhancement Initiative

1	Competencies	*Skills:* *Experience:* *Belief system:*	analytics, cloud, robotics, machine learning, AI, RPA, digital twin prior implementation, execution or consulting experience that the technology is proven and can work in present context
2	Tools	Analytics platform, cloud infrastructure, development platform for AI, robotics and machine learning, robotic process automation systems, digital twin software	
3	Governance	*Roles:* *Policies:*	digital PMO, Innovation Lead, Task Force, DAB, architects, programmers *Reporting structure* *Responsibilities and accountabilities* project management guidelines, management update rhythm

How to Source Digital Capabilities?

'Thanks; that makes it clearer for me,' said Eknath. 'However, exactly how do you propose that we acquire these capabilities? Is it as simple as hiring and training? Should we extensively work with service providers? What else should we keep in mind? Another thought that came to my mind as you were speaking was these terms and phrases sound familiar to what I used to hear from our ex-CIO. What's different What's different about digital capabilities?'

'According to McKinsey,[2] digital capabilities are not a luxury, but a prerequisite for a company that wishes to compete and lead,' replied Dillon. 'Yet, many corporations embarking on a digital journey lack clarity on how to acquire IT and digital organizational structures, tools and talent—in other words, the "capability" as we just defined it—required in order to support a long-term digital strategy.

'A critical component of our digital strategy, of course, is digital capability. The most important question we need to address is *how to source the capability*. Do we just hire, at least most of the time? Should we mostly outsource? Is it even reasonable to expect that these resources will be available in-house?

'First of all, is *digital sourcing different from IT sourcing*? The answer is yes. The following picture will clarify the major differences,' said Dillon, as he projected a picture on the whiteboard. 'Although the sourcing phrases and concepts are similar in digital compared with those in IT, there are important differences owing mainly to the relative newness of the field.'

IT Sourcing	Digital Sourcing
Established for nearly 30 years	Evolving—only been around since 2011
Focus mostly on cost, since sourcing practices are settled and mature	Focus more on talent and less on cost since field is evolving
Project scope mostly fixed, which means....	Project scope changes rapidly, which leads to...

IT Sourcing	Digital Sourcing
Commercials feature complex SLAs but little, or no, outcome-driven payment agreements	Simple SLAs with outcome-oriented payment agreements for up to 50% of deal value
Market contains relatively fewer, larger players	Fragmented players in smaller niches

'How about the talent?' asked the CEO.

'Since digital is a new field that can provide quantum jumps in revenue and profitability,' replied Dillon, 'in my experience, it's worth it to spend 20–25 per cent more in order to hire "top talent." It can lead to up to 10 times more productivity.[2] Why? Because the talent market is not "settled." Being willing to pay for premium talent in such a situation greatly enhances our chances of success.'

'You still haven't addressed my point, outsourcing,' chimed in Falguni.

'Consider me a fan of outsourcing,' replied Dillon. 'There is one important reason why outsourcing makes sense for digital. It's because the *scope keeps changing in digital*. If the talent is mostly outsourced, it's easier to ramp up, or down, as required. However, we need to be deliberate; in other words: outsource repetitive, non-value-add roles, but not that are strategically important.'

'I get it now,' said the CFO. 'Is it accurate to say that most of the execution and delivery activities may be performed by external vendors, while customer-facing activities such as end-user interactions, contextual inquiring and requirement gathering may be performed by in-house teams?'

'Precisely,' replied Dillon.

'I'll go back to a statement you just made: why does scope have to change?' asked Hari. 'I've not heard of anything similar in Finance or HR.'

'The reason is complexity,' asserted Dillon. 'For example, UX, an important digital requirement, is an evolving concept, which means, requirements may be incomplete or poorly defined.[4] In my experience, one time an influential leader required an intranet project to be completely revamped because he became involved as a user—providing detailed functional requirements—and not just as a sponsor. Why? Because employees using the intranet portal had to have "just the right experience."'

'I have a concern,' said Prabhat. 'If the scope is changing, how does that impact your team's deliverables? Assuming your product timelines are a few months long, say, six or nine months, won't we end up wasting a lot of time and resources in putting something out there that doesn't quite do what users want it to do?'

'Excellent thought, Prabhat,' responded Dillon. 'The operating philosophy that precludes that possibility is *rapid, customer-centric innovation using agile DevOps* models and CI and CD.'

'You'll need to translate that into English for me,' said Prabhat, smiling.

'Of course,' assured Dillon. 'For the moment, assume that we have a way to rapidly develop digital products in an iterative fashion that allows users to test and validate the feature in a matter of day, not months. Therefore, the chances are low that our efforts would go to waste.

'In summary,' concluded Dillon, 'if we build an explicit framework of activity and accountability separation between vendors and in-house teams, accept the chaos and uncertainties in project scope and the inevitability of outsourcing, we can source all the necessary elements of our digital capabilities successfully.'

Elements of a Long-Term Digital Strategy

'Given that our Phase 1 digital initiatives are well underway in terms of execution,' said the CEO, 'there must be nuggets of wisdom we've picked up along the way, which paves the road ahead for us, in terms of our medium- and long-term digital strategy. Would you like to elaborate on a few of the more important elements of our long-term strategy, Dillon?'

'Sir, the first element is to *build digital capability*. I already explained the point, so I won't belabour it. Suffice it to say that, as the organization moves ahead in the digital journey, digital know-how will need to be embedded in the culture of the corporation, as a sort of a "do-it-yourself" philosophy, rather than a culture of complete dependency on partner resources or employees possessing a certain skill set.

'You can't keep digital separate from the rest of the business. The days when you could say, "Here's my tech guy, go talk to him", are over. In the industrial company of the future, there won't be a separate IT or digital department. Top leaders will understand digital innovation in the same way they understand finance and accounting today. They will design digital technology into their products and their practices.

'The second element is to *integrate people, processes and technology, and create uniform visibility of digital throughout the organization*. What this means is twofold: first, adopt a "digital-first" philosophy for all new or redesigned processes, forge ahead with the digital journey and align people—as in, objective-setting, performance management and rewards and recognition (R&R). Second, talk up digital in a number of forums within and outside the organization, and ensure that everyone knows what the corporation is up to in the digital space. Creating mottos and slogans or catchphrases, running hackathons, conducting all-day technology events, are all ways to go about doing this. The idea is, if you grab a random employee from any department and ask him or her what our digital vision is, we should receive an intelligible response.

'The third important element, one that's not very well understood because it's somewhat technical, is *establishing a single source of truth and driving IT and digital systems off that version of the truth*. This is known as MDM, commonly effected by specialized MDM software. Now, MDM is a big challenge because as go the data, so goes your insight from the data: crap-in, crap-out. Data are the raw material for analytics, IoT and digital twin applications, among others.

Organizational risk is very high even if 10 per cent of the data are not good. For example, you may have incorrect, duplicate customer master data. All the data that are derived in combination with that 10 per cent of the data are also bad. It's probably best to explain this in the form of this picture,' Dillon said as he projected the following picture.

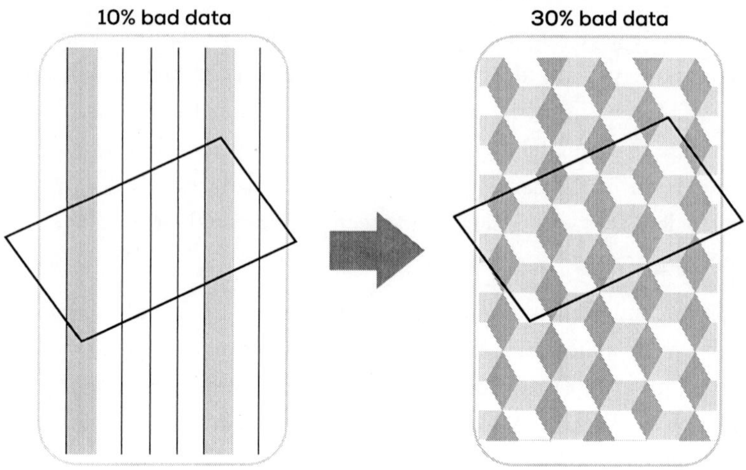

'You see,' Dillon continued, 'the picture on the left represents a data set that has 10 per cent "bad data", that is, data that are erroneous, blank or duplicate, in the form of the grey column. In the data set on the right, due to slicing and dicing of the "bad data" with clean data, we have a larger percentage of "bad data" to the tune of 30 per cent. This shows why it's super important to cleanse the data and maintain a "single source of truth" as it were.

'The fourth, and final, element, of a long-term digital strategy is *establishing a self-sustaining organization*. What I mean is the incubation and innovation aspects of the organization should be such that ideas should be getting generated on an ongoing basis. You won't need to hold ideation or brainstorming sessions; the process of idea generation and execution, as well as the R&R mechanism, should operate like a finely tuned machine. The idea incubation centre should possess the technical capability and budget to carry out pilot projects and build prototypes. In addition, the governance and reporting aspects should be bulletproof. Since we covered these aspects in the digital capability discussion, I'm not going to elaborate.'

'Question,' said Falguni. 'As the CFO, I have to validate the financial soundness of any digital strategy. How would you ensure that the RoI, or payback, remains strong?'

'By a combination of two things,' replied Dillon. 'First, by ensuring success by building a successful PoC or prototype before entering into the project. Second, by tying a large percentage of the partner payment, say 50 per cent, to the successful achievement of an outcome.'

'How long would it take for us to execute these four components of a long-term digital strategy?' asked the CEO.

'Building digital capability is a multiyear effort,' said Dillon thoughtfully, 'but going by the sense of urgency under which we're operating, I'd say we should have a firm long-term digital strategy in place by the time two years are up, counting from the day I was hired.'

Avoid the Biggest Cultural Pitfall—Egos versus Ideas

'Any other pointers, Dillon?' asked the CEO. 'We have about 10 minutes to go before we break for lunch.'

'Well, there's one more point. I won't call it so much as a piece of digital strategy as a pitfall. It's to do with culture. *Forbes* magazine says culture can make or break an organization. "Culture is a living, breathing aspect of your business that develops and changes as you grow. It also extends to how you work with customers and partners and even how stakeholders and potential hires perceive you."[5]

'We've all heard the adage: "Culture eats strategy for breakfast". I've spoken quite forcefully elsewhere about how important culture is to success, so I won't belabour the point, but, in summary, I believe it can be the biggest driver of, or impediment to, corporate achievement in the technology space. In fact, it's said that corporate culture is the most important factor in driving innovation.[6]

'Silicon Valley taught me a secret. I had the good fortune of living and working in Silicon Valley, where the best and the brightest tech minds from around the world come together to build companies that scale up to global proportions. Think Apple, Google, Tesla, Facebook, eBay, Intel, HP, Netflix, etc. What makes Silicon Valley unique? Is it the moderate Mediterranean climate? Or the ready access to top-class education? Or perhaps the adventurous gold rush culture? Close, but not quite. Here's Silicon Valley's secret sauce: *the primacy of ideas over ranks and hierarchies.* No one says, "I'm the leader, and I know best". The best ideas come as often from the chairman as from the new intern. From the early days of start-ups, HP and Intel, folks with the best ideas were heard, respected, rewarded and promoted. Managers in the best companies know how to generate ideas; they are collaborative, not "command and control" type leaders. In other words, ideas rule. Titles don't.

'Which brings me to my point, which is that *the primacy of ideas over egos must be protected at all* costs.'

'Agree,' said the COO. 'Sounds to me like we have to perform a mental rewiring at the higher levels of management. An open culture encourages employees to get excited and work collaboratively in order to seed ideas into innovative products. It also helps create and execute a strong go-to-market strategy.'

'There's another aspect of culture,' said Hari, 'that may be important to success in digital, as it is indeed to any other function within our company: the *culture of speaking up, even at the cost of hurting a leader's ego*. In my prior role, I was at a leadership meeting where a senior manager questioned a specific piece of strategy put forward by the chairman. The chairman, clearly irked, responded: "It's my company and I'll run it the way I please!"

'I've experienced situations,' continued Hari, 'where a CxO, MD, chairman or senior manager would snap at employees who ask questions or offer alternate ideas. And then we wonder: "Why aren't our employees speaking up?" Well, it's because employees watch leaders for cues on what counts as acceptable behaviour and what doesn't. Speaking up is a culture that needs to be protected, nourished and encouraged. As leaders, we should be wary when our people toe our line without question. Dissent should be tolerated, nay embraced, if we seek progress, innovation and breakthroughs, which are especially important so far as digital technology is concerned,' concluded Hari.

'Well said,' asserted the CEO. 'When our head of HR and technology are aligned, it speaks well of our enlightened leadership. I feel, culturally, our digital program is in good hands.'

Evaluating Progress—The DSC

'One more thing before we disperse,' added the CEO. 'How do we track progress? How do we monitor and review ongoing projects?'

'Good question,' chimed in Prabhat. 'I remember we have a DAB. Can we utilize the same governing body for the purpose to which the CEO is alluding?'

'Let's take a step back,' replied Dillon in a measured tone. 'Let's first establish the need for what we call a digital steering committee (DSC), and then discuss....'

Om, the COO, cut Dillon off. 'Sorry, but we already have too many committees, and far too many meetings. I'm not comfortable with throwing another committee into the mix!'

'I'm with Om on that one,' said the CFO.

'First of all,' began Dillon, 'the DAB is not the same as a steering committee. The DAB advises the CDO on technology feasibility and execution. Second, a primary function of the DAB is to provide the CDO with a working team to start making progress even before key positions get hired into the digital organization.

'On the other hand, the purpose and operating rhythms of a DSC are quite different. Here are a few primary functions of the DSC[7]:

- Ensuring that the objectives and the outcomes of selected digital initiatives meet the requirements

- Monitoring risks and reviewing projects regularly, commonly at monthly intervals
- Ensuring that the prioritization of the initiatives is in line with the organization's vision and objectives
- Providing policy or regulatory direction to the project
- Suggesting escalation techniques and corrective actions in case unexpected issues delay ongoing projects'

'I guess I have a problem with this arrangement,' said the COO. 'I think the DSC would end up controlling the digital program. Most committees, in my experience, feel a compelling need to be the controlling influence, or an adult supervisory influence, over what they view as out-of-control behaviour by technology teams.'

'Point taken,' said Dillon in a friendly, persuasive tone. 'In my experience, steering committees do tend to exert "controlling" forces over projects when they perceive that nobody else is doing it, and there's a need for it. However, if we get an excellent project manager who's focused on keeping the project on track, the DSC won't interfere. The DSC is primarily concerned with ensuring that there's focus on the execution, that roadblocks, if any, have to be removed, and that other internal or external events, such as market changes, M&A or critical leadership changes, are taken into account and "managed."

'I view steering committees as a valuable resource. Use it to your benefit and succeed,' Dillon concluded.

'How often should the steering committee meet?' asked Falguni. 'As I said earlier, there are already too many meetings to which executive council members are invited. While I do agree that DSC has a vital role, we need to ensure that there are as many meetings as we must have, but not more. I'm just making it clear that I'm not a big fan of committees.'

'That is determined by the size and scope of the project,'[8] responded Dillon. 'Let's support we have a smaller project. In that case, it may be adequate to meet a few times at strategic points in the project life cycle;

let's say once at the planning or initiation stage, then again at the 50 per cent point of the project to monitor progress, and then finally, near the end of the project in order to assess the outcomes of the project and assess whether the project met its objectives.

'On the other hand, for larger projects, the DSC may want to plan its meetings with relation to the key milestones of the project. What I've seen work best is that the DSC sets dates for the meetings in advance and encourage the committee members to attend the meetings. Typically, the committee meets once a month to discuss the larger projects in some detail.'

'Which brings us to the question,' chimed in Hari, 'of who should be part of the committee.'

'What I'd suggest,' answered Dillon, 'is that we invite members of the executive council, and leaders one level below. Unlike the DAB, which also consisted of engineers and other junior employees in order for idea generation, the DSC simply needs senior leaders with considerable experience of oversight. We may want to invite to these leaders and, in addition, ask for alternates who can attend in their place in case they can't make it. Not every member can make it to every meeting, but I'd expect all the senior members to have attended the majority of the DSC meetings through the course of the year.'

The Big Party at Home

'But being fashionably late is par for the course, especially in India!' protested Prabhat's wife, Pratima.

It was the big year-end party at Dillon and Kavya's bungalow, at the north-west corner of Siruseri. About a dozen close friends, a half-dozen senior leaders from Dykstrand India and their families had been invited. Although the party started at 6:30 p.m., Prabhat and Pratima had walked in at 7:15 and had to endure some leg-pulling.

'I guess "fashionably late" means different things to each one us,' said Kavya, laughing, as she ushered Pratima into the family room where the other ladies were sipping on tea. A resplendent spread of snacks awaited Pratima. She noticed an array of tasty Indian snacks on the left of the oblong dining table: samosas, *bondas,* chaat, *momos* and a number of others. On the right were staple Western snacks such as sandwiches, salad, slices of fruit and boiled corn. Kavya loaded up a plate with a sample of everything and handed it to Pratima who, after holding up her hand in mock protest, accepted the food.

In the meantime, Dillon was explaining punctuality, Indian style, to the men assembled in the drawing room.

'In the USA, punctuality is a virtue, but Americans refuse to be defined by it,' he started. 'They accept delays of a few minutes if the circumstances are genuine. On the other hand, Germans are extremely particular about punctuality, and can appear stern—even rude—to visitors who don't understand what the fuss is about if they're late by a few minutes to a meeting.

'But when we moved to India, I realized we needed to reset our expectations. In our first week here, we were invited to the Daulats' party in their farmhouse on the outskirts of Siruseri. I believe Hari and Punit were also invited. Anyway, the party was supposed to start at 7, and we reached promptly at 7. No one greeted us because no one was available to greet us. We found the place to be in a state of last-minute unpreparedness, with about 15 workers hauling things and decorating.

'A few of the workers surrounded me, asking for instructions on the decorations. At this time, the caterer's van pulled in to the back of the party room, which itself was on the rear end of the sprawling property, and workers began unloading the food items. The delivery man walked up to me and asked, "Sir, how should we arrange the items?" It was then I realized why all these workers had surrounded me. They'd mistaken me for the host!

'It was only around 7:45 when Mr Daulat, the host, and his wife, entered the party hall, profusely apologizing for their delay. Amazingly, not a single one of the other guests showed up before 8, and the party properly began at 8:30. It was then that we realized what the official starting time of 7 p.m. meant.'

'Welcome to India,' said Punit, laughing heartily. 'Of course, you've now been here for a year, but I guess relocating to a small town straight from the USA presented your family with some unique cultural challenges.'

In the meantime, in an adjoining room, the kids were being entertained by a magician. Eknath, the CEO, wandered over to check on his grandson, 7, who was sitting spellbound as the magician, the famous Ramesh, pulled a small rabbit out of his hat.

Eknath ambled back to where the rest of the men stood, and remarked to Dillon, 'It's been an eventful year for us, but especially so for you and your family. Relocating to India after so many years in the USA was certainly challenging, but you seem to have pulled it off quite well. Any lessons learnt?'

'A big lesson for me, personally, was that peace at home was an essential prerequisite to success at work,' asserted Dillon. 'I must say it was an area where I was found wanting, but thanks to friends like Srini, I weathered the storm and here we are, celebrating a wonderful first year back in India.'

'Srini?' enquired the CEO, looking puzzled. 'I didn't know you moonlighted as a counsellor, although, I must admit in hindsight, out of all the senior managers, you were the one who could have been a friend and a mentor to Dillon.'

'Thanks, sir,' said Srini, 'although I must say Dillon applied what I suggested to him.'

Presently, the party ended, and the guests began to leave. Eknath's grandson exited the kids' room, excitedly clutching a balloon and a gift. Srini's daughter walked out, smiling, looking calm and at peace. The other kids, too, came out, some running, in order to show to their mothers the gift they'd received.

'It's been a most wonderful party,' said Srini, as he shook hands with Dillon and his family stood ready to get into the car. 'Thanks.'

'Thanks for coming to this party and into my life,' said Dillon earnestly. 'If not for your advice, I don't know if we'd all be here today, laughing and eating, and having a great time together.'

The Perfect Family

'Please come in,' said Mrs Raman, the principal of SK International, Aaron's school. 'Give me a moment while I sign this document and hand it over to my assistant.'

It was a Friday afternoon, and Dillon and Kavya were at the principal's office. The note to Dillon from the office had been cryptic. 'The Principal would need to speak with you in private. Please make sure to bring your wife along for a face-to-face meeting.' Kavya had been worried. 'Did Aaron get into trouble?' she'd wondered. 'Hush,' Dillon had responded. 'Don't even think so. The other day he received an award for being the breakthrough performer of the year, remember?'

Presently, the principal wrapped up what she was doing and looked up at the couple sitting across from her. She smiled. 'Can I get you both something to drink?'

'No,' Kavya responded. 'What's this all about? Did Aaron commit any mischief?'

'Oh no,' assured the principal, laughing heartily. 'I see—the note wasn't too clear, was it? I couldn't quite explain this in a note. You see, we live in a world gone wrong. Families are dysfunctional; kids are neglected and addicted to devices and substances; materialism is rampant. Most families don't have a "true north"—a value system that guides their individual lives and moulds them into model human beings. People are craving for simple answers to complex questions.

'I notice the confusion writ large on your faces,' continued Mrs Raman. 'What's all this got to do with you? Please bear with me for a moment. Ever since we had our school annual function—in which your son took home the biggest award of the night—I've been thinking about how to promote real-life role models that kids, and even their parents, can aspire to emulate. You know, the father that performs his work unselfishly and gives his time and energy, the mother who holds it all together and provides the encouraging and positive environment at home and the kid who makes the most of his or her abilities and the resources that are provided at home and at school.

'We thought about the "role model" bit and evaluated the top dozen families in this town. Our criteria were simple, and the checkboxes were pretty much what I described to you just now. You'll be glad to know that we picked your family—specifically you both—to be the role model for our kids,' concluded Mrs Raman.

'I.... I don't know what to say,' stammered Dillon, usually not the one to be at a loss for words.

Kavya smiled broadly. 'This is most gratifying,' she said. 'Thank you! But what does this entail? What does the school expect us to do?'

'If you accept the role,' explained the principal, 'we'll create a six-month-long program, entitled, "Raising the Perfect Family", where you both would need to come in once a month and speak at workshops on relationships, creating a positive environment at home and developing the growth mindset. We'll have teachers to assist you, of course, but you'll have the leeway to design the workshops and full freedom on the content.

'Will you do it?'

'Of course,' said Dillon, glancing at his wife before continuing, 'it's our privilege to give back in any way to this wonderful school that's been a pillar of development for our special needs child.'

'Thank you, Mr Dillon,' said the principal. 'We'll get back to you on the schedule and work with you in the coming weeks. We certainly appreciate your serving attitude, and the quick decision-making. When we look at you, Mrs D'Souza,' continued the principal, 'we feel you're the embodiment of the modern woman: confident, educated, unselfish and very strong. And Dillon, we appreciate the values you stand for, of success, growth and giving. When we evaluated the families, it didn't take too long for us to realize that your family was special. Every family has challenges, but your family is indeed the "perfect family" if there was ever one.'

Kavya smiled. *If you only knew,* she thought. *It wasn't that long ago that we were thinking of a separation.* 'Thank you, Mrs Raman,' she said sincerely. 'If I told you how we devised our "perfect marriage", you won't believe it. Suffice it say that we feel blessed and extremely grateful.'

'Consider us signed up,' she said as Dillon and she got up and prepared to leave.

References

[1] Hemerling, Jim, Vikram Bhalla, Diana Dosik and Stephanie Hurder. 2016, June. 'Building Capabilities for Transformation That Lasts.' BCG White Paper. Available at https://www.bcg.com/publications/2016/transformation-people-organization-building-capabilities-transformation-that-lasts.aspx (accessed on 22 April 2019).

[2] Daub, Matthias and Anna Wiesinger. 2015, March. 'Acquiring the Capabilities You Need to Go Digital.' *McKinsey Digital*. Available at https://www.mckinsey.com/business-functions/digital-mckinsey/our-insights/acquiring-the-capabilities-you-need-to-go-digital (accessed on 22 April 2019).

[3] Fosty, Vincent and Yves Van Durme. 2015, June. 'Building Your Digital DNA, Digital Transformation in Progress.' Deloitte White Paper. Available at https://www2.deloitte.com/content/dam/Deloitte/be/Documents/technology/deloittedigital/Deloitte-Digital-BE_Building-your-digital-DNA_download_HR.pdf (accessed on 22 April 2019).

[4] Phelps, Robert. 2017, November. 'Five Top Causes of Project Change.' Dell EMC. Available at https://infocus.dellemc.com/robert_a_phelps/five-top-causes-of-project-change/ (accessed on 22 April 2019).

[5] McClain, Mark. 2017, November. 'How Corporate Culture Can Make (or Break) Your Organization.' *Forbes*. Available at https://www.forbes.com/sites/forbestechcouncil/2017/11/06/how-corporate-culture-can-make-or-break-your-organization/#63a3d42e6d27 (accessed on 22 April 2019).

[6] University of Minnesota. 2008, November. 'Corporate Culture Is Most Important Factor in Driving Innovation.' *ScienceDaily*. Available at https://www.sciencedaily.com/releases/2008/11/081118122057.htm (accessed on 22 April 2019).

[7] Vascellari, Andrea. 2013, October. *Digital Steering Committee.* Available at http://www.andreavascellari.com/2013/10/digital-steering-committee/ (accessed on 22 April 2019).

[8] Law and Justice Foundation of New South Wales. *Implementing a Project: The Role of a Steering Committee.* Available at http://www.lawfoundation.net.au/ljf/site/templates/resources/$file/SteeringCommittee.pdf (accessed on 22 April 2019).

13

The Best Three Years of My Life

'Aaron's a teenager already? Gosh,' shouted Dillon from the master bedroom. Kavya had just informed him that she was going to participate in a meetup of parents of teenagers, which had confounded Dillon because, in his mind, Aaron was still just a kid. 11? 12 maybe, but certainly not a *teenager*!

'Yep, that's the right number,' shouted back Kavya from the kitchen. Presently, Dillon emerged. 'So that means it's been *three* years since we came here to Siruseri?' 'Yes,' replied Kavya. She smiled before continuing, 'Most moms know the age of their kids to the month and week, as in, Aaron is 13 years, a month and a half old. Most dads scratch their heads when asked about their kids' age, as in, "Let me see now—which year was he born in again?"'

'Of course, tease away, dear,' Dillon said as he hugged his wife. '*Of course*, I knew he was approaching 13,' he added rather unconvincingly. 'It's all your fault, though. We should've thrown a birthday party like Aaron wanted. When you celebrate the birthday, the dad won't usually forget the number.'

APAC Digital Leader of the Year

'What's this award again, Dillon?' asked Srini at work that day, when Dillon informed him about his trip to Delhi to accept the prize. 'Of course, the CEO announced the award at the executive council meeting on Thursday, but I'm not sure I'm not thinking, "yet another trophy", to bookend the dozen others you've accumulated in the last couple of years!'

'I acknowledge the leg-pulling,' agreed Dillon, smiling. 'It's been an exciting three years at Dykstrand India, and the dozen trophies you're referring to has been the result of many long nights and weekenders that the team has pulled off. External validation isn't the only prize the team was after, of course, but it excites the team and keeps the energy levels up. This particular award is called "APAC Digital Leader of the Year" and goes to the leader who's created the greatest direct value for business.'

The next evening, at a glittering event at New Delhi's Asian Bellagio Hotel, Dillon walked up the 10 steps to get on the stage to receive the award from Mr Suresh Ekale, India's federal commerce minister. Mr Ekale congratulated Dillon and, warmly shaking him by the hand, asked him to "say a few words on this occasion."

'Thank you, Mr Minister,' said Dillon as he took the microphone and surveyed the audience of nearly 800 people.

'What I appreciate the most,' he started, 'is that this award comes from my peers. My team believes in me and the senior management at Dykstrand is firmly behind what we're trying to accomplish. However, when the recognition comes from you, my peers, whom I've come to know and admire in the last few years, it means the world to me. Thank you! I'd just like to say that my team of developers, architects and product managers is the real winner, and that I'm simply representing that team on this magnificent stage!'

'Mr Dillon, can you please take a minute to explain the background of the award-winning project?' whispered Mr Natarajan, the organizer who stood right next.

'Of course,' Dillon nodded. 'Three years ago, when I joined Dykstrand India's Siruseri plant, we had a problem on our hands. Business had to maintain 30 days' worth of inventory levels, since our market leading footwear product lines suffered from unpredictable demands, and we never wanted to disappoint our distributors. Naturally, too much cash was locked up in maintaining a 30-day inventory. We needed to increase our FCF by reducing the inventory levels from 30 days to 20 days.

'In order to tackle this business challenge, we broke down the problem into two. First, we'd devise and implement a forecasting consolidator, which would automate demand forecasting across our plants in the country, so that production could be aligned to the real demand, and not an imaginary worst-case emergency. Second, we'd use advanced analytics tools in order to provide real-time inventory levels at various plants, through dashboards, to manufacturing executives.

'A number of fascinating insights quickly emerged from the data. For example, we found we had 25,000 pieces of a component—trimming—lying at a plant in North India and another 32,000 pieces of the same component lying in a plant in the eastern part of the country. Since these two plants used separate systems to track and monitor inventory levels, managers didn't realize just how much extra inventory they had. By getting to know what they had in their hands, they were quickly able to cut the numbers.

'Here's what excited the team. Our initial target was to cut the inventory levels to 20 days, but in eight months' time, we found we'd reduced the levels to 17 days, and devised a second iteration of the system that would reduce the inventory to 12 days. Cutting the inventory level from 30 to 12 days would free up about $600M of cash, which would directly impact our FCF.

'In addition, we've reduced our maintenance costs by 28 per cent of our biggest equipment, namely pattern-making and finishing machinery, using predictive asset maintenance. We've also increased production by 6 per cent by the use of process modelling, IoT and digital twins. We have set up a 30-member strong Digital Centre of Excellence, and our digital product pipeline is very strong, with a visibility of 10 quarters.'

Shortly thereafter, Dillon left the stage to a standing ovation.

Moving on Is the Toughest Decision

'I've never seen you more relaxed,' said Kavya. It was the Wednesday after the award ceremony. Aaron had retired to his room for studies after father and son played a game of soccer in the backyard. Grabbing a drink of a Panchgani-inspired Mojito, Dillon settled on the sofa with a contented look.

'Really, I wear my emotions so visibly?' inquired Dillon. 'Honestly, though, I don't mind admitting that I do feel at peace.'

'Even the night before you spring the big surprise on your boss?'

'Not sure it would be much of a surprise.'

'But you've never discussed it with him!'

'Agree, but at his level—I mean, at the chairman and managing director level—he'd be foolish not to have a succession plan chalked out for all his senior leaders. As I've said many times before, there shouldn't be anyone in the organization who's the sole possessor of specific knowledge, no matter where they are in the chain of command. I have a successor in mind; it just remains to be seen if the CEO goes along with my recommendation.'

'I hear you. Although the CEO may be prepared, he'll still be surprised, I bet.'

'Let's see.'

'Sir, I need to share something else with you,' said Dillon, the next morning, when he'd shared a quick overview of his work with the CEO. The CEO nodded. 'Go ahead,' he said.

'It's been a pleasure working with you and the management team at Dykstrand India,' began Dillon. 'I can't tell you how much I've appreciated the open embrace, coming from the USA after so many years and settling down in India.'

The CEO smiled. 'You're not telling me you're moving on, are you?' he asked.

'I am,' concurred Dillon. 'After three years in Siruseri, we've decided to move on to live in Bangalore. The schooling opportunities are just a lot better over there for my son, Aaron, as he moves on to middle and then high school. At a personal level, I'd like to take a few months off and write a memoir, perhaps. Or just travel. My wife, too, wants to hit the refresh button professionally and explore a different profession after a little break.'

'I must say I did have an inkling,' said the veteran leader, smiling.

'Really?' Dillon looked puzzled. Aside from Kavya and himself, he'd informed no one. Although he did expect the CEO to be ready to handle the news, he'd expected him to be somewhat surprised.

'I couldn't help noticing how you were positioning your Digital PMO, Narain, as a successor, at the last couple of executive council meetings,' observed the wily CEO.

'I see,' Dillon concurred, smiling. 'I guess some words don't need to be spoken. In my mind, of course, I've been preparing and guiding Narain for nearly two months. I just didn't realize it would be so transparent.'

'But didn't you say Narain was temperamental, that he needed more seasoning in terms of leadership?'

'I did, sir, and in the last two and half years that he's been here, he's made rapid progress. I did have a succession planning program in place for the last year, not only for my own role but also for the other senior roles within the group. Here are the steps of the *succession planning program* I instituted for Narain.

'First, *EQ*. Narain came from a strong technology leadership background. Tech leaders are notoriously weak in terms of feelings, that is, how do they feel about themselves and others? What feelings are driving some of their team members' behaviours? I was glad to notice that Narain was quick on the uptake on his EQ training and now has established himself as a leader who has a firm grasp of the emotional pulse of his team and internal stakeholders. He doesn't get worked up over details and gives the slack to his team in order for it to perform at a high level.

'Second, *financial fluency*. Although Narain had a command over the fundamentals, he lacked the understanding of capital investment decision-making, cash positions and balance sheets. This wasn't a weakness that we were going to turn into a strength. Instead, we agreed it was an area that needed to be shored up so that it didn't end up being a liability. Once that happened—and it did—Narain could always depend on the CFO's team in order to help with the deeper analyses and decision frameworks.

'Third, *communication skills*. Narain was always quite strong in this topic, but a couple of areas we focused on were advanced presentation techniques and executive presence. As a result, he's been able to speak powerfully and influence leaders by understanding their working styles. A key requirement of success in digital is influencing skills, which is where Narain is now quite strong.'

'I appreciate the detailed update,' said the CEO, approvingly. 'Although I can't say I'm glad to see you go, given your reasons, I can say I'm not despondent. I've lost some great leaders over the years, and I've remained their loyal friend and mentor even after they've left. It's a tribute to your own leadership greatness that you've developed a worthy successor while establishing a digital CoE from scratch and delivering on the core agenda of digital.

'There're undoubtedly HR processes you'd need to execute, but let me say this: I'm an admirer of yours, Dillon. I hope to be able to call you a friend as you go conquer new heights.'

'Certainly! I appreciate the kindness, sir,' said Dillon with genuine feeling, as he got up.

Final Takeaways

'Dillon, this is, quite simply, the most exciting opportunity of my life.'

It was a couple of weeks later that Dillon had broken the news to Narain that he'd been picked as the CDO-in-waiting at Dykstrand India, and that, in the due course of time, subject to the approval of the executive council, Narain would be confirmed as the full-time CDO.

Naturally, Narain was thrilled. 'Two years ago, if you'd asked me to apply for a CDO role, I'd have had a hard time convincing *anyone* that I was ready. You know why? Because I couldn't have convinced *myself* that I was ready. And yet, after an apprenticeship of a little over two years, you've given me an opportunity to dream of a CDO role.'

'You've got a good chance of making the dream come true,' Dillon asserted, smiling. 'We've had quite a few coaching and mentorship sessions in the last six months, haven't we? If I didn't feel you were ready, I won't have broached your candidacy to the executive council.'

'I'm really, really thrilled,' said Narain, his face lighting up. 'However, I still have some apprehensions. Not necessarily about my own capability but about the fact that I don't want to mess up. I agree that we all have to make our own mistakes and go through our own journeys in order to become who we're meant to be; however, I'd try to avoid some of the biggies that have pulled many a mighty leader down.

'If you could take your journey as an accomplished digital leader and distil that journey to its essence, what would you consider the three things I mustn't do, and the three things I must do, if I wished to ensure my success?'

'Hmmm... great question,' opined Dillon. He paused and collected his thoughts. The welcome, the hopes, the fraught relationships—at home and at work, the challenges, the sweet successes—the images fleeted past in little more than instant. A drop of tear formed at the corner of one of his eyes. Presently he composed himself.

'Let me start with the *three things you must never do*,' he began.

'First, *you must not let your ego get into the driver's seat.* Let me explain. Leadership, at the end of the day, is about accomplishing stuff, thereby driving your team, your organization and yourself, to greater successes. You can't go there alone; you must ask for, and obtain, the cooperation of other leaders. And you won't always be right. You'll often need to cede the spotlight; in fact, you'll often need to shine the spotlight on others in and outside your team. Make the journey about *them*; not about your ego gratification. Constantly ask yourself, *is my intent selfish?*

'Second, *you must not always be in battle mode.* You must pick your battles. Often, you'll need to lose the smaller battles on pur pose so that you'd win the bigger wars. It's easier to do that when you're in collaboration mode most of the time, not in battle mode. If you're cross with someone, don't wait for an opportunity to get back; instead, look for opportunities to embrace them and move forward in a spirit of collaboration. If you possess a spirit of forgiveness, your biggest detractors will become your greatest champions.'

'Third, *you must not sell out on your principles.* You must stand for what you believe in. While compromises and arrangements are a staple tactic, you shouldn't budge when you're asked to sign off on something that's against your moral beliefs or character, for example, turning a blind eye to an unfair policy or signing off something corrupt because "we all need to fall in line this one time". Stand for integrity; don't compromise on your principles under any circumstances.

'Next, let me describe the *three things you must always do.*

'First, *learn how to negotiate.* If you're going against a detractor at an important meeting, *agree with them* on a minor point early in the meeting. You'll win them over to your side and, in all likelihood, they'll come around to your point of view. Use your personal connects in order to further your agenda, so long as you're doing something for the good of the organization. Personal skills matter tremendously. EQ matters the most in your journey as an influential leader.

'Second, *understand and appreciate your chief responsibilities as a leader, and perform those as though they were scared.* You must establish the meaning of your team's tasks. You must clear the clutter so that your team members can perform their tasks freely. Celebrate small suc-cesses. Define the vision and constantly articulate it. Communicate the strategy early and often. Learn ways to inspire the team. Keep an eye on the culture; be ruthless in rooting out destructive, unprofessional cultural traits.

'Third, *learn, practice and promote a practical digital detox plan for yourself and your team.* Make it an annual practice to get away from electronic devices for a chunk of time all at once, say for a week or two. Spend the time with your family, or in pursuing the hobby you've been putting off. Spend time in nature in solitude. In your journey as a leader and a human being, your growth in the realms of mindfulness and self-discovery will determine your ultimate success, the meaning of your life. Unless you step away from the immediate and the urgent, you won't be able to provide your mind the break it requires in order to uncover the deeper meaning of life.'

'This is beyond my wildest expectations,' remarked Narain after a long pause. 'When I asked you for your greatest learnings, I'd thought of lessons in stakeholder management or governance frameworks. Instead, you've provided me with deep insights on *self-management*.'

'That's because you must lead yourself before you can lead an organization,' asserted Dillon. 'Those who conquer themselves will conquer the world.'

The Interview at a National Daily: What's up with DT 2.0?

'But it's *Digital Review* magazine, Dillon!' It was Hari. He was persistent that Dillon should do an interview, and Dillon wasn't sure he had the time for it.

'The magazine, as you know, is the longest running monthly on digital,' continued Hari. 'Vijay Michael, the editor, is planning to do a cover story on the top 10 digital leaders of India under 40. It's going to be a phenomenal promotional article for Dykstrand India. I've known Vijay since our IIM days. He does the most perceptive interviews, really!'

'All right, I'll do it,' submitted Dillon. 'How long is it going to be?'

'30 minutes.'

Not long afterwards, Dillon and Vijay were sipping coffee at the company cafeteria. The photographer accompanying the editor had shot a few "environmental shots" of Dillon which, he explained, were going to go well with the feature article.

'My first question, Dillon, is as follows. *You're a digital leader of note not only in India but in the entire Asia-Pacific region. What are the three cultural ingredients you'd consider most essential for a successful* DT?'

'The top cultural ingredient,[1] in my view, is the realization that great ideas can come from anywhere within the organization. To be successful in carrying out DT, you have to be open-minded to the possibility that ideas may come from outside your "technology" organization. The way ideas are generated, nurtured and developed has changed. Even though we're a "traditional organization" where senior employees exist with deep footwear expertise and 20–30 years of experience, that background isn't the only one that possesses a monopoly on brilliant ideas.

'The second cultural ingredient I consider essential to a successful transformation is a sense of curiosity, of learning and growing. A leader and a team with a sense of curiosity will never "settle", because you don't settle at any point in a digital journey. Digital technology is changing at a fast pace; typical business leaders are not used to changing. Leaders need to be keenly observant of how they're promoting curiosity as a behavioural trait that's recognized and rewarded. This culture will eventually drive disruption and grow the business exponentially.

'The third cultural ingredient, in my view, is that you've got to be willing to fail. Don't even call them failures; learn as a team to refer to failed projects as mistakes from which you've learnt. Digital is a relatively new field; you'll find yourself in uncharted territories. By adopting an iterative approach towards accomplishment, you've got to create a culture where folks take risks, learn along the way, adjust their plans and eventually succeed.'

'Thanks, Dillon,' said Vijay. *'What are the top three obstacles to management buy-in? How would you suggest that digital leaders overcome the obstacles?'*

'That's an excellent question,' started Dillon. 'Most influential leaders of the organization, that is, the members of the executive council, need to rally behind digital as a strategic priority for the company. The three obstacles for the leaders to buy into your vision are: first, capability: does your team know how to do this? Second, credibility: does your team possess proven success? Third, mentality: as a leader, why should I care about technology?

'The way I'd go about answering these questions is as follows,' continued Dillon. 'First, RoI establishes your team's capability. Understand and speak the CEO/CFO language; the language of financial literacy. Be meticulous in figuring out payback and RoI. Second, achieve quick wins that establish your credibility. Identify one or two key needs of top stakeholders. Identify a proactive leader from your team. Take the help of a partner if needed, and drive quick wins. Third, ride your proactive actions to establish a change in the leadership mindset. You need to own the change of mindset of leaders. You also need to communicate often and establish a personal connection. Lastly, you may want to figure out the psychological barriers and work on them.'

'Time for my last question,' asserted Vijay. 'Digital leaders everywhere are looking for the formula of success in a world that's constantly changing. At any point of time, CDOs are working on dozens of imperatives that would deliver benefits to their organizations.' *What are the top three imperatives CIOs and CDOs need to focus on, in order for the DT to provide the greatest benefit?*'

'In order to establish and grow a digital organization,' responded Dillon, 'CIOs and digital leaders need to focus on the following three imperatives[2]: augmented intelligence, product management and organizational digital twin.'

'Can you explain?,' questioned Vijay. 'Our readers are more familiar with AI than with augmented intelligence. Additionally, while we understand digital twins of equipment or processes, what's an organizational digital twin?'

'Certainly,' replied Dillon reassuringly. 'Normally when we say AI, we mean machine intelligence. By augmented intelligence, we mean that human and machine intelligence combine in order to maximize organizational capability. For example, a production or finance leader first consults with an AI assistant to determine a procedure and augments the course of action with expert human advice.

'Next comes product management, by which we mean a product-centric focus of delivery of digital capability. Digital product management, as opposed to the traditional software product management, brings together the achievement of performance goals, superior UX and new functionality.[2] Product management in the world of digital deals with agility, or rapidity, and data-driven decision-making during delivery.

'Finally, organizational digital twin. Normally, digital twin refers to the maximization of performance and output through the physical and digital modelling of processes and equipment. Here, I'm talking about the digital twin of an organization, that is, the modelling of everything—processes, systems, equipment and human interactions. For example, you can aspire to produce and employ the digital twin of your entire supply chain, in order to optimize costs and complexity.'

'Thanks,' Vijay replied, looking glad that the discussion was substantive. He continued to jot furiously on his notepad.

'I didn't realize we've been speaking for more than an hour,' remarked Dillon, getting up. 'It's been a pleasure talking with you!'

'When you're having an interesting conversation, time flies,' opined Vijay. 'Thank you, Dillon! The pleasure was absolutely ours.'

The Send-Off Party

'It'll just take a minute,' said Hari. It was the Friday before the last week of Dillon's stint. The latter had been cleaning out his desk, putting the souvenirs away in a small box, when the former had knocked and come in. The occasion? To request Dillon's presence to 'give away a long service award to an employee.'

Dillon followed Hari into Himalaya, the largest conference room in the administrative building. *Who's this employee?* Dillon thought. *Must be someone important, if HR has organized an event in this cavernous conference room!*

Hari entered the conference room first, with Dillon a few steps behind. As soon as he stepped in, Dillon realized something was amiss; there was complete silence. Momentary quiet ... and then, pandemonium! A large cry went around the gigantic conference room, *Surprise!*

There were almost a 100 people cramped into the room that could probably sit 40. They were all there—Dillon's team members, functional leaders, executive council members and, at the centre, the CEO, smiling and holding a plaque. The noisiest group was the team of 20-something interns at the back of the room.

'Dillon, please come over here to the front of the room,' said the CEO.

'I.... I mean, this is quite crazy,' admitted Dillon, laughing heartily. 'Hari really played his part well, and I fell for it!'

'This is for our beloved leader and prankster-in-chief, Dillon, who's leaving us next week,' said Eknath, shaking hands with Dillon and handing him a shiny plaque. Dillon glanced at the plaque for an instant, and read something to the effect of, 'inspiring leader and role model.'

Amidst the applause, Sucheta, the HR talent acquisition leader, picked up the microphone and said, 'Indeed. The CEO put it perfectly. Dillon can be the perfectly serious type when he wishes to, but he also plays the most awesome pranks. I remember once when, right after his dental surgery, he came into a meeting wearing something over his teeth that made it appear as though three of his upper teeth were chipped, with the middle one having fallen off! It nearly gave me a heart attack!'

Ishani, the R&D manager, said, 'Dillon would always pull my leg over the fact that I have a few patents to my name. Like this one time when he e-mailed the entire R&D team about a "new patent assigned to Ishani" that read like the perfectly legitimate article, except that it said I'd had the patent issued in my name for "having invented a beer container lookalike that can completely fool a guest wishing to pick up a glass of beer. When the guest picks up the container and attempts to drink the beer, he or she will be embarrassed because there's no beer inside." The reason it was hilarious was because I don't drink and have no interest in beer or wine, and Dillon knows it, plus I'd never invent such a contraption and actually attempt to patent it.'

Hiren, the engineering manager, spoke next. 'Lest it should be concluded that Dillon was only interested in pulling pranks, I can assure everyone here that Dillon was a leader who gave his teams the freedom to choose their path. When I got on one of the many digital projects, I knew I was going to have a great time because I could use my ingenuity and passion, and Dillon would never micromanage. He would empower us and get out of the way.'

Gagan, the financial analyst, said, 'What I remember the most about Dillon's leadership was how he got us to care about what we were doing, so that we'd do it the very best way we knew. He cared deeply about quality. If his name was going to be on something, he wanted it to be world class. It rubbed off on us in a big way. Whatever we did had to be *awesome*. When we'd be staring at defeat, his quiet words of encouragement would often make the difference. He believed in us long before we ever began to believe in ourselves.'

Cyril, the maintenance engineer, took the microphone, but paused. He seemed emotional. Finally, he managed to speak. 'Dillon was a great leader because he sacrificed for us. I've had bosses who'd throw their people under the bus if it fit their needs. Dillon was a great boss because he'd take the bullets for us. He'd pull his people from the bus's path before they realized they were in danger. The accolades we received from senior management, the awards, the recognition—he was the driving force behind all of that, and yet, he never hogged the credit or the limelight. I can unequivocally say this on behalf of the team that *these were the best three years of my life*. What a ride!'

Falguni, the CFO, spoke. 'I'll miss my dear friend, Dillon. When he came in, we butted heads often. We'd fight over issues small and big.

Over time, I realized I wasn't fighting him; I was fighting against my own prejudices against technology and tech leaders. Subsequently, I realized my own mistake and made the smallest of concessions; I extended my hand of friendship. To his credit, while I just extended a hand, Dillon fully embraced me as a friend and colleague, without the least bit of resentment or grudge. He who can forgive and truly embrace his opponent, is, in my view, the greatest leader.'

Hari, the head of HR, spoke at the end. 'Unforgettable leaders are human, as was Dillon. And he wasn't afraid to show it. He was personable and easy to relate to; he was warm. He was everyone's friend. When you spoke to him, he *heard you.* Too many of us are not listening; we're merely thinking of what to say next. However, Dillon always heard you because he genuinely cared about your opinion. I've often said that a high EQ will take an average leader to greatness, and I don't know of anyone who embodied that more than Dillon did.'

Dillon was quite teared up at this point. For once, he stood speechless. 'I appreciate all the kind words,' he said finally. 'However, I believe in that wise man who opined, "When things are going well, you're not as good as they say you are. And when things are not going well, you're not as bad as they say you are." I stand here, humbled, as you shower praises. Memories flash into the brain in a jumbled mass. I remember those days when the team was struggling, when our funding for the IoT project was cut off after three months of back-breaking effort. I also remember when the same IoT project eventually got funded and went on to win the ITNAM award.

'Through the last three years, this team has made tremendous strides. The self-belief, and the capability, are sky-high, as are senior management's expectations from the team. I believe Narain will take the program to a higher level. I count on all your support to make that vision a reality.

'It's been a heck of a roller-coaster of a ride and a perfect privilege for me. Now it's time to say goodbye. I love you, and I'll miss you all.'

A Last Secret to Success

'I knew you'd be busy, even on your last day here,' said Srini. It was the Friday of Dillon's departure. He'd started the day by attending the executive council meeting, where he'd brought all the leaders up to speed on the status of Dykstrand India's DT journey. He'd taken along Narain, his successor, so that he'd have a chance to familiarize himself with senior management.

Now it was afternoon, and Srini had dropped by, expecting Dillon to be tidying up his office and collecting his personal effects. However, Dillon was still busy in the conference room next to his office, providing his input to a team of young engineers on a critical AI-related project that was going live in a couple of weeks.

'I'm about done,' Dillon acknowledged to Srini. 'Can you please give me, say, 10 minutes? If you don't mind, please step into my office and I'll join you soon.'

Srini entered Dillon's office, which was now completely empty, save for a plaque hanging in a corner that was as cryptic as it was intriguing. It said, BIG PICTURE on one line, and CONSISTENCY on the second. And that was it.

In about eight minutes, Dillon walked in, Narain in tow.

'What's this plaque all about?' asked Srini. 'And why haven't you packed it?'

Dillon smiled. 'It's for the next guy. For Narain, and perhaps he'll leave it behind for the person who succeeds him.'

Now Narain was intrigued too. 'Tell us what's so special about this plaque.'

'Personal relationships and job-related emergencies used to cause the biggest stress in my life,' began Dillon. 'For example, a tiff with my wife late at night or early in the morning caused me great heartache. My little son, "terrible two", as they call it, would throw a major tantrum, shattering the quiet peace of the household. A call from a colleague, informing me of an upset client, would fill me with anxiety and set the stress alarms ringing.

'The solution came to me much later, after I'd begun talking with Srini. It was to take a step back and ask myself: 'is this going to lead to the end of civilization as we know it?' If the answer is no, then take a deep breath, thank God for his grace and get back to work. I found that that what I considered to be a cataclysmic event was but a speck of dust in the grand scheme of things.

'One afternoon in Goa, where I lived for the first nine years of my life, my dad and I were visiting a large bookstore, one of the biggest and most modern in town. We looked over many shelves of books. Dad and I could count on this bookstore to enjoy a few moments of quiet and peace, looking over a biography here and a leadership book there.

'We returned home that night, ate and went to sleep. The household was awoken at about three in the morning to loud screams from my mother. My father had gotten up to go to the bathroom, and upon returning to the bedroom, had collapsed on the floor. I can never forget the prostrate figure on the ground, face upwards, eyes open but a vacant expression on his face, was my father! He'd passed away—my father, my playmate, my best friend—the one with whom I'd spent a most enjoyable evening merely hours earlier.

'My dad's passing away touched me in a personal way and stressed me for years afterwards. I realized a couple of years ago, finally, that I should appreciate that life was precious, that it could be taken in an instant. All around us, people were dying every day in accidents, of disease and in wars. And I got stressed because of an irate customer, an unreasonable colleague or a complaining wife or child?

'I resolved to always take a step back and reflect on the big picture: that I loved my wife and an occasional bickering or two won't have any lasting effect. That I loved my son and that throwing tantrums and behaving inexplicably some of the time was part of the process called growing up. That the irate colleague was not necessarily upset with me; she was taking out on me her frustrations due to some other unrelated reason.

'That's what BIG PICTURE means to me. Don't get too caught up in work-related setbacks and always focus on the big picture. My favourite affirmation is "I have no fe ar; I ha ve no agitation. I ha ve no stress, because God is in charge. I'm but his instrument. I'll not worry about things I can't control."

'And now about the second line. I have to take you back to something that happened over two decades ago, but which only made sense to me as I grew in my career.

'"I have to be better than you to be considered as good as you", said my classmate and fellow baseball player, Trinath, one evening 21 years ago. I'd just been picked to the college baseball team, and more than one classmate thought that I'd been picked primarily because I was related to a well-known faculty member of the college. And in my heart of hearts, I thought they were right, because I didn't believe in myself enough to believe that I'd been picked solely on my merits. One of the players not picked, Trinath, communicated exactly how rotten he felt about his non-selection.

'*I'll show them,* I pledged to myself. *I may not be very talented, but I can be the most consistent, committed player!* During t he s ummer b reak between my first year and second year in college, I started a practice I would continue until my last day at college: I would hit a baseball for hours every day. I took a ball, put it into a sock, hung it from a branch of the huge jackfruit tree in the backyard and then just hit the ball with a bat as the ball swung back and forth. I did this for at least 10 minutes every day, and sometimes as long as two hours.

'Months passed. When the second season started, I was one of the better batters on the team. Next year, I was the best batter on the team. During my senior year, I was not only the best batter, but also helped my team win the coveted annual tournament of 32 college teams. In the final, I scored a home run, and played with vigour and enthusiasm. We beat the heavily-fancied G. M. College in a nail-biter.

'It capped the proudest moment of my life. Not just a great day—it was the best day of my life. Why? Because I'd overcome my self-doubt, and others' skepticism, to demonstrate that determination and consistency will take you where talent may not. And I'd helped my team win! Most people quit if they can't see or measure progress. For example, I didn't see any progress on my batting ability after a week, even after a month. However, I stuck with it because, deep down, I believed that consistency was going to do it for me.

'I learnt, a few years ago, as much at a leadership event[3]: just like a relationship, leadership is the direct result of the accumulation of a number of little things that are done over and over again, *consistently*. Consistency, indeed, is most important factor in building relationships and in becoming a great leader.'

Narain spoke up. 'This is very cool. Now that you've explained the background of this plaque, it'll continue to occupy an important spot on the wall and, more importantly, in my heart.'

'I've got to go,' said Dillon. 'It's been nice knowing you, Narain. And Srini, what can I say? You've been the friend, philosopher and guide I always needed in my life, though I didn't realize it, someone who cared about me, and had the wisdom to be able to make a difference. I'll never forget you. Keep in touch!'

The two men hugged. Srini patted Dillon in the back, but didn't say anything. He didn't have to.

Finding Happiness in One Another

'We've come really far,' said Dillon, six months later, to the receptionist at the stupendous hilltop resort. Dillon and family had driven for over seven hours in order to reach the famed hilltop town of Ooty. The resort, carved out from the jagged edge of the *Nilgiris*, offered spectacular views.

'How far, sir?' inquired the clerk.

'400 km,' offered Dillon, 'but I wasn't thinking about that when I remarked to you that we've come far. My thought was how far, as a family, we've come in the last three years.'

The clerk scratched his head.

Later, when Dillon and Kavya were relaxing by the poolside, each holding a glass of the lime-and-mint Mojito for which Ooty is famous, Kavya remarked, 'You know what Aaron said to me as he changed into his sporting gear in order for rope climbing?'

'What did the young man say?' asked Dillon, sipping his drink.

'I don't know if you'd still call him a young man after I tell you,' smiled Kavya. 'He asked me, "Mom, do I have to get married to find a perfect mate and all that?"'

'Reasonable question for a 13-year-old.'

'Quite so. I told him it was going to be his decision when he grew up, but then, I told him I was curious why he asked.'

'And?'

'You won't believe what he said. He said, "Because when I see you and dad being so happy in each other's presence—which in turn makes me very happy—I couldn't stop wondering how you'd found each other. Most of my friends tell me their parents often quarrel, which is why those friends of mine have made up their mind never to marry. Since you never fight, I figured you may have found each other not by marriage but perhaps by some other means."'

Dillon smiled.

'So I told him, "You're right, son. We didn't find each other through marriage. We found each other when we lost ourselves and started focusing on the other. It took us about 10 years, but it was worth every bit of it."'

'And what did he say?'

'Nothing,' replied Kavya. 'He just hugged me and ran out to the rope climbing area.'

'Now that we're alone,' said Dillon as he turned towards his wife, 'what do you think of the CDO opportunity in Mumbai for KTV Steel?'

'We just moved to Bangalore last year, honey! Are we ready to go through another mass troop movement?'

'Here's why Mumbai may make sense, Dear. Let me tell you about ... '

References

[1] Burns, David. 2018, June. 'CIO Thoughts on Digital Transformation.' Internal address by GE Aviation CIO David Burns.

[2] Scheibenreif. 2018, December. 'From Digital Transformation to Continuous Next.' Gartner Research Notes. Available at https://blogs.gartner.com/don-scheibenreif/2019/01/17/from-digital-transformation-to-continuousnext/ (accessed on 10 June 2019).

[3] Sinek, Simon. 2018, November. *Why consistency matters in Relations and Leadership*. Available at https://www.youtube.com/watch?v=njeAb4CLQeI (accessed on 23 April 2019).

Epilogue

As you've gone through the book, naturally, a question on your mind may be: Is there a way I can get my hands on the complete list—in one place—so that I won't have to go back again and again, and make notes?

Here it is: a handy list of steps for your reference, a quick guide containing the steps of your business transformation journey using digital. We are confident that it will prove to be a useful reference list during your own transformation journey, one that you can customize for your organization.

Step No.	Description	Remarks
1	Define 'what is digital' for the organization and also 'what is DT'	It's important that everyone in the organization speaks the same language and is well acquainted with these basic questions. Elaborate details on the elements of an organization's transformation: people, process, technology, mindset and culture.
2	Conduct digital maturity assessment	Conduct an assessment on parameters of leadership, technology, culture, process and ecosystem partners—in order to determine where the organization is at the start of the journey.
3	Set the digital vision	Set the North Star by aligning the digital vision with business vision.
4	Establish a methodical approach to the DT journey	At the start of the journey, create and broadcast within the organization the approach and the methodology and adhere to those at every stage.

(continued)

(continued)

Step No.	Description	Remarks
5	Set up the digital organization	Diverse roles are needed in the digital organization, for example, CDO, a team of digital evangelists, an experienced program manager, an analytics expert, a IoT champion and a technology architect. CDO's key responsibilities include: navigates the internal maze, works with IT and Commerce, is a translator and possesses interpersonal skills and result orientation. Other organizational elements include the following: • Steering Committee (senior management) • DAB (middle management and young talent) • Taskforce of shared resources (junior management, young enthusiasts)
6	Establish a governance model	Setting up a governance model is crucial to the success of the digital journey. Set up regular review meetings at various levels with a monthly Steering Committee, followed by weekly Advisory Board meetings and daily connects, as applicable, for smooth implementation, feedback and reporting.
7	Conduct value discovery workshops	Conduct workshops organization-wide across functions to identify business challenges and gaps, the outcome being a list of most important business challenges that are expected to be resolved with intervention of digital technology.
8	Identify digital themes and the list of initiatives	List down the current environment and landscape: functions, processes, systems, tools, etc. Identify current issues and pain areas and business challenges. Determine potential areas for technology intervention, process changes, etc.
9	Prioritize	A comparative evaluation of ideas is needed under the organization's financial, time and resource constraints. The evaluation is on the basis of strategic fit with business, ease of implementation, ease of adoption, time taken to realize benefit, cost of implementation and degree of stakeholder buy-in. Classify the resulting initiatives into quick wins and long-term projects.
10	Digital road map	An output of the above step is a road map of 'what' to do and 'when' to do it. 'How' to do is the next step, following which the execution journey can begin. Determining future state of TA is part of the digital road map.

Step No.	Description	Remarks
11	Prepare and float RFPs/ RFQs	Do a thorough requirement gathering of prioritized projects and write down the RFQ (or proposal) with details such as: • Problem statement • Scope of work • Inclusion and exclusion • Timelines • Deliverables • Legal terms and conditions • Non-disclosure agreement
12	Prepare EAN	Prepare a 'note,' which contains the capital outlay and the value proposition of the project. Three broad sections of the document: • Project background • Financials • Acceptance and approvals by heads of the relevant business functions, the CFO, CIO or CDO and the CEO
13	Determine a digital budget	At the beginning of the financial year, during the annual budgeting exercise, prepare a budget for the prioritized initiatives for capital expense (CapEx) and operating expense (OpEx) spend, as appropriate. The budget can be 'owned' either by the CDO or the relevant functional head.
14	Apply the 6-step solution co-creation model to each identified initiative	Designing a solution consists of: • Business problem • Empathy map • Pains and gain • Features • Prioritization • MVP schedule
15	Adopt an Agile digital project delivery philosophy	The PMO ensures that detailed project plans have been made and projects executed in a series of Sprints employing the Agile methodology. Agile requires a mindset change.
16	Keep the transformation journey on track	Keep the overall journey on track using the following steps: • Right team and right strategy in place • Structured reporting in the organization with respect to the program • Clear assignment of roles and responsibilities

(continued)

(continued)

Step No.	Description	Remarks
17	Keep in mind the TA	Keep in mind that: • The TA goes hand-in-hand with digital road map implementation • Key decisions on core/non-core and platform solutions determine the speed and effectiveness of digital implementations.
18	Determine your approach to the AI journey	Factors to consider in the AI journey: • Where to start? • How to start? • Alternate to AI? • Infrastructure requirements to run AI
19	Perform 'digital detox' periodically	It's important to perform the following steps on a regular basis: • Get away from electronic devices • Spend time with family • Pursue a hobby • Practice mindfulness
20	Exhale, rest and repeat	Digital is not a one-time deal. A 'transformation' is the means, not the end. Celebrate your victories, rest and recuperate, and be ready to get going with the next phase of your digital journey!

Glossary

API (application program interface): A set of functions and procedures allowing the creation of applications that access the features or data of a computer construct, for example, an operating system or an application.

CapEx (capital expenditure): The funds a firm spends to buy, maintain or improve its fixed assets, such as buildings, software systems, vehicles, equipment or land.

DT (digital transformation): The profound transformation of business, along with a shift of mindset and organizational activities, processes, competencies and models to fully leverage the changes and opportunities offered by a mix of digital technologies.

EBITDA (earnings before income, tax, depreciation and amortization): A measure of a company's operating performance, a way to evaluate a company's performance without having to factor in financing decisions, accounting decisions or tax environments.

ENIAC (Electronic Numerical Integrator and Computer): The world's first general-purpose computer.

EPC (engineering, procurement and construction): Form of contracting arrangement used in some industries where the contractor is made responsible for all the activities from design, procurement, construction, commissioning and handover of the project.

ERP (enterprise resource planning): Business process management software that allows an organization to use a system of integrated applications to manage the business and automate enterprise functions such as sales, finance and HR.

GPS (Global Positioning System): Global navigation satellite system that provides geo-location and time information to a receiver anywhere on or near Earth.

MDM (master data management): A comprehensive method of enabling an enterprise to link all of its critical data to a common point of reference, or a system.

PLC (programmable logic control): Digital device which controls manufacturing processes such as assembly lines or robots.

PLM (product life cycle management): The process of managing the entire lifecycle of a product from inception, through engineering design and manufacture, to service and disposal.

PMO (program management office): Department within a business, government agency or enterprise that defines and maintains standards for project management within the organization.

RDBMS (relational data base management system): A commonly-used type of database whose data can be manipulated by use of the SQL (structured query language).

RFID (radio frequency identification): Technology whereby digital data encoded in smart tags or labels are captured by a reader via radio waves.

RPA (robotic process automation): Business process automation technology based on the use of software robots in order to perform routine, manual tasks.

SAP HANA: An 'in-memory' relational database management system developed and marketed by SAP SE.

SLA (service level agreement): A contract between a service provider and the customer that documents the service standards the provider is obligated to meet.

TCO (total cost of ownership): A financial estimate intended to help buyers and owners determine the direct and indirect costs of a product or system.

WC (working capital): The capital of a business which is used in its day-to-day trading operations, calculated as the current assets minus the current liabilities.

About the Authors

Amitabh Mishra is an international technology executive with 25 years of experience in the USA, Europe and Asia in a variety of industries such as high-tech, automotive, aerospace defence, aviation, metals and mining, and pharmaceuticals. He has over 10 years of experience in transformation and organizational turnaround in engineering, manufacturing, operations and maintenance with some of the world's largest companies. He obtained a master's degree in computer science from Texas A&M University and management education from MIT Sloan School of Management. He has served as Chief Ambassador at Toastmasters International and is a Distinguished Toastmaster (DTM). He has been featured on TV, in journals and at international trade conferences. His blogs and articles have garnered over a million views. He has also delivered keynote addresses at technology conferences in India, the USA and the Middle East. He is a three-time winner of 'India's Top Change Agents' and 'CIO 100' awards. In his spare time, he loves to dabble with his guitar and write stories.

Ashish Ranjan is a digital transformation executive with over 15 years of experience in natural resources, steel, manufacturing and automotive industries. He operates at the interface of business and technology, and has led DT from strategy to execution in companies in India, the USA, China, the Middle East and Asia-Pacific a cross i ndustries i n n atural resources and steel. He holds a bachelor's degree in engineering from Birsa Institute of Technology (BIT) Sindri, Jharkhand and a master's degree in business administration from K. J. Somaiya Institute of Management Studies and Research, Mumbai. In his spare time, he loves to read or indulge in sports.